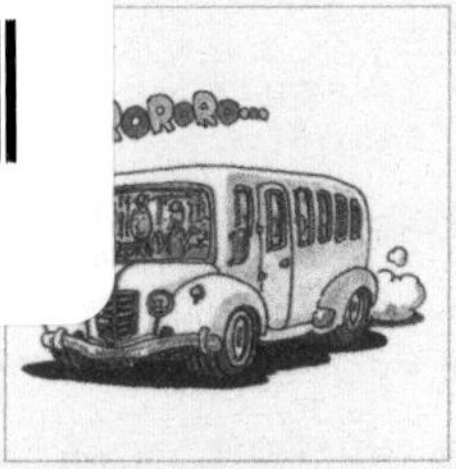

尾田栄一郎

Hello and thank you for taking our bus tour. We're heading toward the 100th chapter of *One Piece*. On your right, you can see the thumbs held up high. There's plenty more action and adventure ahead!

-Eiichiro Oda, 1999

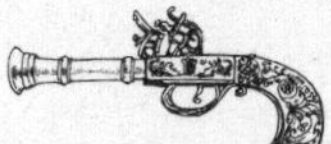

Eiichiro Oda began his manga career at the age of 17, when his one-shot cowboy manga **Wanted!** won second place in the coveted Tezuka manga awards. Oda went on to work as an assistant to some of the biggest manga artists in the industry, including Nobuhiro Watsuki, before winning the Hop Step Award for new artists. His pirate adventure **One Piece**, which debuted in **Weekly Shonen Jump** in 1997, quickly became one of the most popular manga in Japan.

ONE PIECE VOL. 11
EAST BLUE PART 11

SHONEN JUMP Manga Edition

This graphic novel contains material that was originally published in English in **SHONEN JUMP** #39–41.

STORY AND ART BY EIICHIRO ODA

English Adaptation/Lance Caselman
Translation/JN Productions & Michie Yamakawa
Touch-up Art & Lettering/Mark McMurray, Vanessa Satone
Additional Touch-up/Josh Simpson
Design/Sean Lee
Editor/Yuki Takagaki

Printed in the U.S.A.

Published by VIZ Media, LLC
P.O. Box 77010
San Francisco, CA 94107

20
First printing, July 2006
Twentieth printing, November 2023

viz.com

SHONEN JUMP MANGA

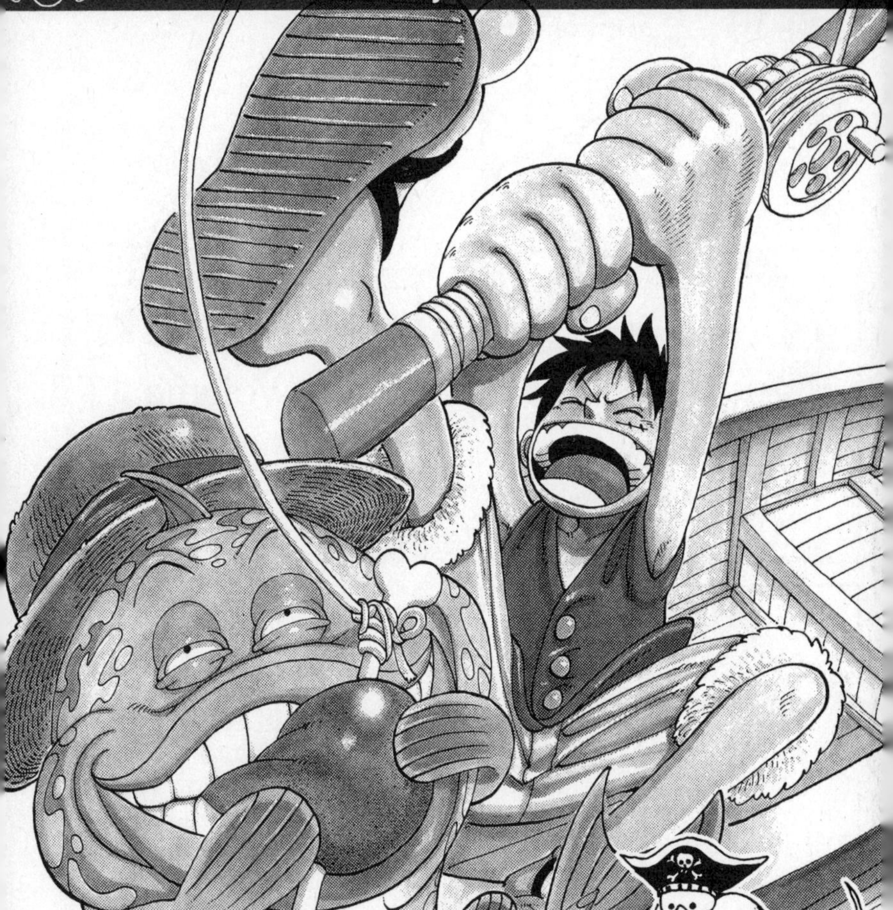

ONE PIECE

Vol. 11

THE MEANEST MAN IN THE EAST

STORY AND ART BY

EIICHIRO ODA

THE STORY OF ONE PIECE

Volume 11

Monkey D. Luffy started out as just a kid with a dream—and that dream was to become the greatest pirate in history! Stirred by the tales of pirate "Red-Haired" Shanks, Luffy vowed to become a pirate himself. That was before the enchanted Devil Fruit gave Luffy the power to stretch like rubber, at the cost of being unable to swim—a serious handicap for an aspiring sea dog. Undeterred, Luffy set out to sea and recruited some crewmates: master swordsman Zolo, treasure-hunting thief Nami, lying sharpshooter Usopp, and Sanji, the high-kicking chef.

Arlong

Nami
A thief who once specialized in robbing pirates. Although she hates pirates, Luffy convinced her to be his navigator.

Monkey D. Luffy
Boundlessly optimistic and able to stretch like rubber, he is determined to become King of the Pirates.

Usopp
His penchant for tall tales is matched by his accuracy with a slingshot. His father, Yasopp, is a member of "Red-Haired" Shanks's crew.

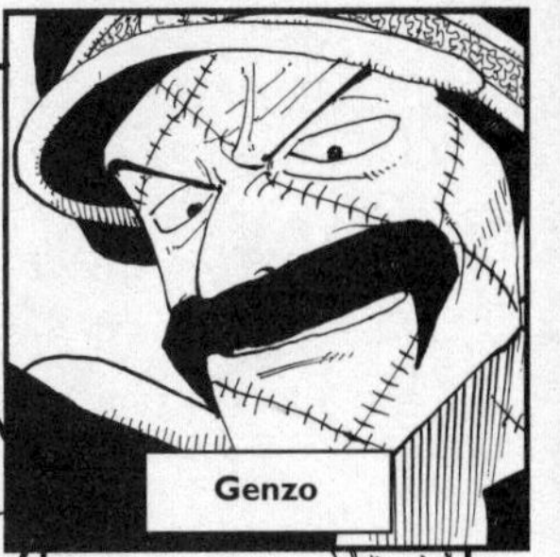

Genzo

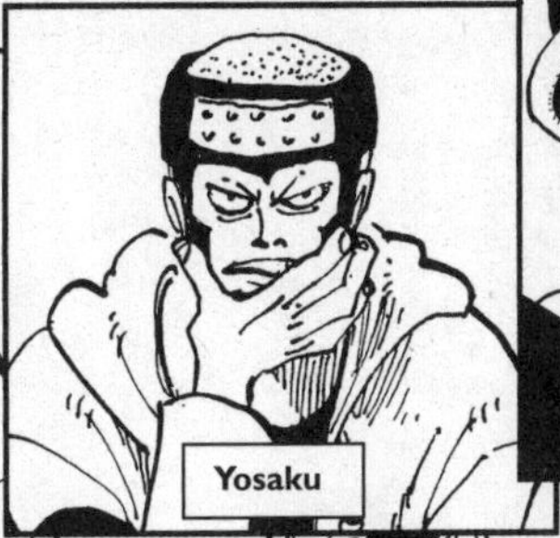

Yosaku

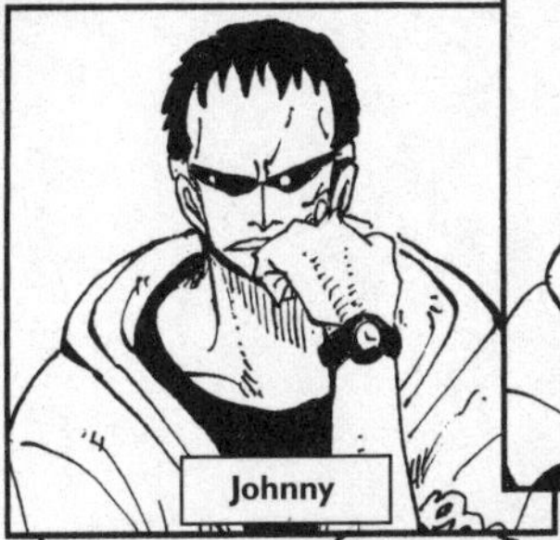

Johnny

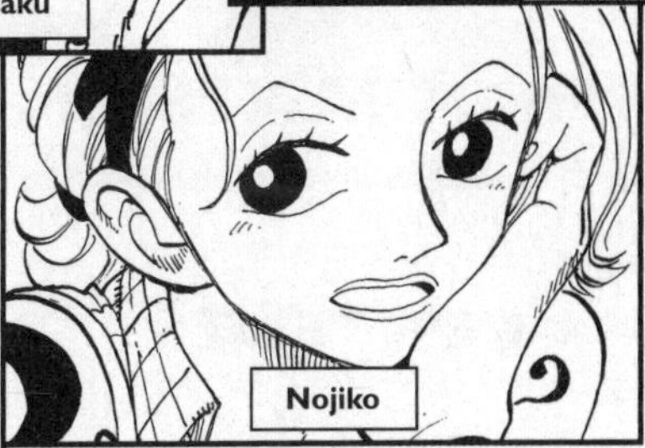

Nojiko

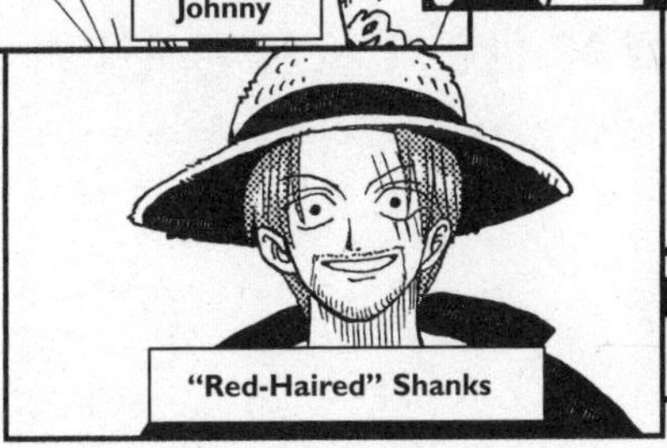

"Red-Haired" Shanks

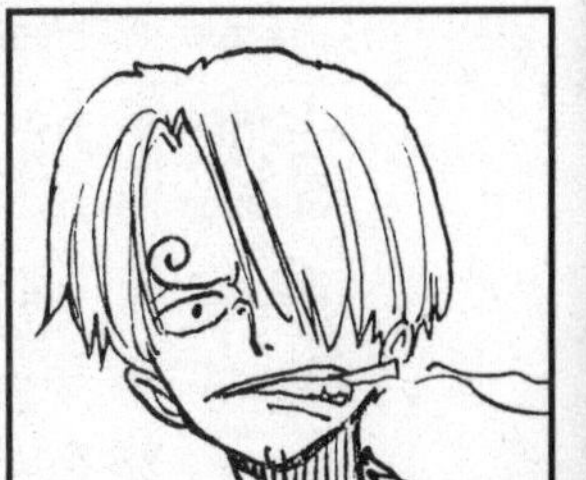

Sanji
The kind-hearted cook (and ladies' man) whose dream is to find the legendary sea, the "All Blue."

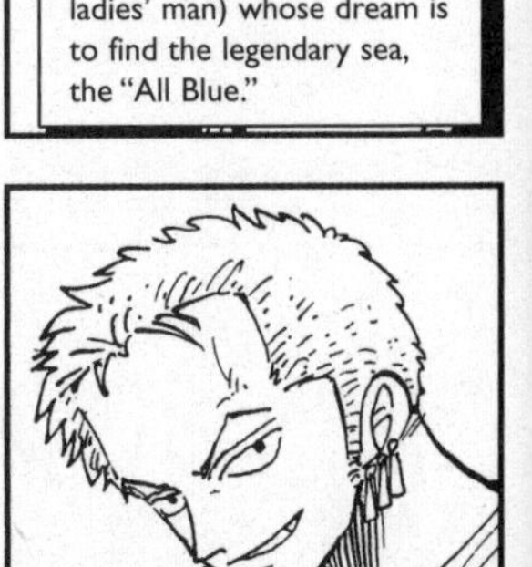

Roronoa Zolo
A former bounty hunter and master of the "three-sword" fighting style. He plans to become the world's greatest swordsman!

Searching for Nami, Luffy and his crew head to Arlong Park, stronghold of the ferocious Fish-Man Pirates, only to discover that Nami herself is one of them! They learn the story of Belle Mère and the origin of Nami's hatred of pirates from Nami's stepsister, Nojiko, who also explains how Nami swallowed her hatred and went to work for Arlong, gathering loot to buy her village's freedom.

Moved by Nami's secret suffering, Luffy goes toe to toe with Arlong, but is hurled into the ocean! Sanji and the others fight and defeat Arlong's men and rescue Luffy. But they still have to contend with the most terrible foe of all—Arlong himself!

Vol. 11
THE MEANEST MAN IN THE EAST

CONTENTS

Chapter 91: DARTS

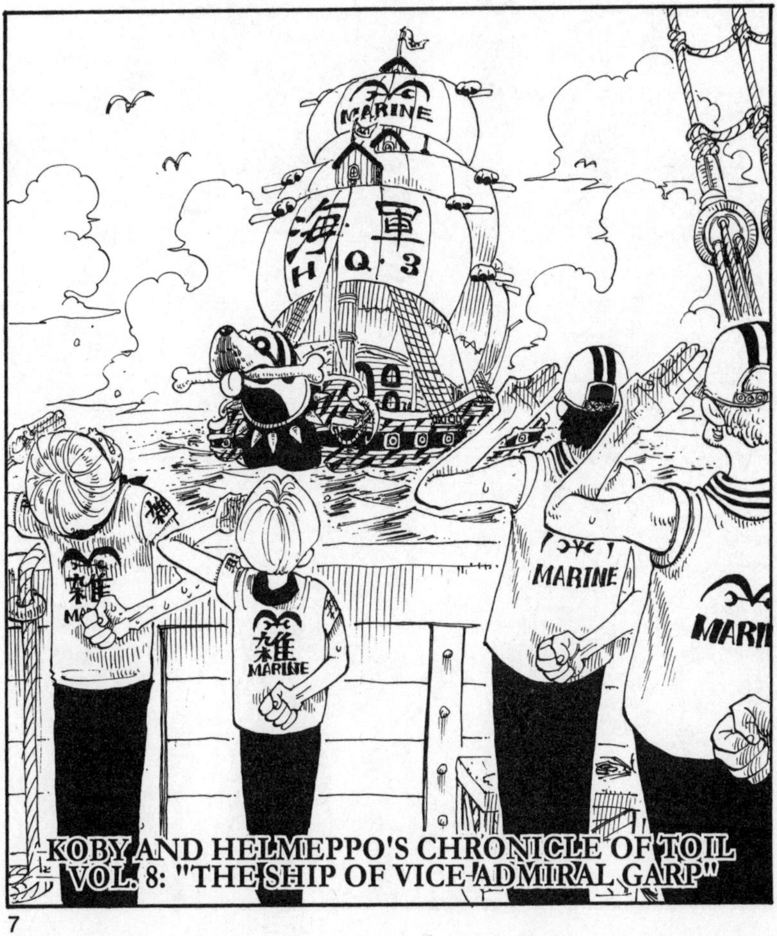
MARINE
海軍
H Q 3
MARINE
MARINE
MARINE
KOBY AND HELMEPPO'S CHRONICLE OF TOIL
VOL. 8: "THE SHIP OF VICE-ADMIRAL GARP"

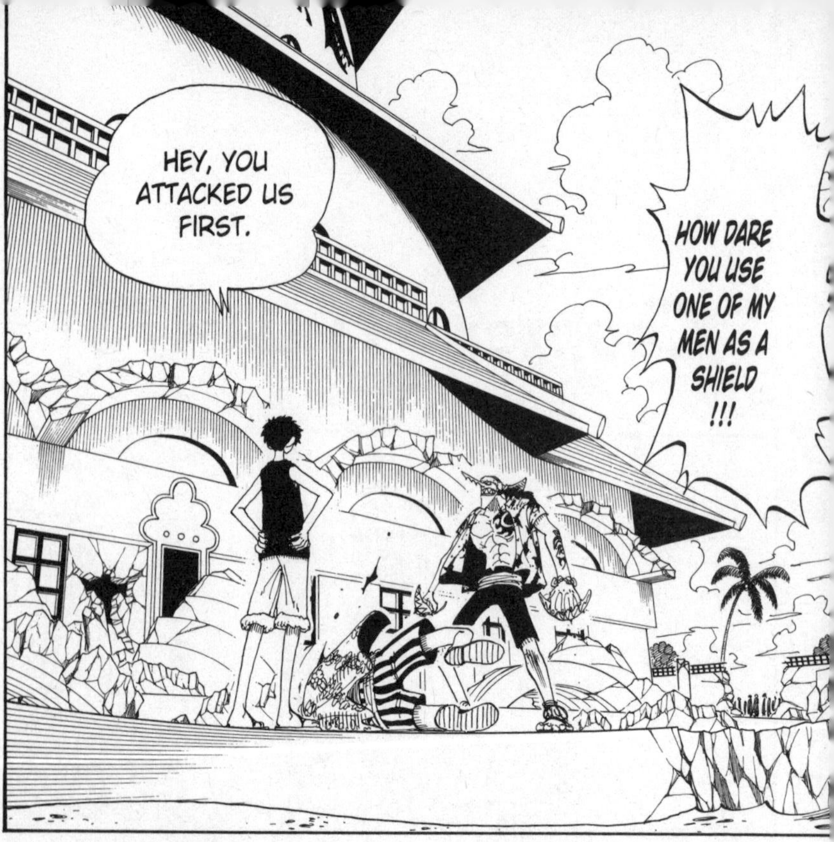
HOW DARE YOU USE ONE OF MY MEN AS A SHIELD !!!
HEY, YOU ATTACKED US FIRST.

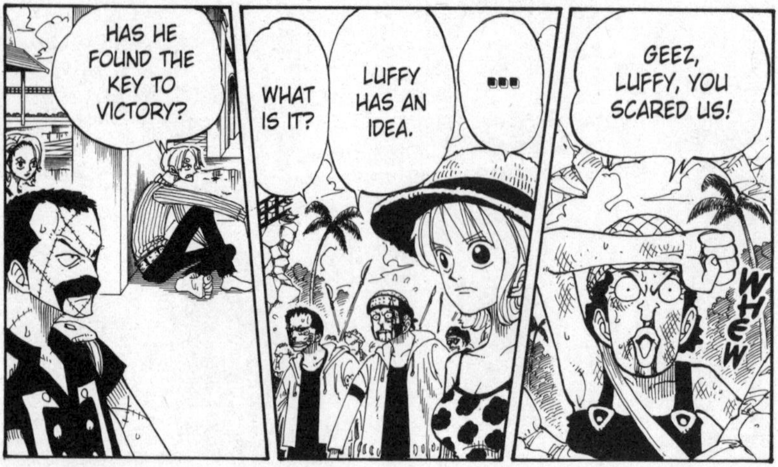
GEEZ, LUFFY, YOU SCARED US!
WHEW
...
LUFFY HAS AN IDEA.
WHAT IS IT?
HAS HE FOUND THE KEY TO VICTORY?

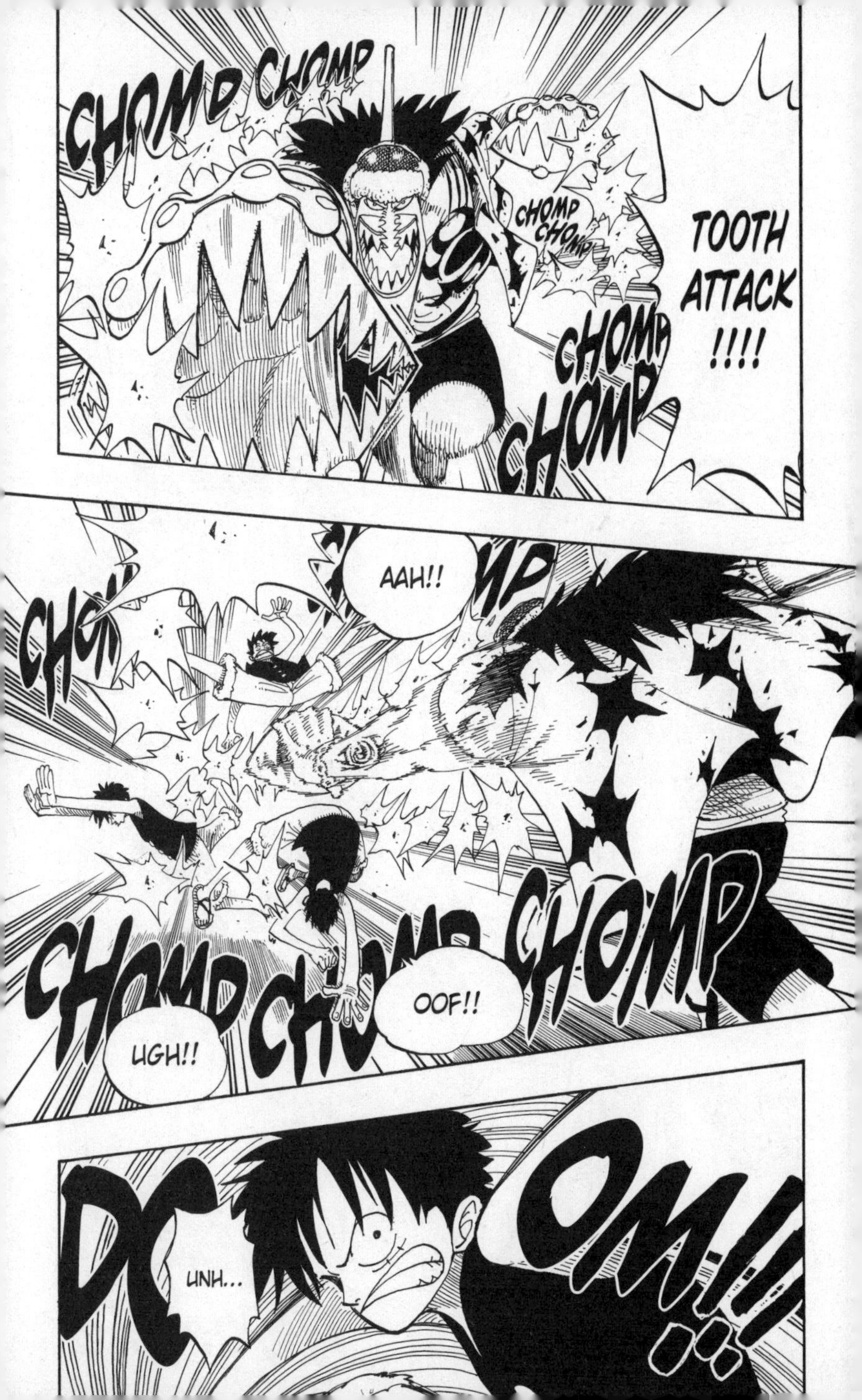
TOOTH ATTACK!!!!
CHOMP CHOMP
CHOMP CHOMP
CHOMP CHOMP
AAH!!
CHOMP
OOF!!
CHOMP CHOMP
UGH!!
UNH...

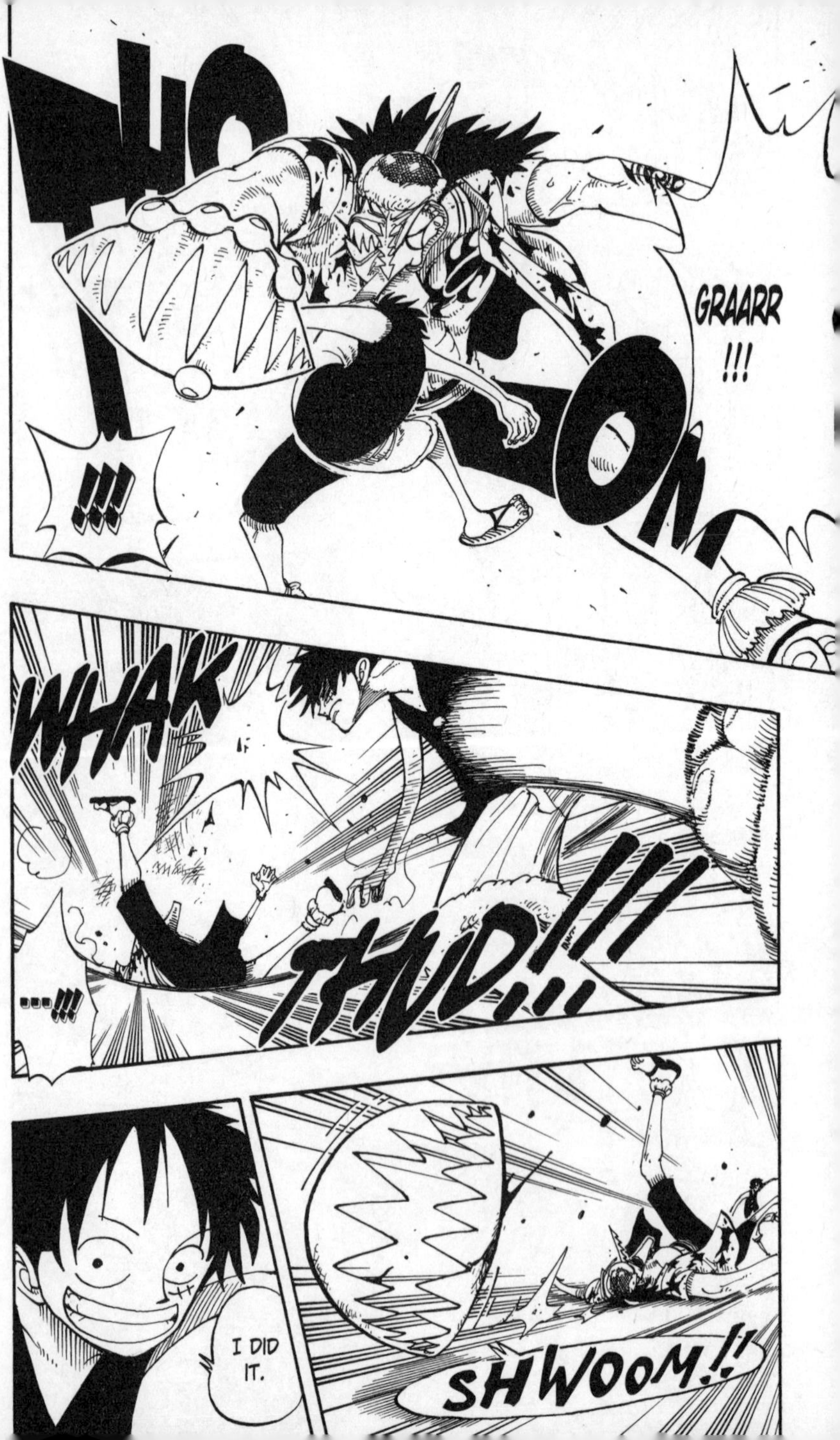
GRAARR !!!
THOOM
!!!
WHAK
THUD!!!
...!!!
SHWOOM!!
I DID IT.

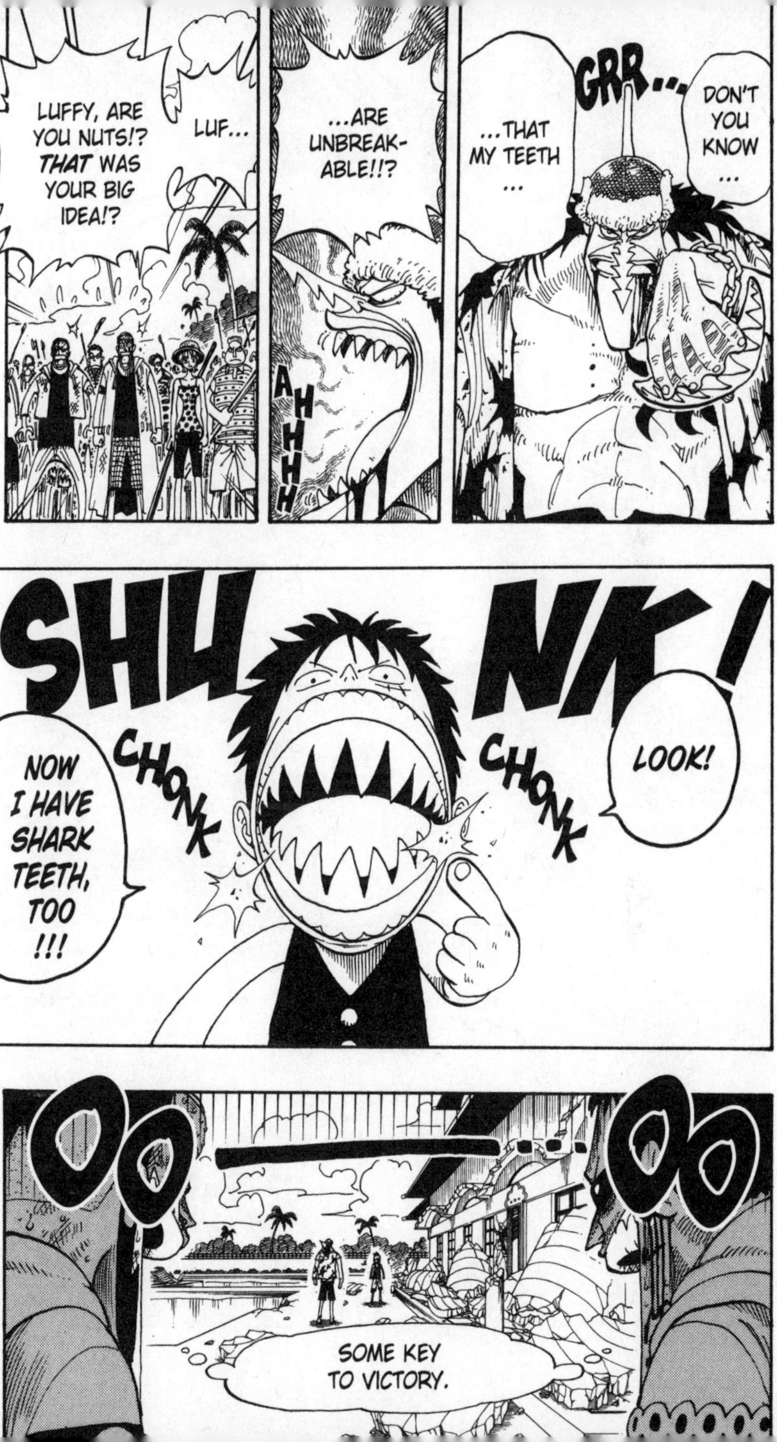
GRR...
DON'T YOU KNOW ...
...THAT MY TEETH ...
...ARE UNBREAK-ABLE!!?
AHHHH
LUF...
LUFFY, ARE YOU NUTS!? *THAT* WAS YOUR BIG IDEA!?
SHUNK!
LOOK!
CHONK
CHONK
NOW I HAVE SHARK TEETH, TOO !!!
OO—OO
SOME KEY TO VICTORY.

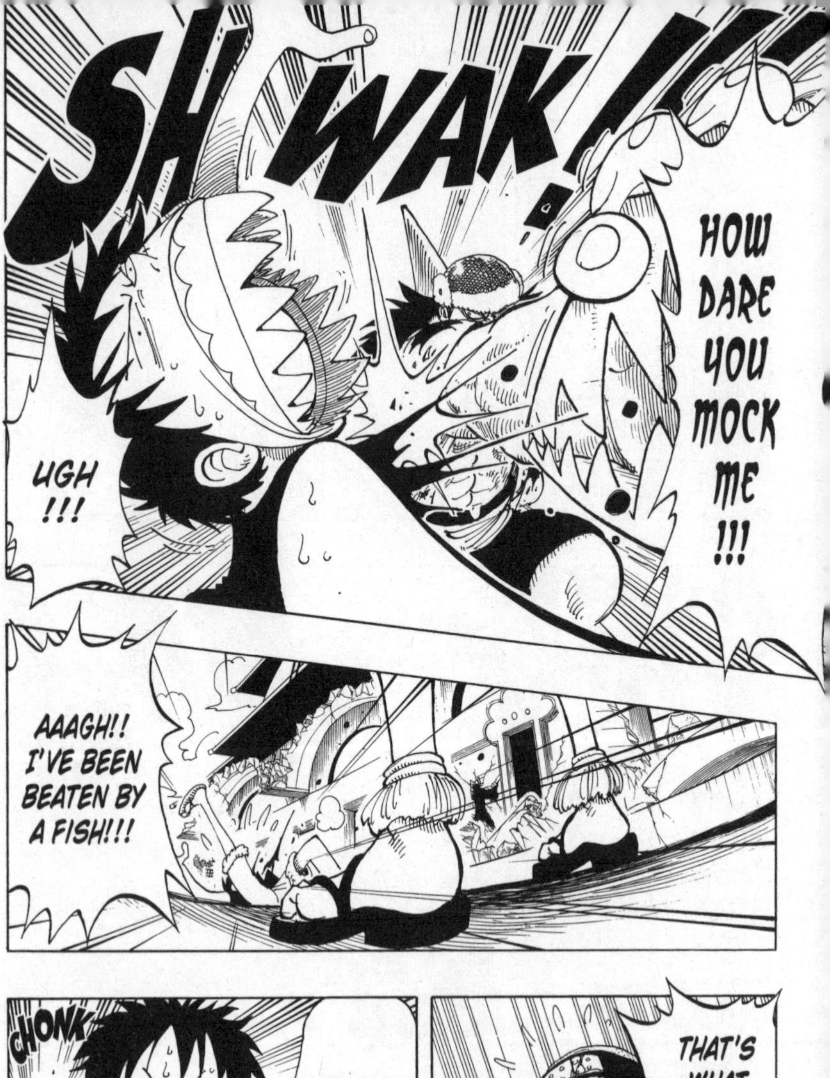
SHWAK!!
HOW DARE YOU MOCK ME!!!
UGH!!!
AAAGH!! I'VE BEEN BEATEN BY A FISH!!!
THAT'S WHAT YOU GET FOR FOOLING AROUND!!!
CHONK
I'M NOT FOOLING AROUND!!
CHONK
!!

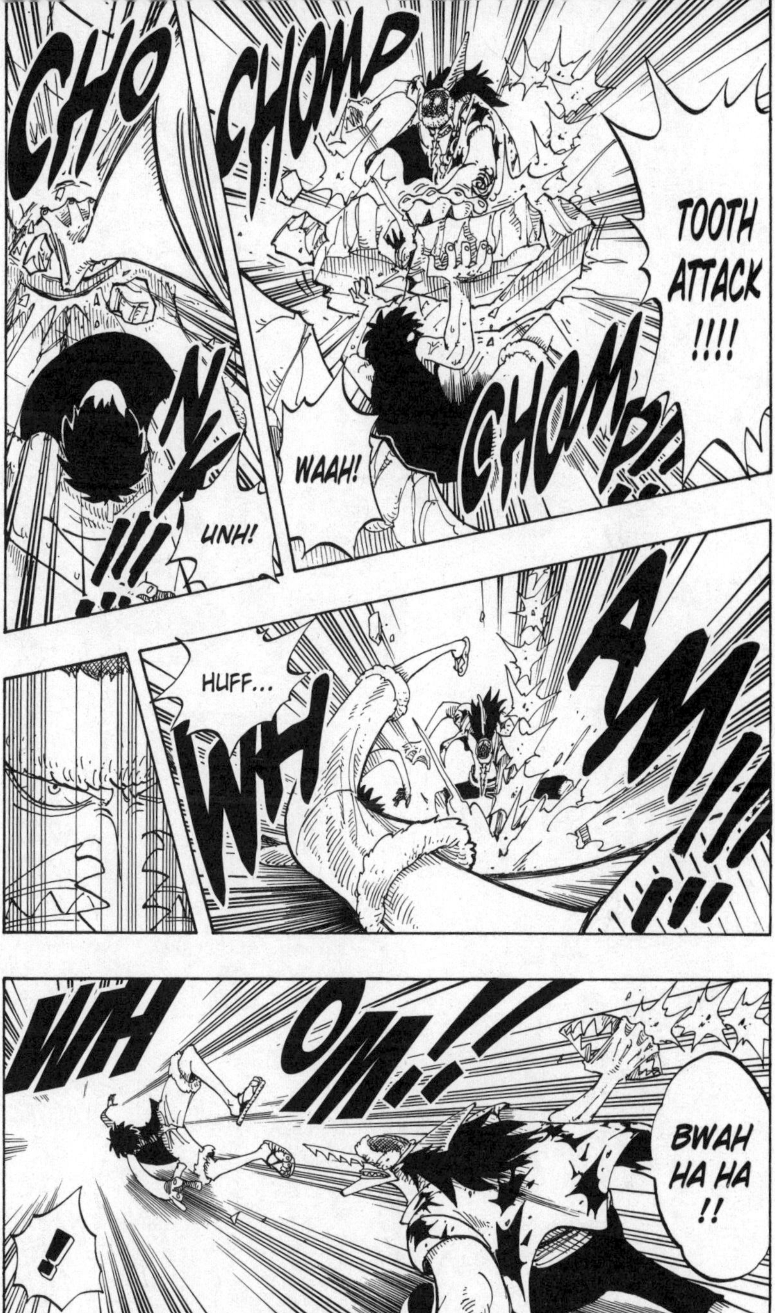
CHOMP
TOOTH ATTACK!!!!
CHOMP!!
WAAH!
CHO
NK!!!
UNH!
AM!!!
WH
HUFF...
BWAH HA HA!!
WH
OM!!
!

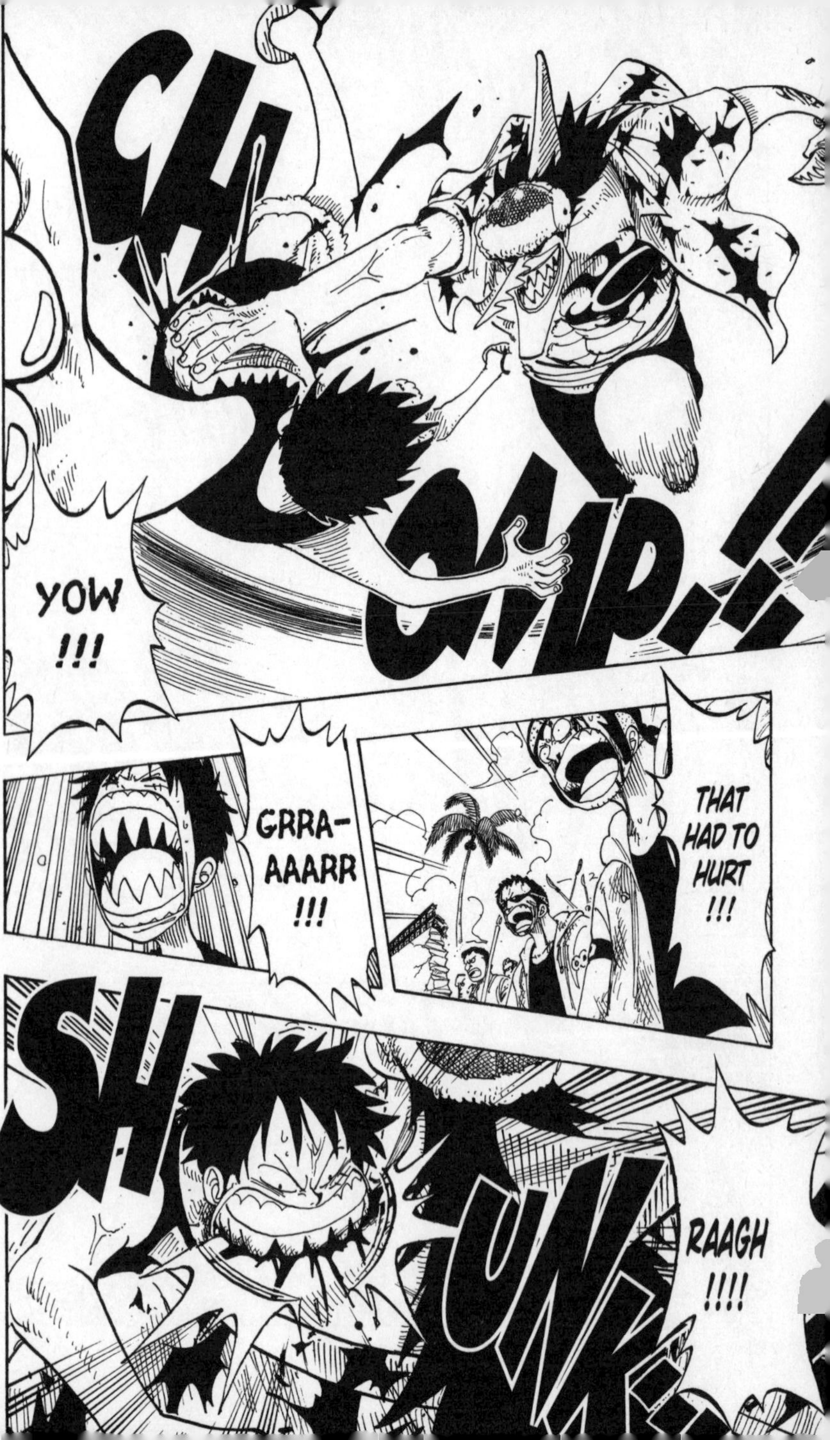
CHOMP..!!
YOW !!!
THAT HAD TO HURT !!!
GRRA-AAARR !!!
SH-UNK...
RAAGH !!!!

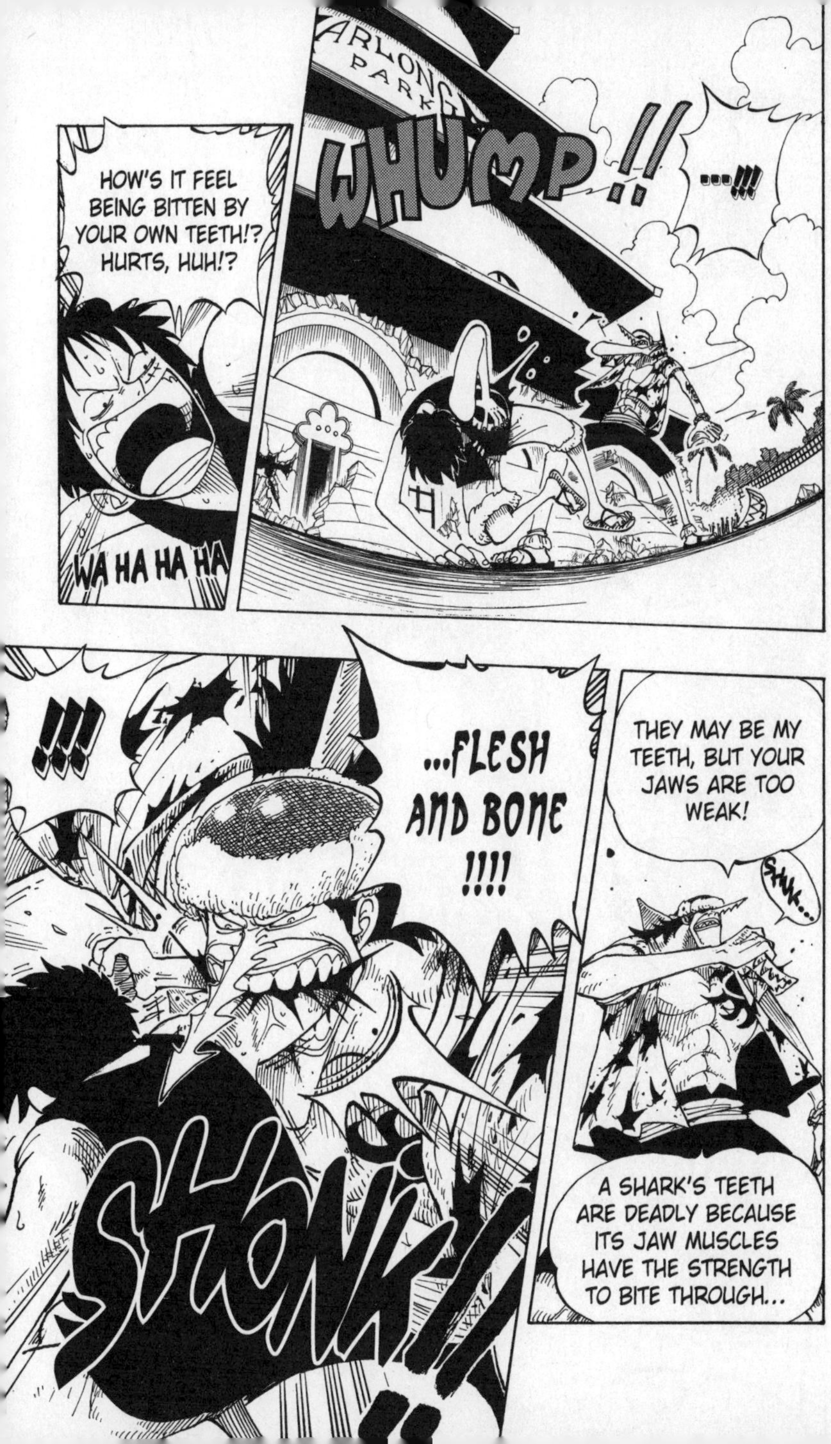
ARLONG PARK
WHUMP!!
...!!!
HOW'S IT FEEL BEING BITTEN BY YOUR OWN TEETH!? HURTS, HUH!?
WA HA HA HA
THEY MAY BE MY TEETH, BUT YOUR JAWS ARE TOO WEAK!
SHNK...
A SHARK'S TEETH ARE DEADLY BECAUSE ITS JAW MUSCLES HAVE THE STRENGTH TO BITE THROUGH...
...FLESH AND BONE !!!!
!!!
SHONK!!

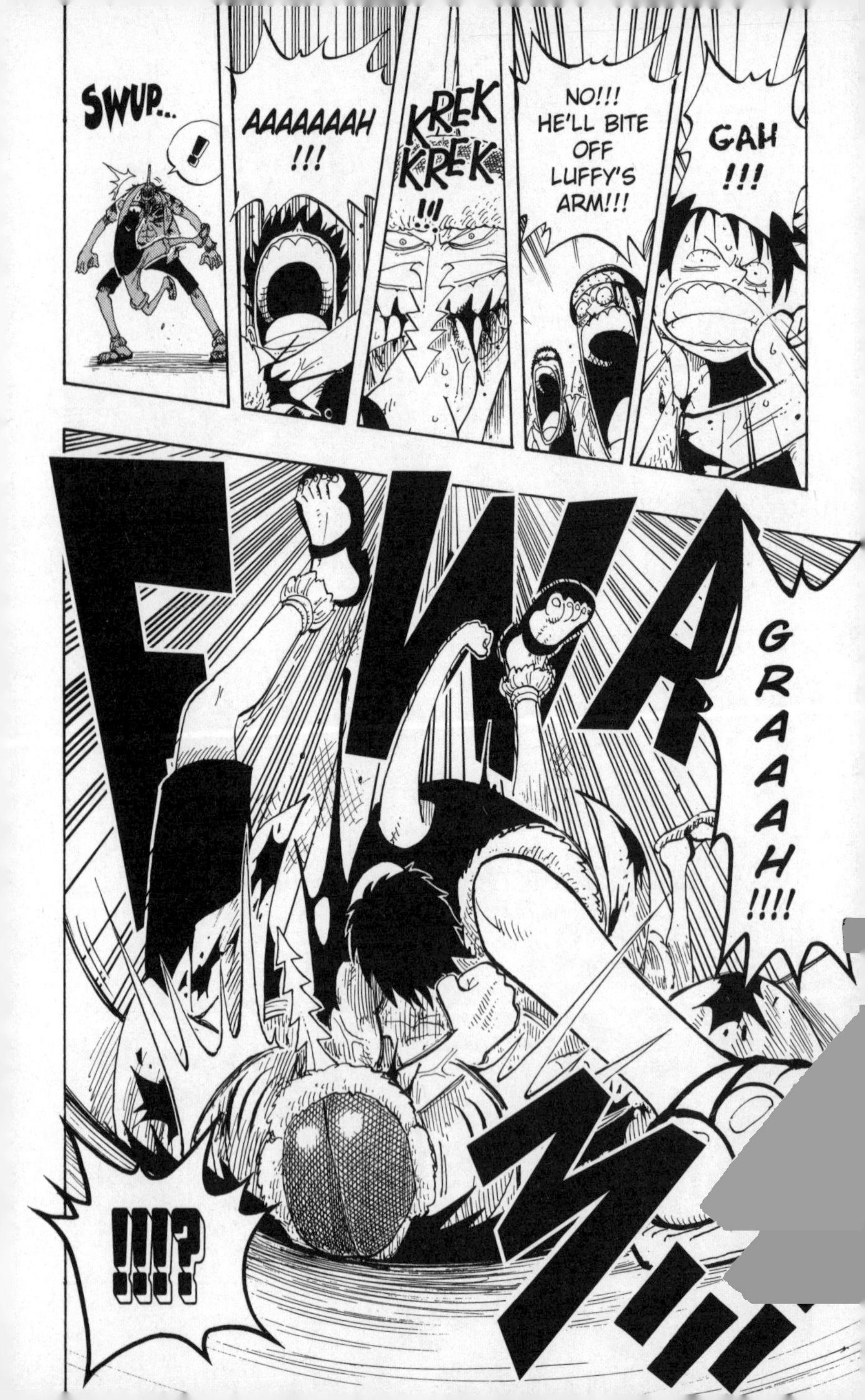
GAH !!!
NO!!! HE'LL BITE OFF LUFFY'S ARM!!!
KREK KREK !!!
AAAAAAAH !!!
SWUP...
!
GRAAAH!!!!
FWA
!!!?
ZN

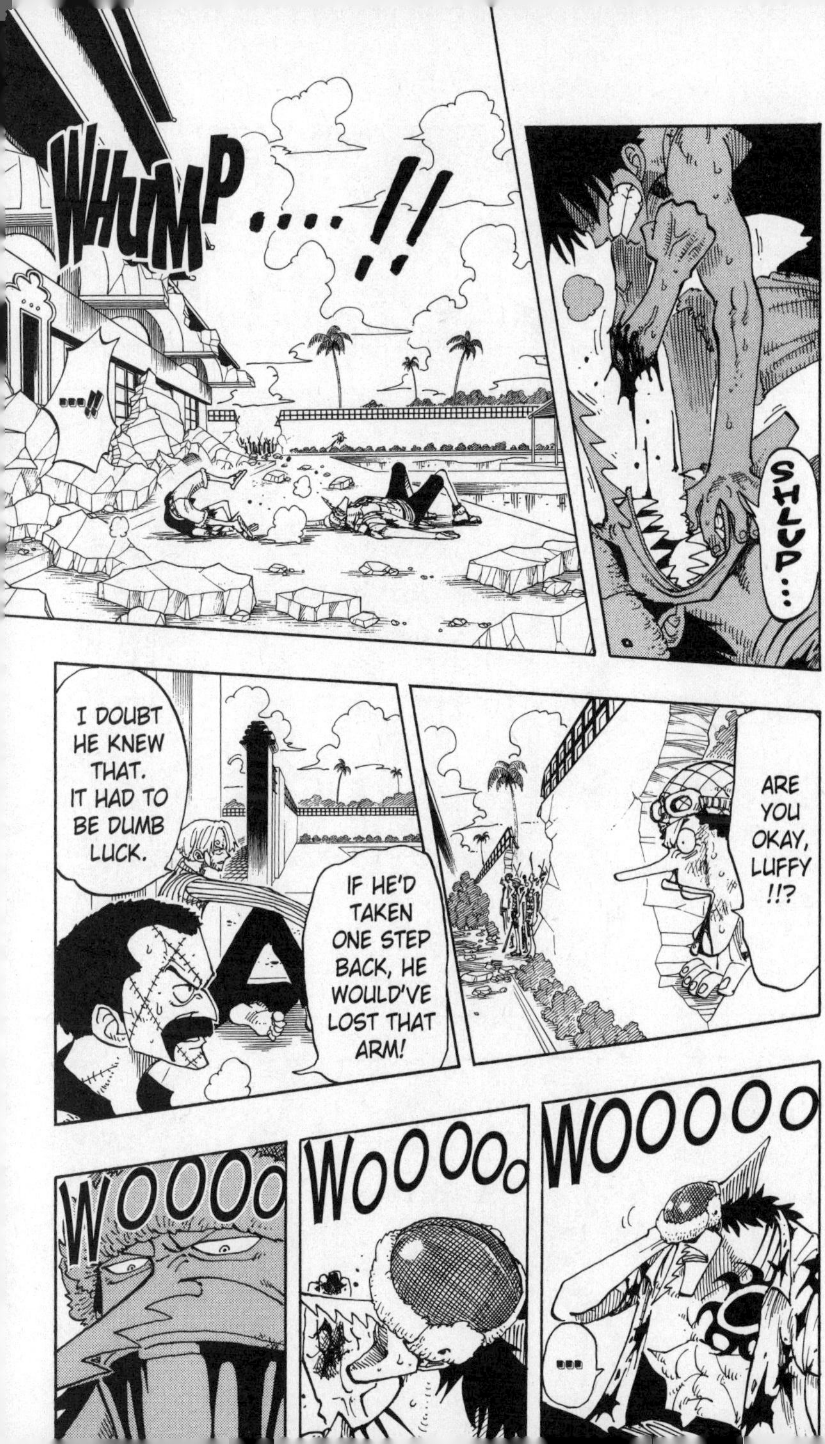
SHLUP...
WHUMP
....!!
...!!
ARE YOU OKAY, LUFFY!!?
IF HE'D TAKEN ONE STEP BACK, HE WOULD'VE LOST THAT ARM!
I DOUBT HE KNEW THAT. IT HAD TO BE DUMB LUCK.
WOOOOO
...
WOOOOo
WOOOO

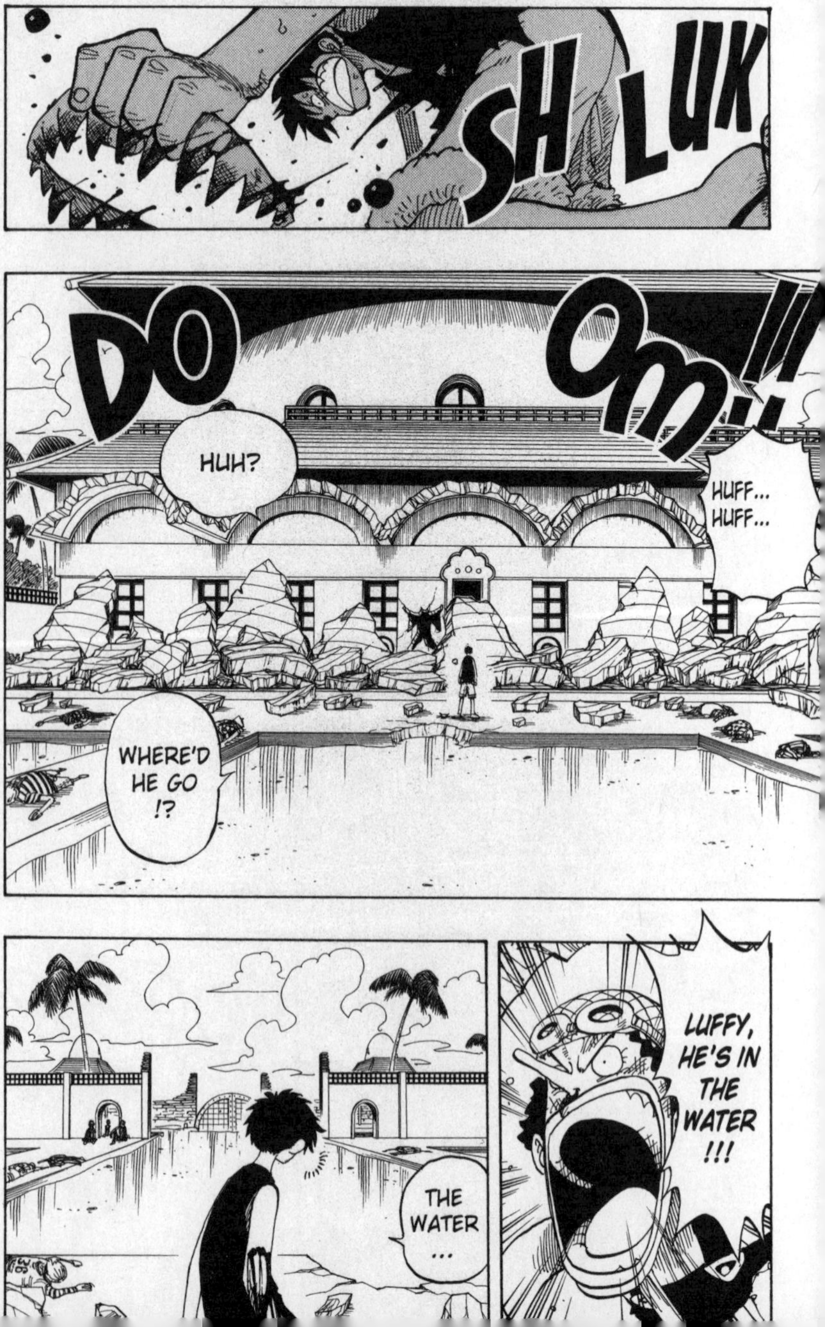
SHLUK
DOOM!!!
HUFF... HUFF...
HUH?
WHERE'D HE GO !?
LUFFY, HE'S IN THE WATER !!!
THE WATER ...

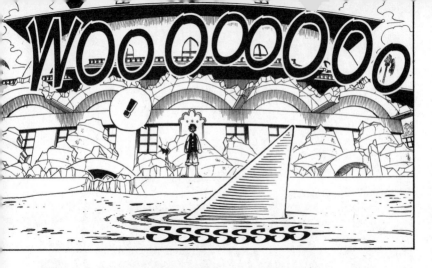

WOOOOOOO

SSSSSSSS

WHAT?

HE WENT UNDER.

GURGLE...

IT'S ARLONG!!!

HEY, A SHARK!!!

WHUP!

NOBODY CAN BEAT ME IN THE WATER! I'M EVEN FASTER IN MY OWN ELEMENT!!!

GLUP

GLUP

?

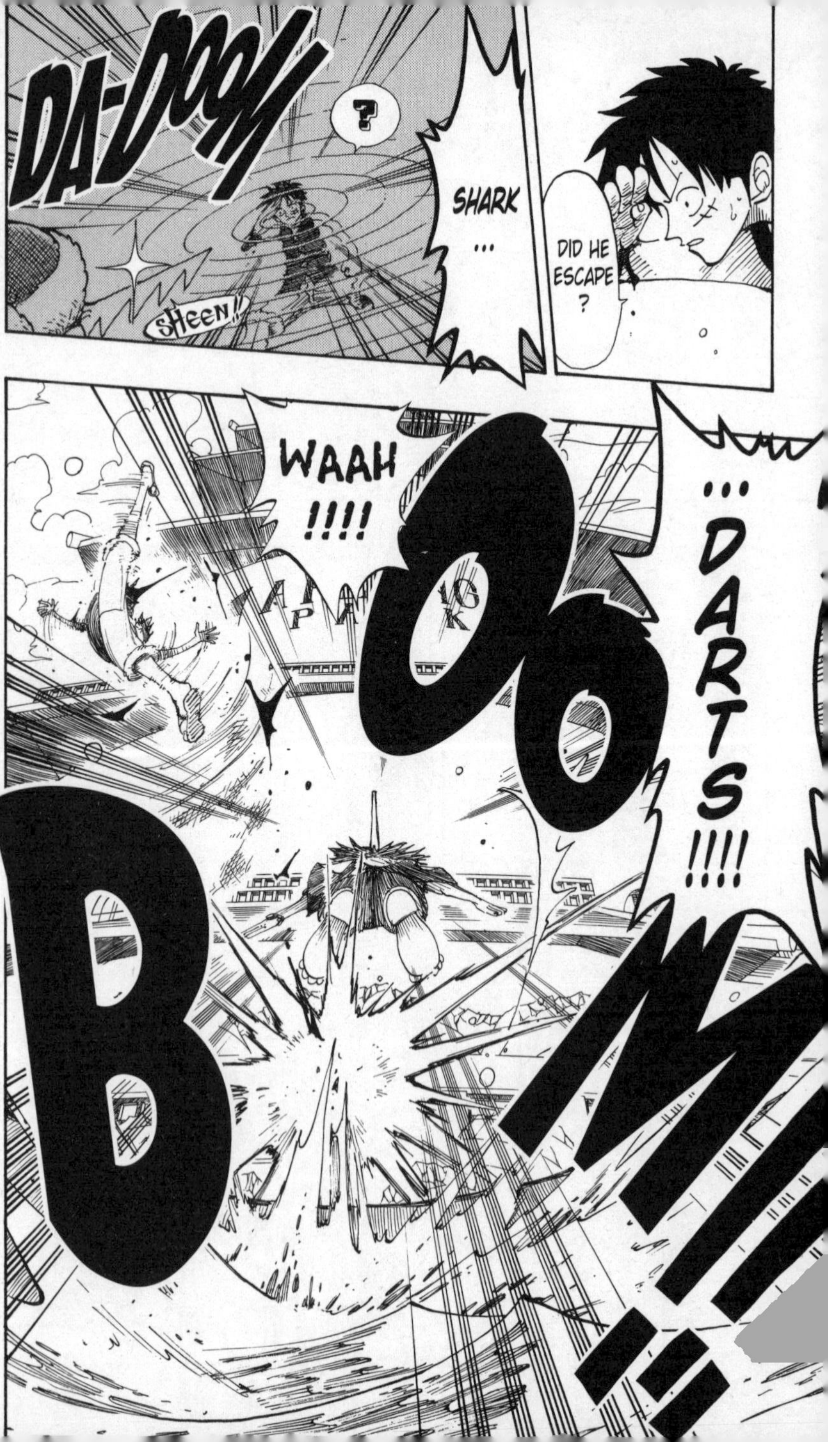
DID HE ESCAPE ?
SHARK ...
?
DA-DOOM
SHEEN!!
WAAH !!!!
...DARTS !!!!
BOOM!!

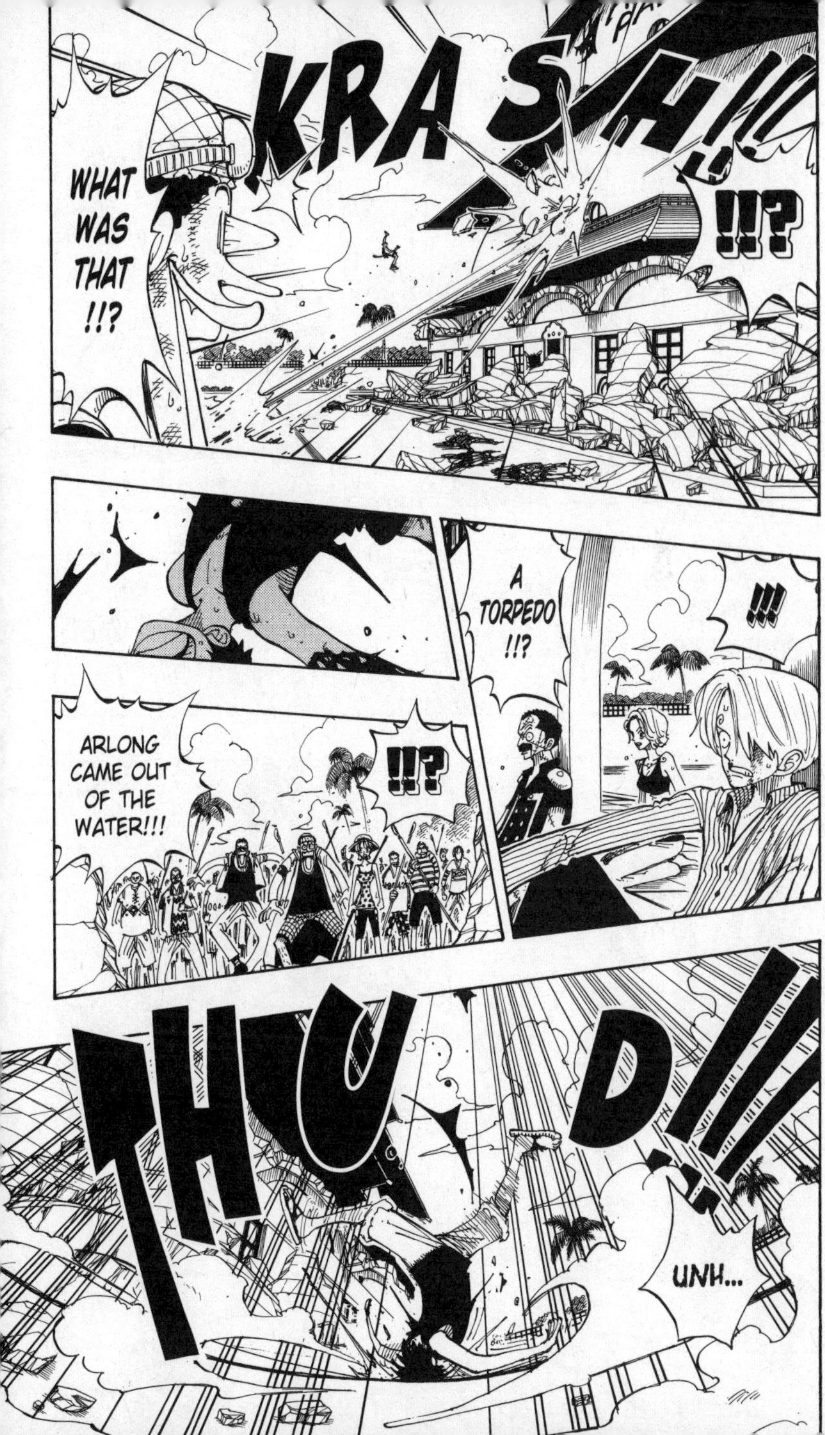
KRASH!!
!!?
WHAT WAS THAT!!?
!!!
A TORPEDO!!?
!!?
ARLONG CAME OUT OF THE WATER!!!
THUD!!
UNH...

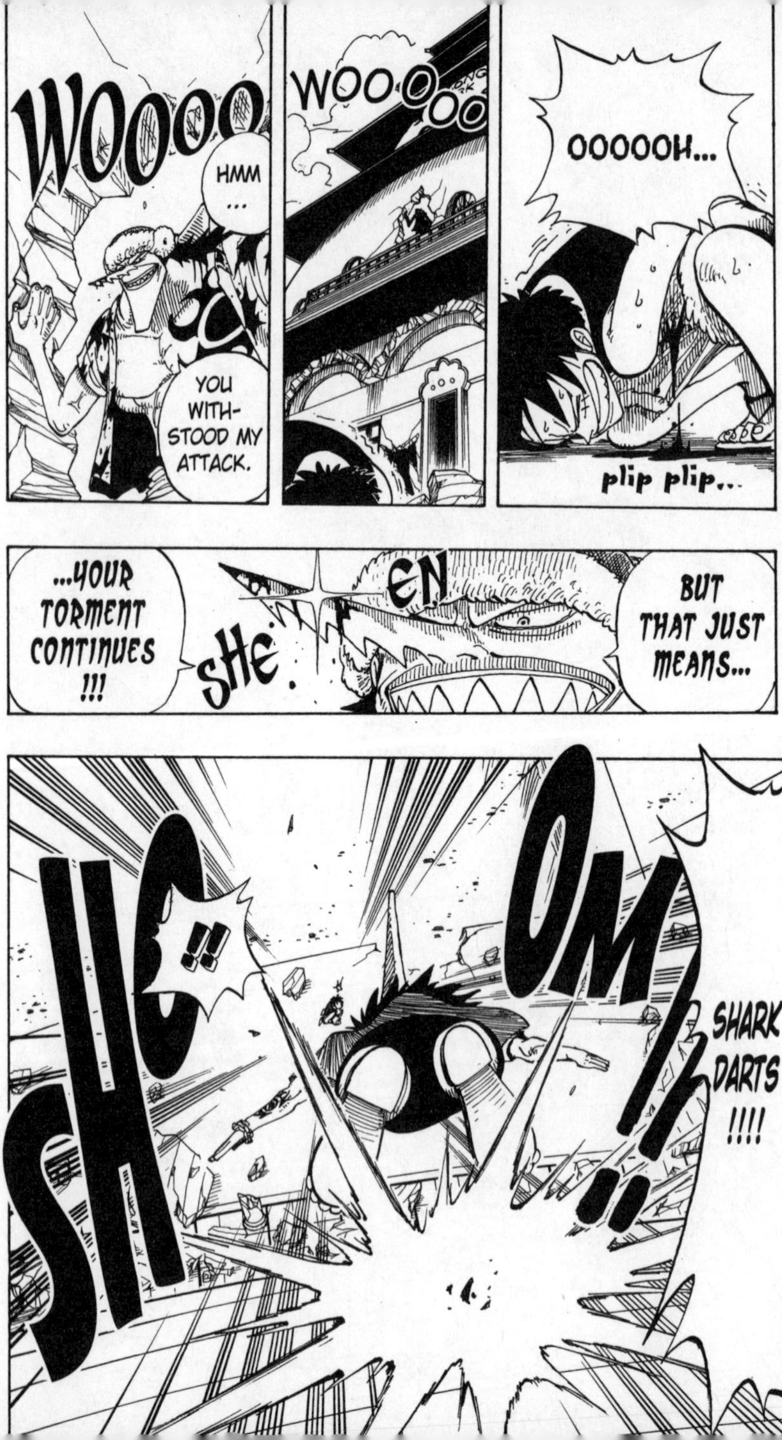
OOOOOH...
plip plip...
WOOOOOOO
WOOOO
HMM ...
YOU WITHSTOOD MY ATTACK.
BUT THAT JUST MEANS...
SHEEN
...YOUR TORMENT CONTINUES!!!
SHARK DARTS!!!!

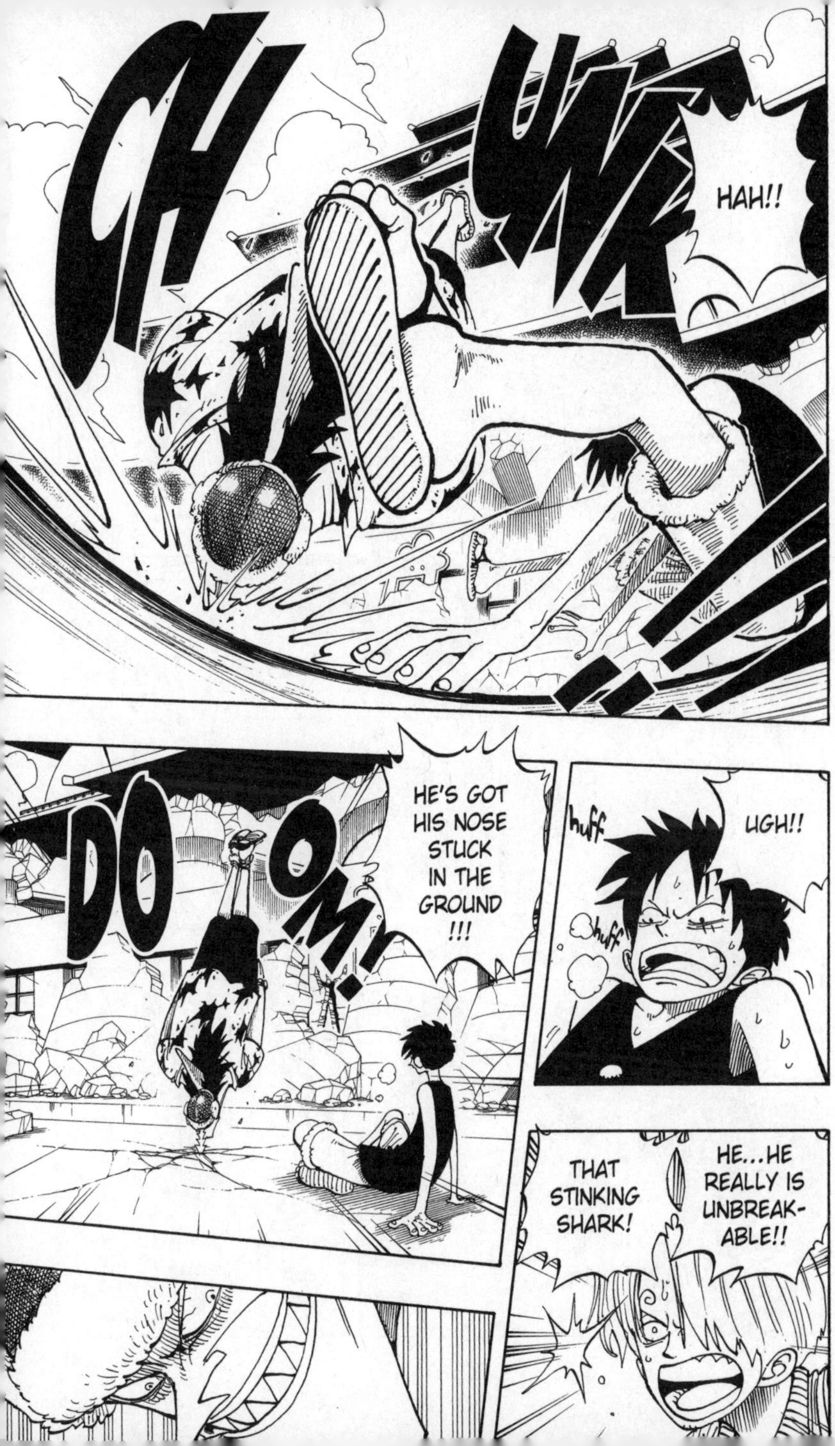
HAH!!
CHUNK!!
huff
UGH!!
huff
HE'S GOT HIS NOSE STUCK IN THE GROUND!!!
DOOM!
HE...HE REALLY IS UNBREAK-ABLE!!
THAT STINKING SHARK!

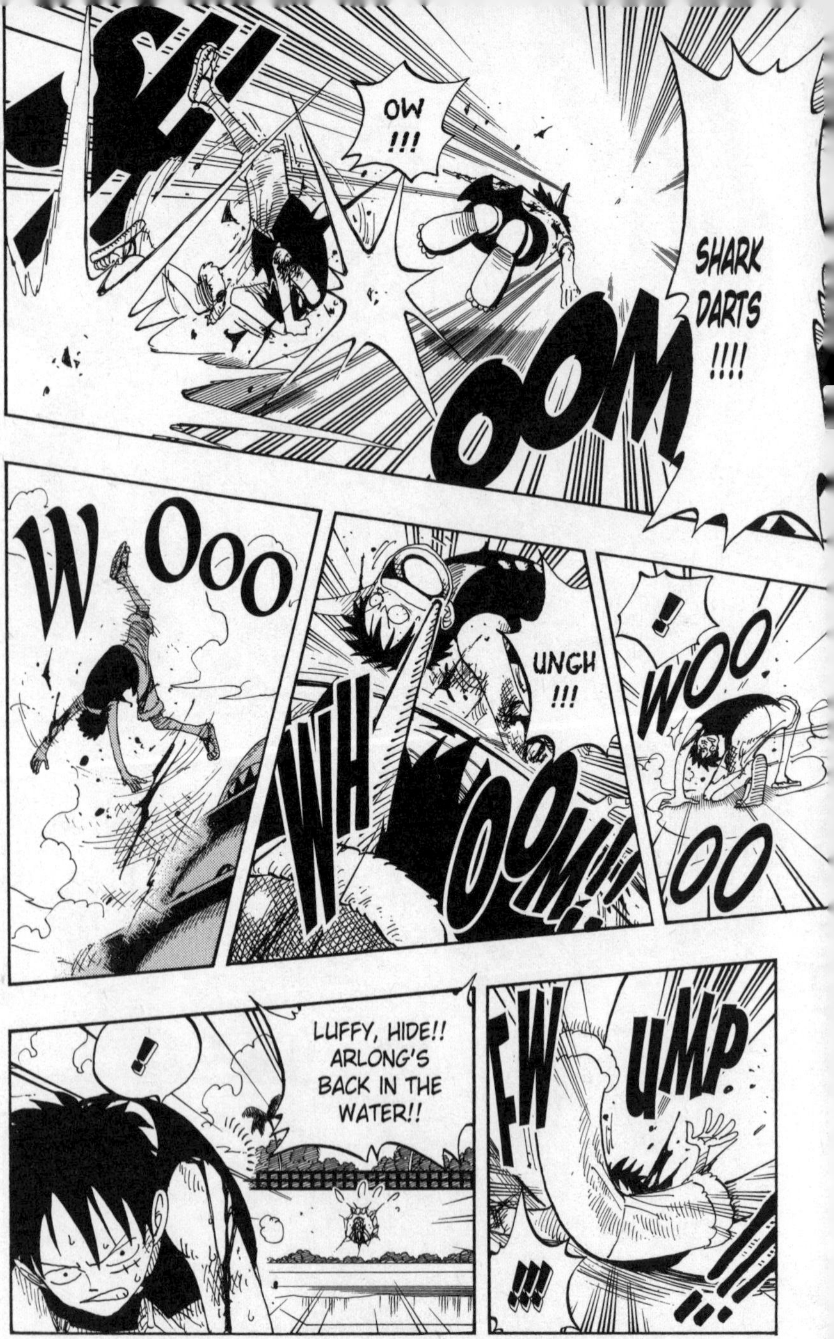
SHARK DARTS !!!!
OOM
OW !!!
!
WOO
OO
UNGH !!!
WH
OOM!!
W OOO
FW UMP
!!!
!!!
!
LUFFY, HIDE!! ARLONG'S BACK IN THE WATER!!

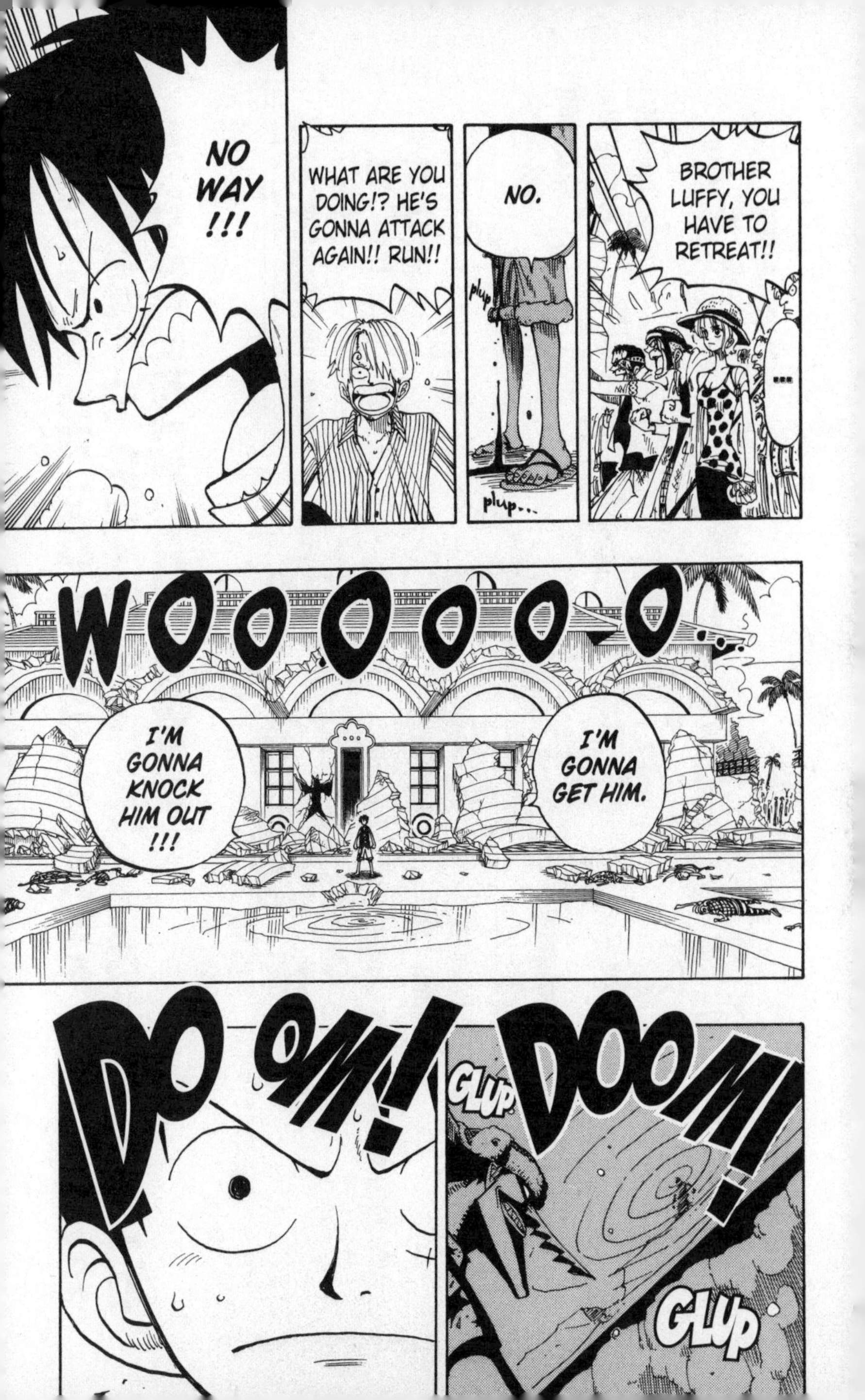
BROTHER LUFFY, YOU HAVE TO RETREAT!!
...
NO.
plup
plup...
WHAT ARE YOU DOING!? HE'S GONNA ATTACK AGAIN!! RUN!!
NO WAY!!!
WOOOOOOO
I'M GONNA GET HIM.
I'M GONNA KNOCK HIM OUT!!!
DOOM!
GLUP
GLUP
DOOM!

INSTEAD OF THE SBS QUESTION CORNER, HERE'S A CUT-AWAY VIEW OF LUFFY'S SHIP, THE *MERRY GO*. A LOT OF READERS HAVE ASKED ABOUT IT.

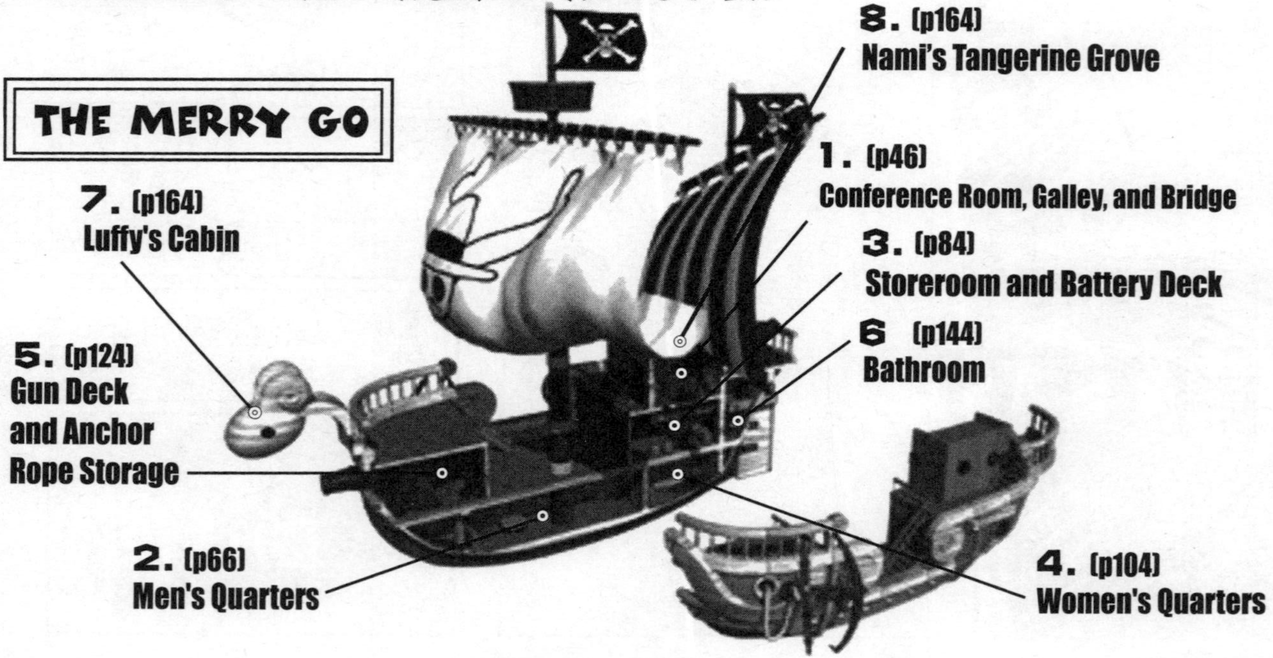

THE MERRY GO
8. (p164)
Nami's Tangerine Grove
1. (p46)
Conference Room, Galley, and Bridge
3. (p84)
Storeroom and Battery Deck
6 (p144)
Bathroom
7. (p164)
Luffy's Cabin
5. (p124)
Gun Deck and Anchor Rope Storage
2. (p66)
Men's Quarters
4. (p104)
Women's Quarters

Chapter 92: HAPPINESS

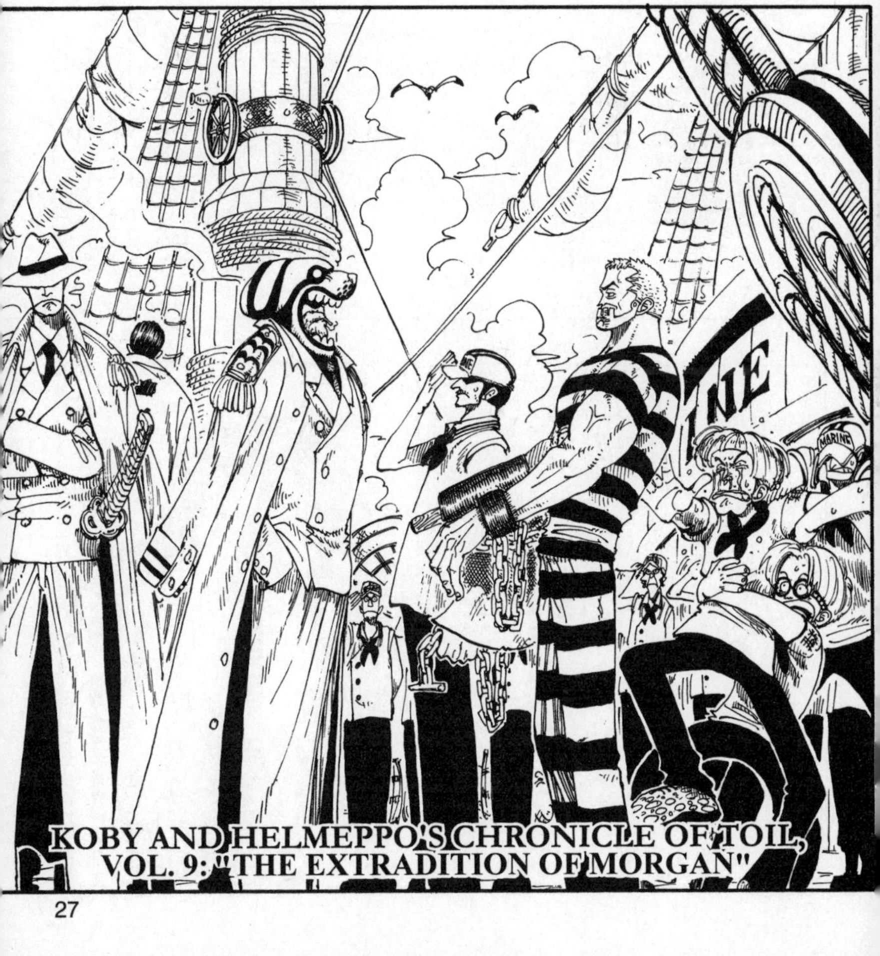
KOBY AND HELMEPPO'S CHRONICLE OF TOIL,
VOL. 9: "THE EXTRADITION OF MORGAN"

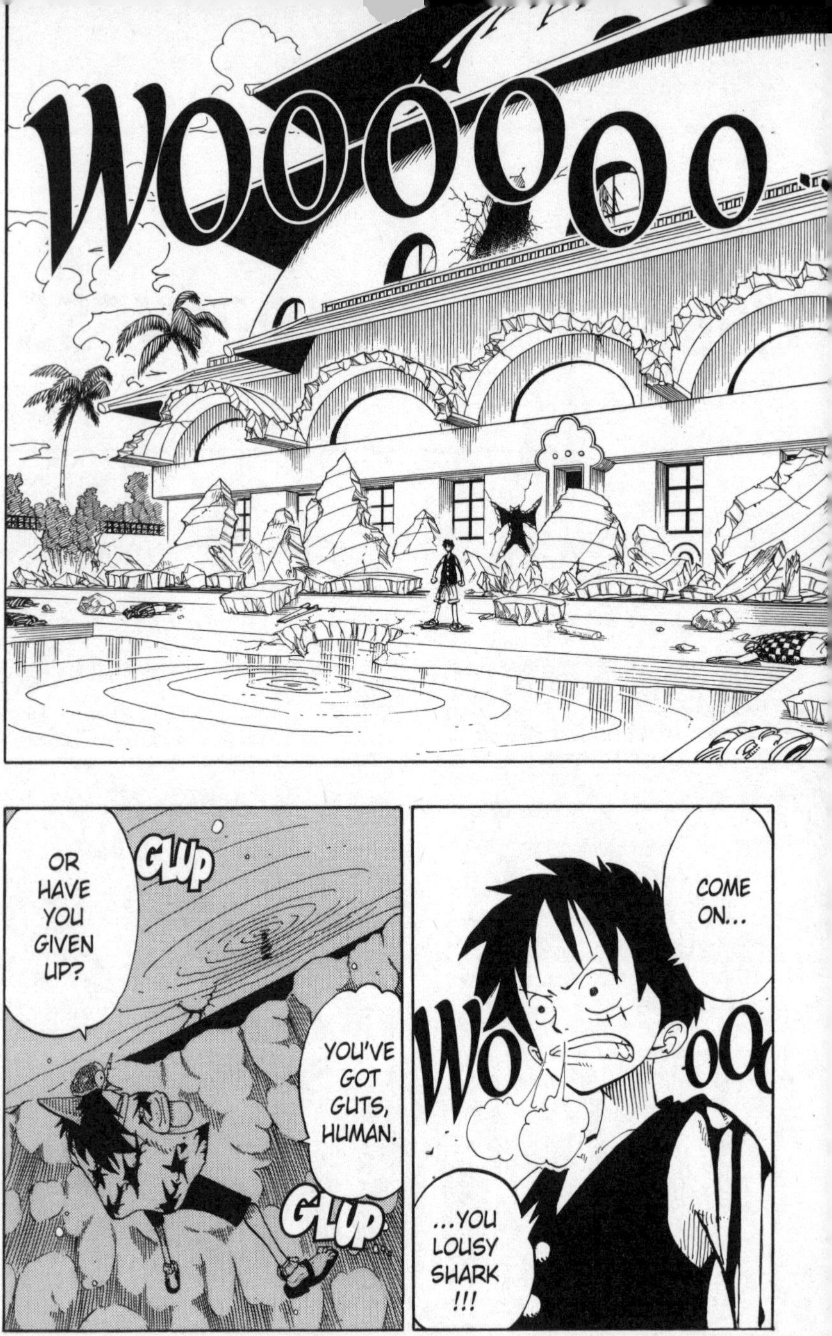
WOOOOOO...
COME ON...
WOOO
...YOU LOUSY SHARK !!!
GLUP
OR HAVE YOU GIVEN UP?
YOU'VE GOT GUTS, HUMAN.
GLUP...

READ THIS WAY

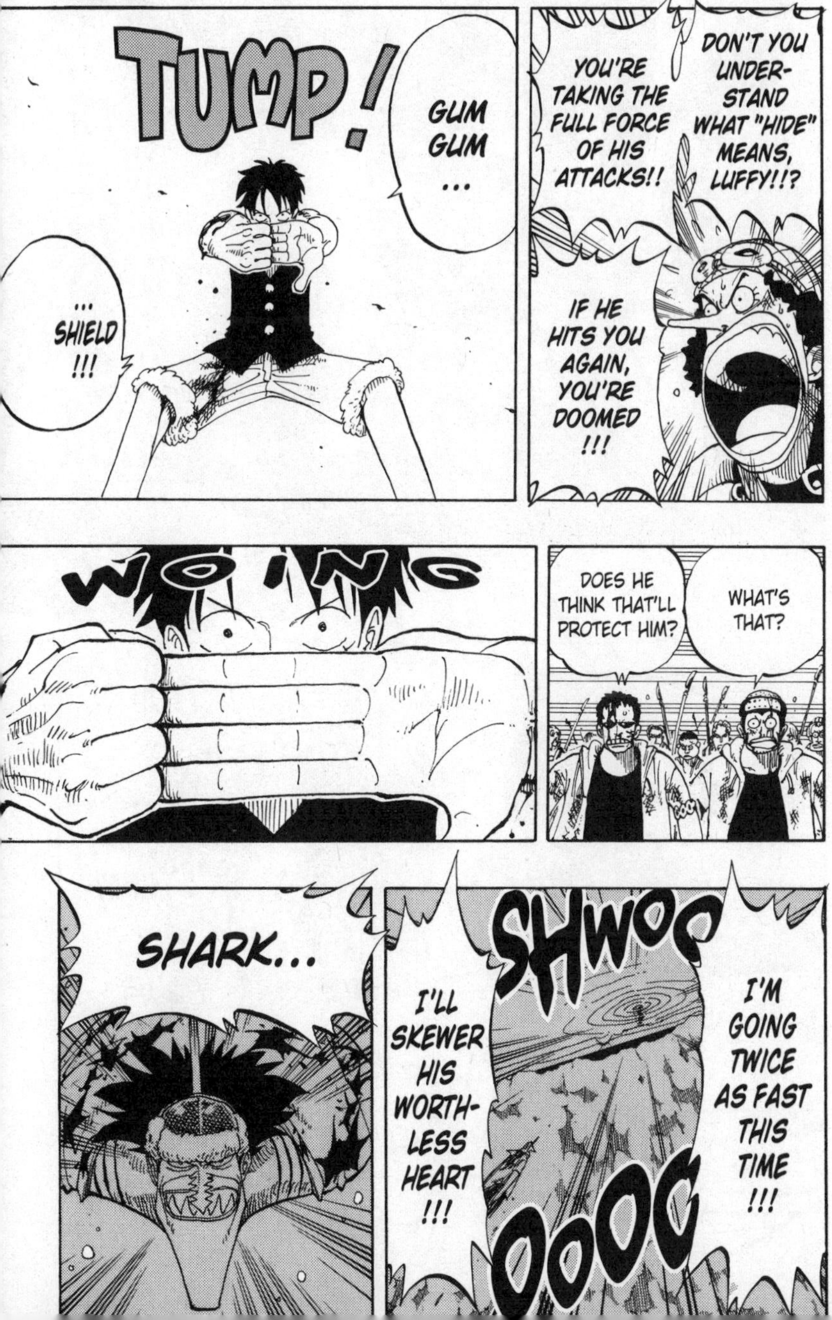
DON'T YOU UNDERSTAND WHAT "HIDE" MEANS, LUFFY!!?
YOU'RE TAKING THE FULL FORCE OF HIS ATTACKS!!
IF HE HITS YOU AGAIN, YOU'RE DOOMED!!!
TUMP!
GUM GUM ...
... SHIELD!!!
WHAT'S THAT?
DOES HE THINK THAT'LL PROTECT HIM?
WOING
SHWOO
I'M GOING TWICE AS FAST THIS TIME!!!
I'LL SKEWER HIS WORTHLESS HEART!!!
OOOC
SHARK...

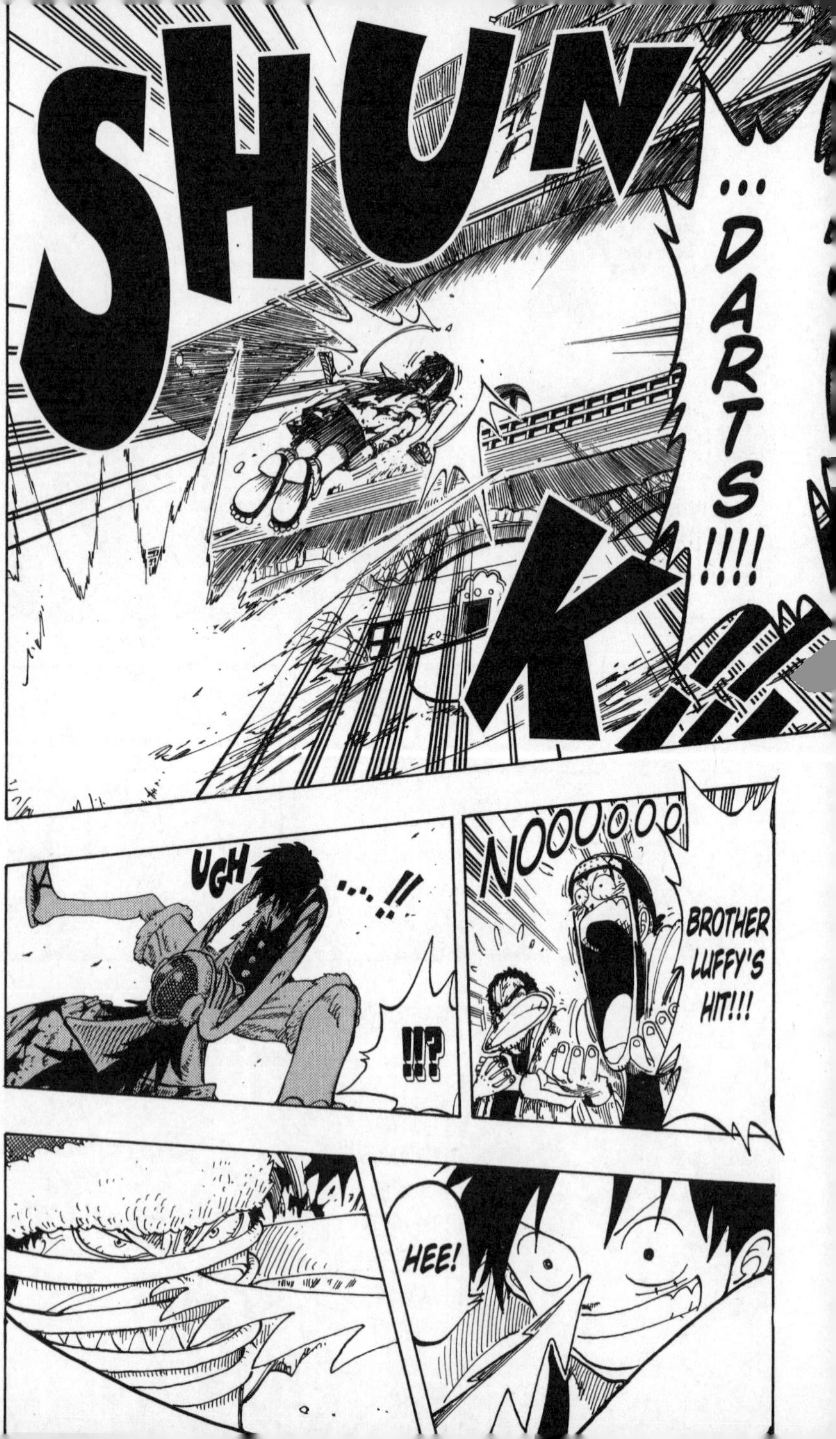
SHUN
...DARTS!!!!
K
NOOOOOOO
BROTHER LUFFY'S HIT!!!
UGH
...!!
!!?
HEE!

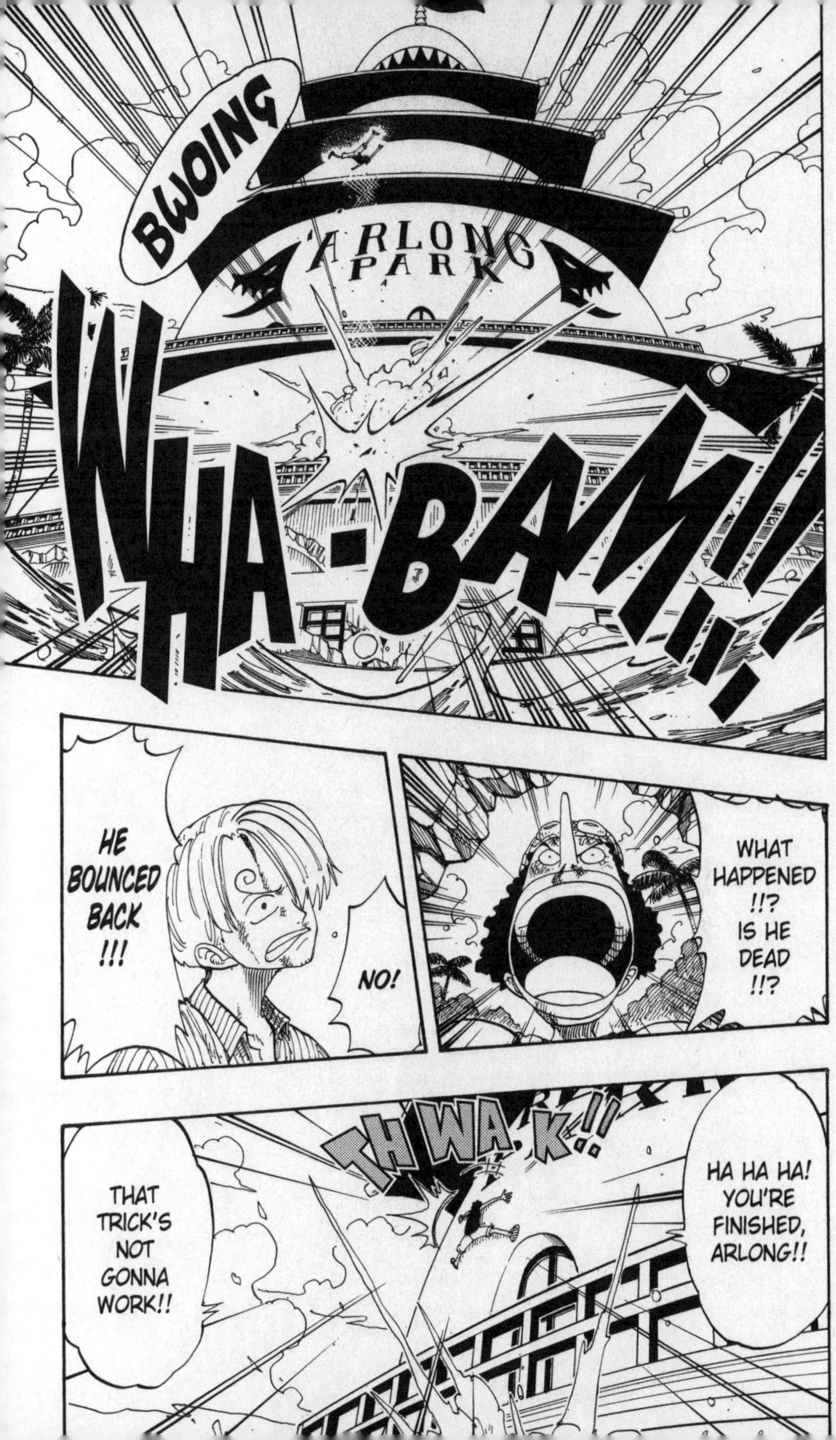
BWOING
ARLONG PARK
WHA-BAM!!!!
WHAT HAPPENED!!? IS HE DEAD!!?
NO!
HE BOUNCED BACK!!!
HA HA HA! YOU'RE FINISHED, ARLONG!!
THWAK!!
THAT TRICK'S NOT GONNA WORK!!

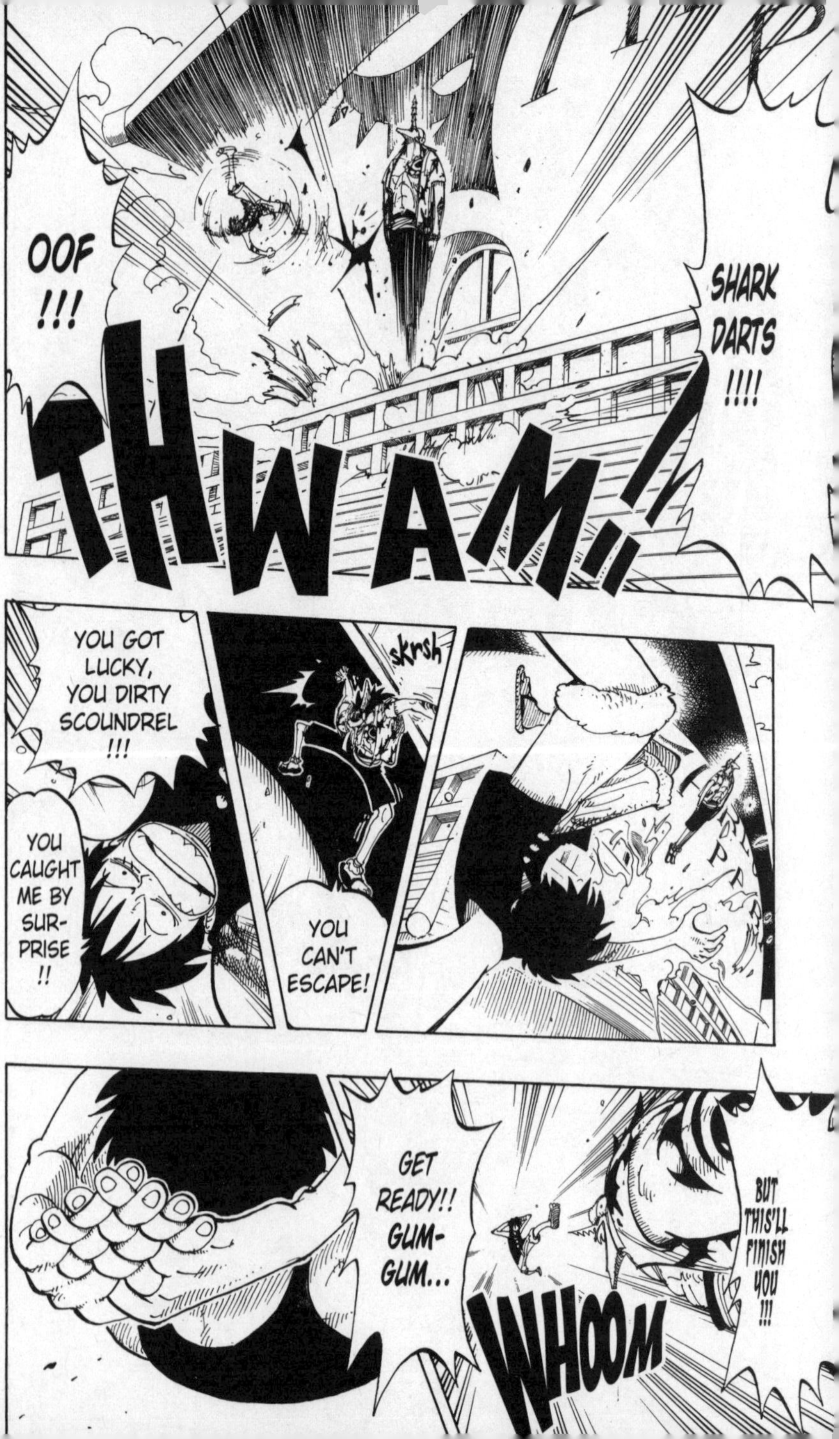
SHARK DARTS !!!!
THWAM!!
OOF !!!
skrsh
YOU CAN'T ESCAPE!
YOU GOT LUCKY, YOU DIRTY SCOUNDREL !!!
YOU CAUGHT ME BY SUR-PRISE !!
BUT THIS'LL FINISH YOU !!!
WHOOM
GET READY!! GUM-GUM...

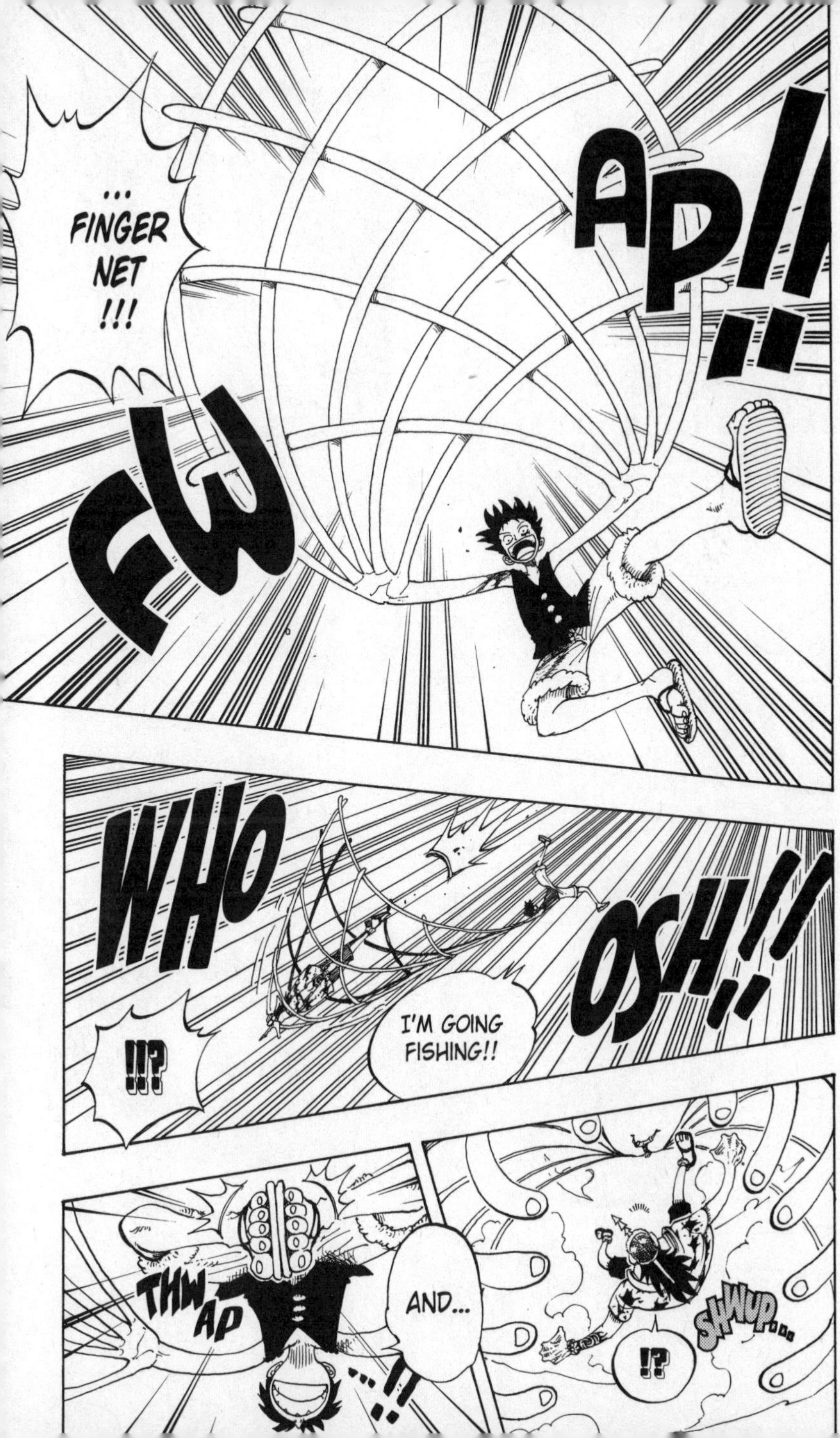
... FINGER NET !!!
FWAP!!
WHOOSH!!
I'M GOING FISHING!!
!!?
!?
SHWUP...
AND...
THWAP
...!!

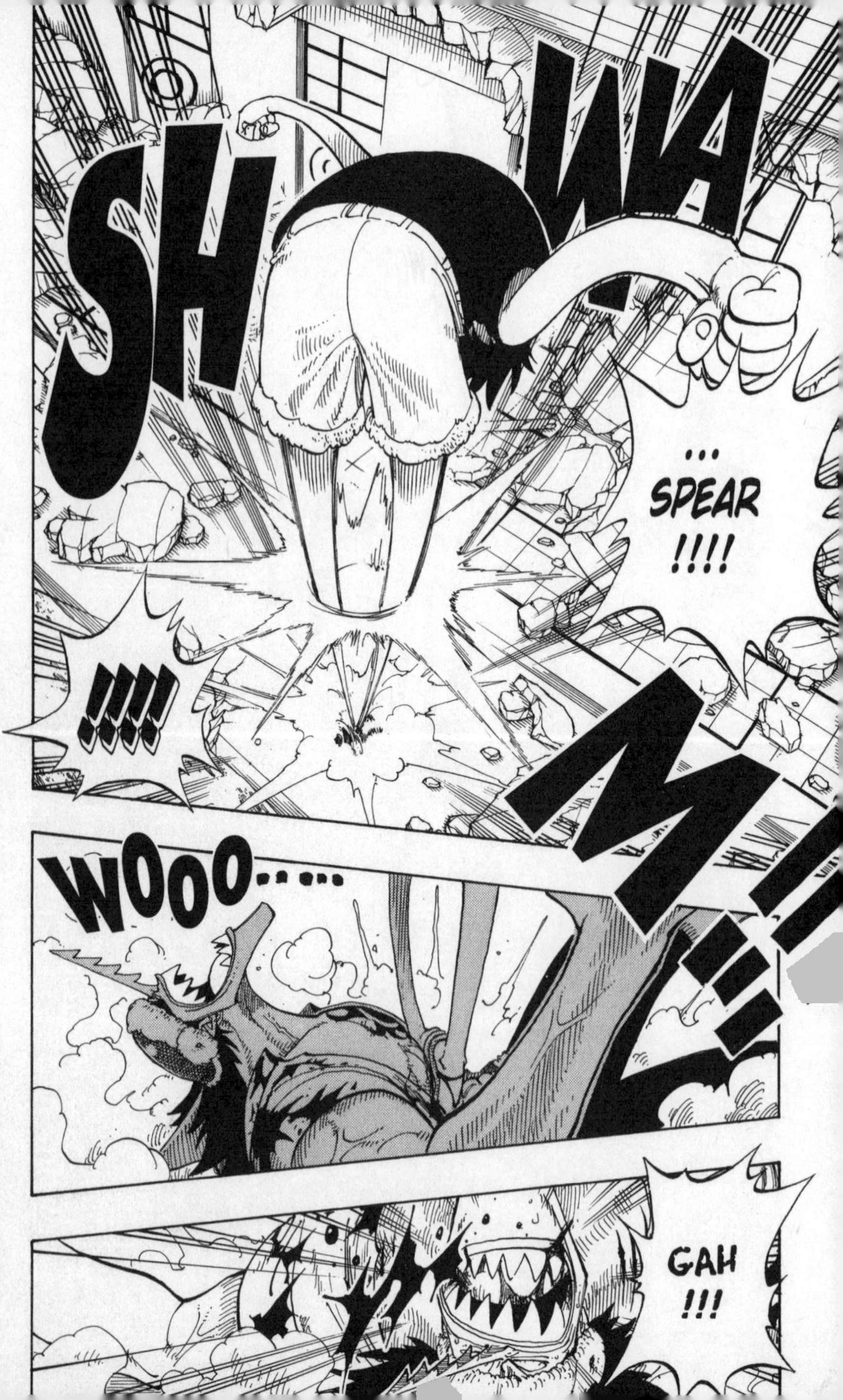
SHWA
... SPEAR !!!!
!!!!!
WOOO...
M!!!
GAH !!!

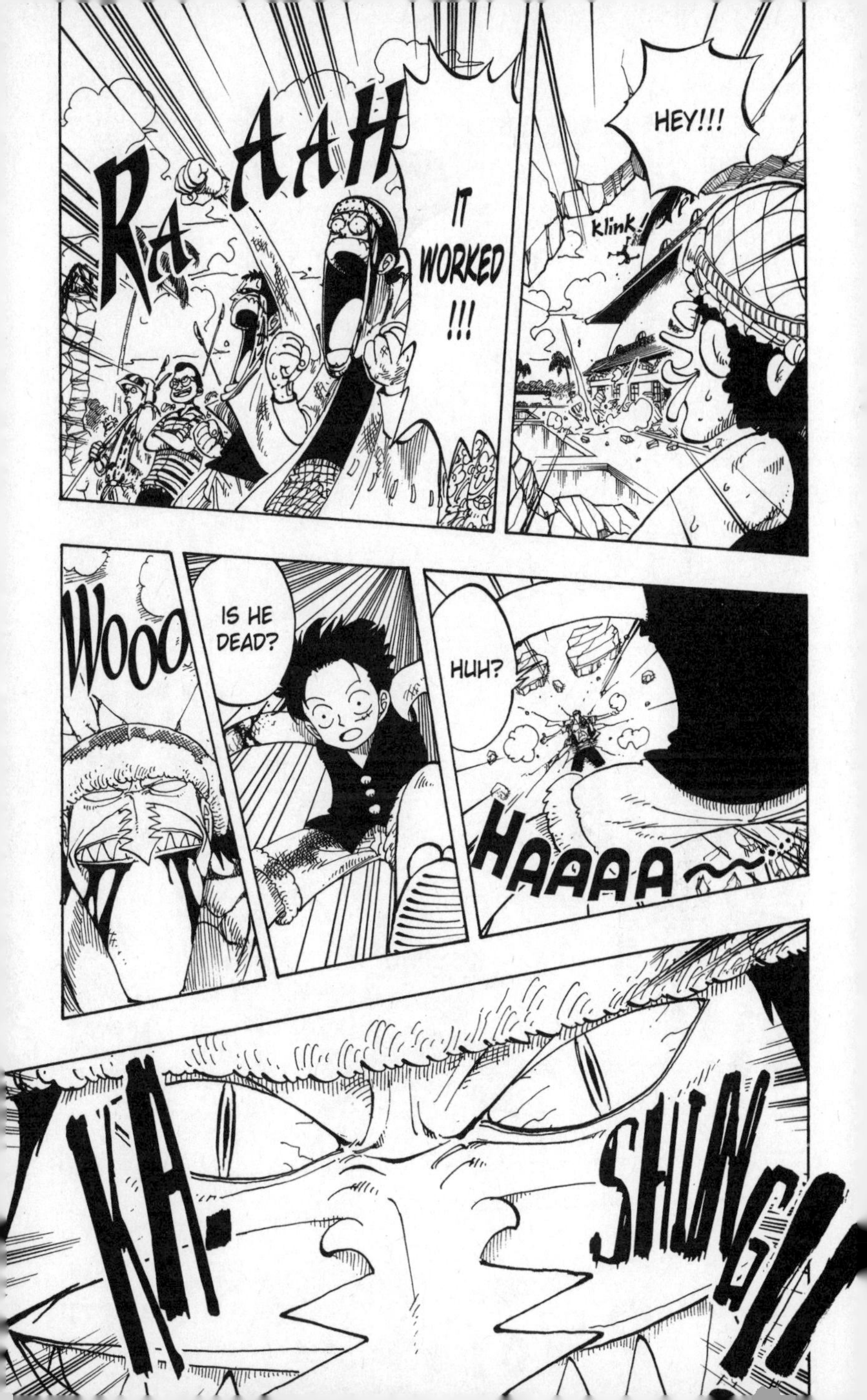
HEY!!!
klink!
RA-AAH
IT WORKED!!!
HUH?
HAAAA~~
IS HE DEAD?
WOOO
KA-SHUNG!!

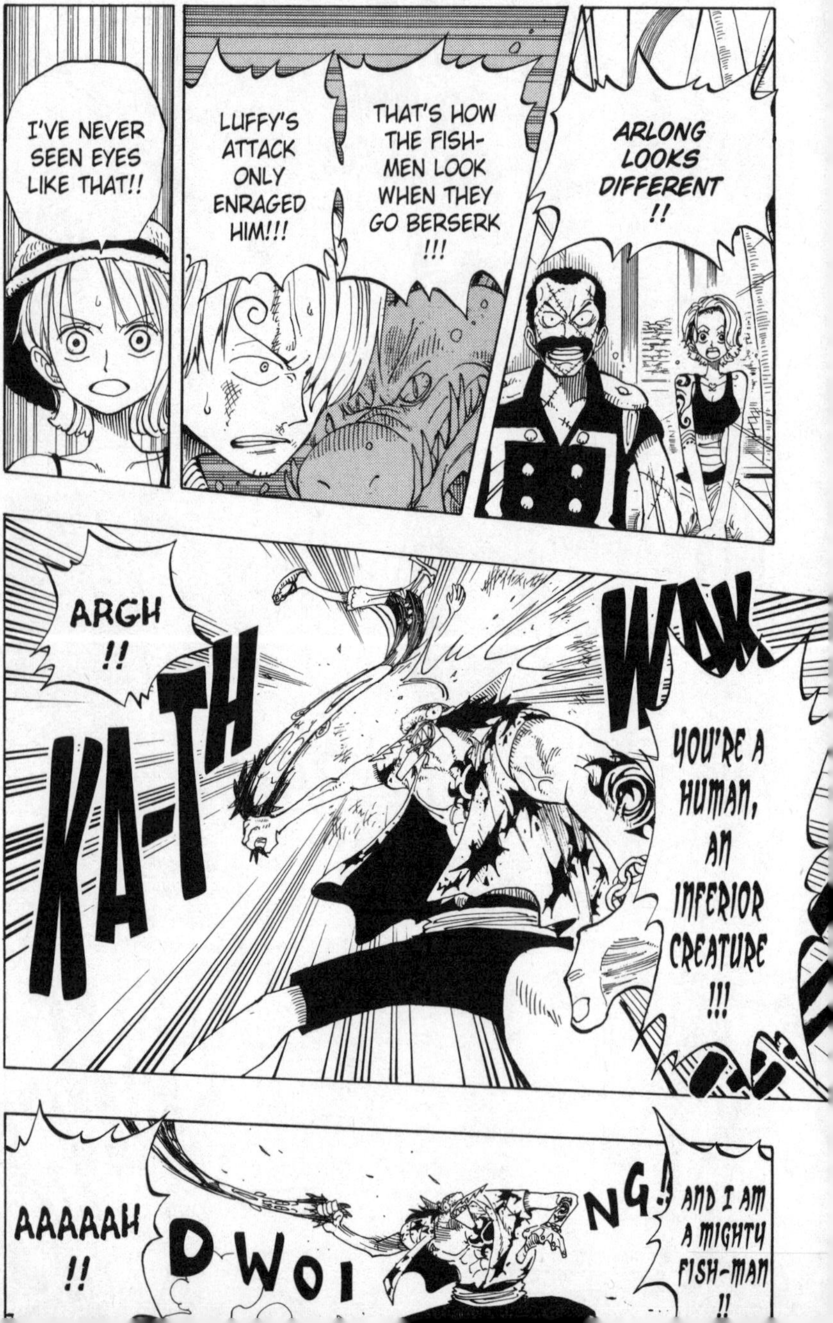

ARLONG LOOKS DIFFERENT !!
THAT'S HOW THE FISH-MEN LOOK WHEN THEY GO BERSERK !!!
LUFFY'S ATTACK ONLY ENRAGED HIM!!!
I'VE NEVER SEEN EYES LIKE THAT!!
WAK
YOU'RE A HUMAN, AN INFERIOR CREATURE !!!
ARGH !!
KA-TH
AND I AM A MIGHTY FISH-MAN !!
DWOING!
AAAAAH !!

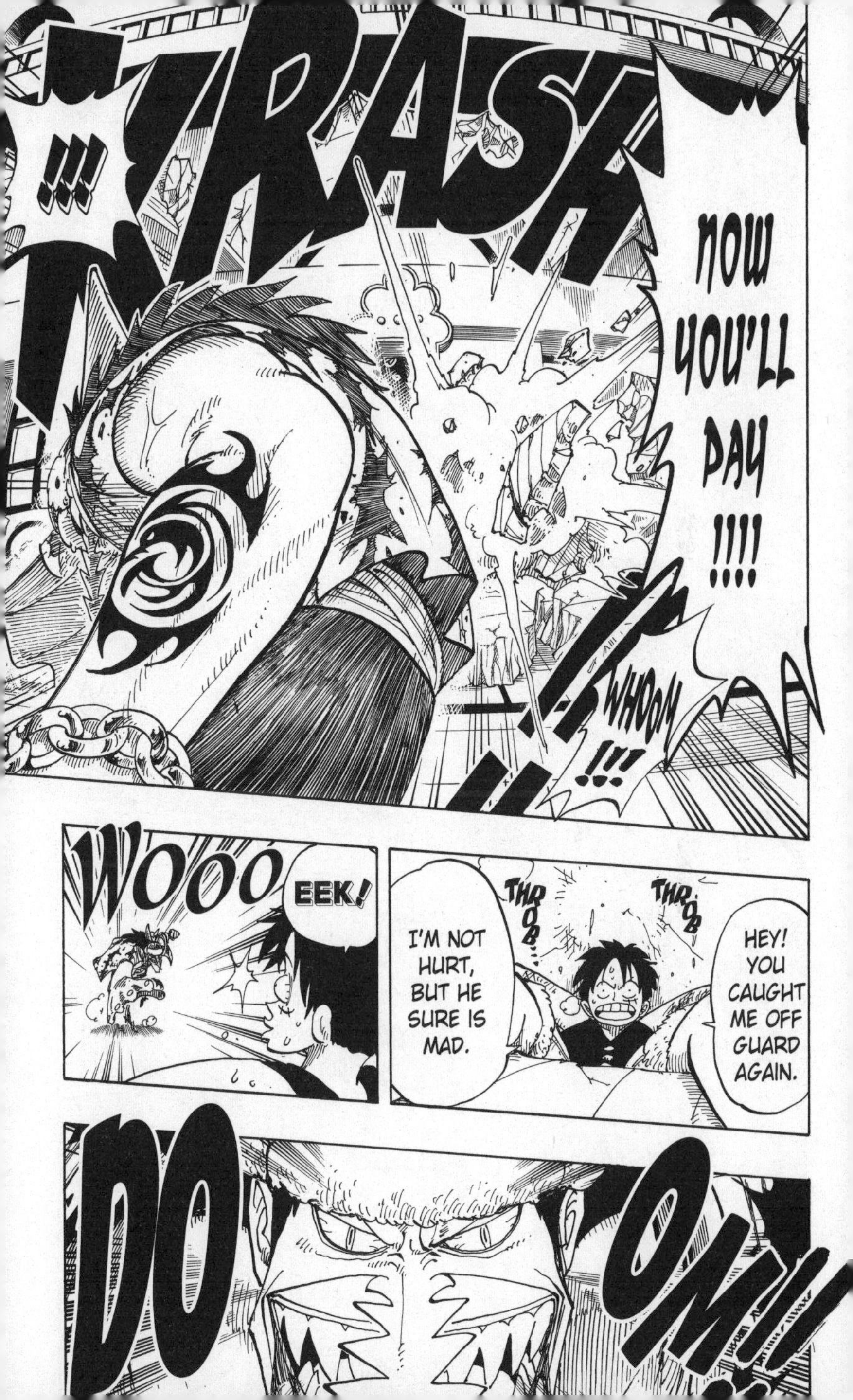
CRASH!!!!
NOW YOU'LL PAY!!!!
WHOOM!!!
HEY! YOU CAUGHT ME OFF GUARD AGAIN.
THROB
THROB
I'M NOT HURT, BUT HE SURE IS MAD.
EEK!
WOOO
DOON!!

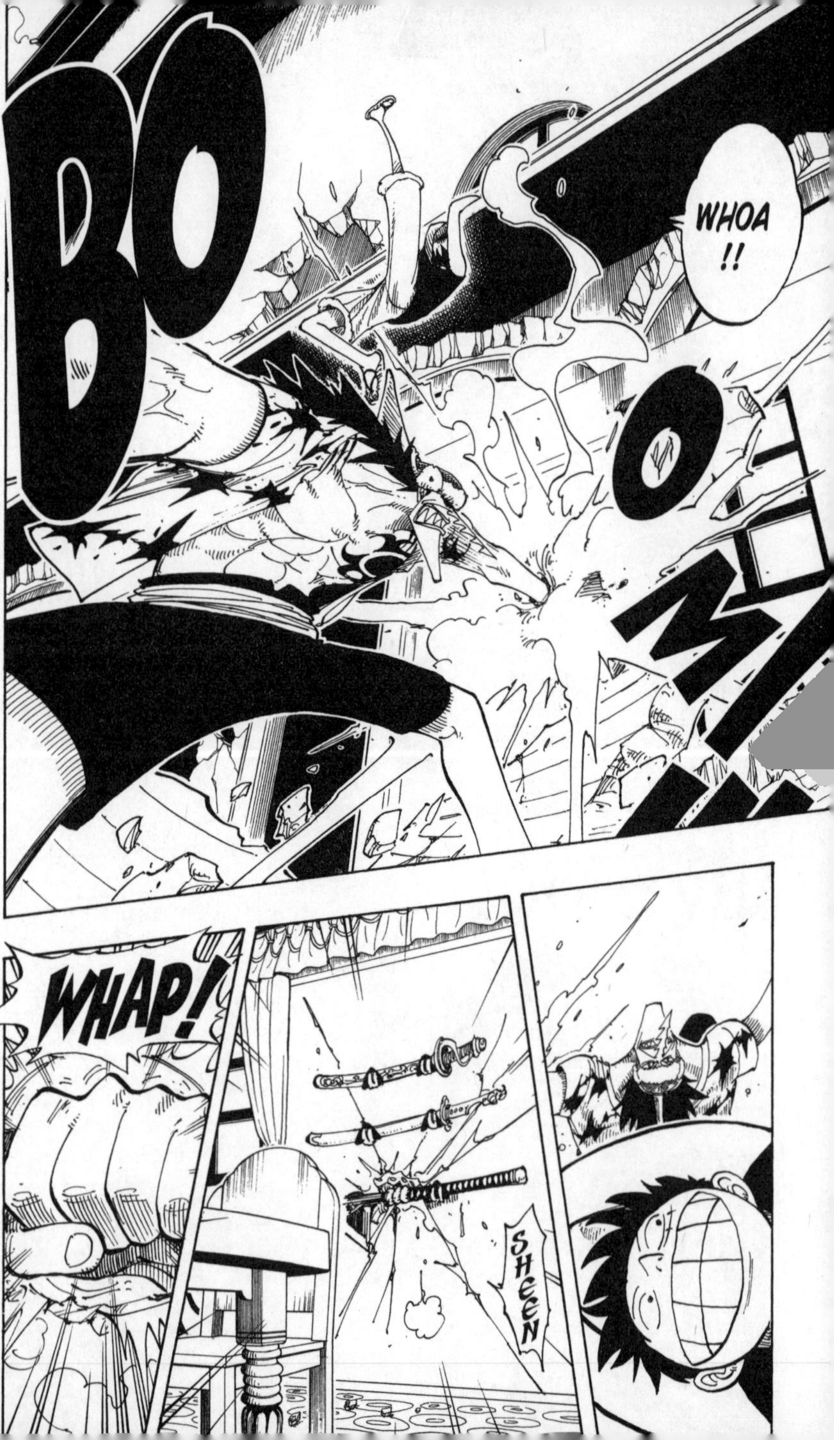
WHOA !!
BOOM
SHEEN
WHAP!

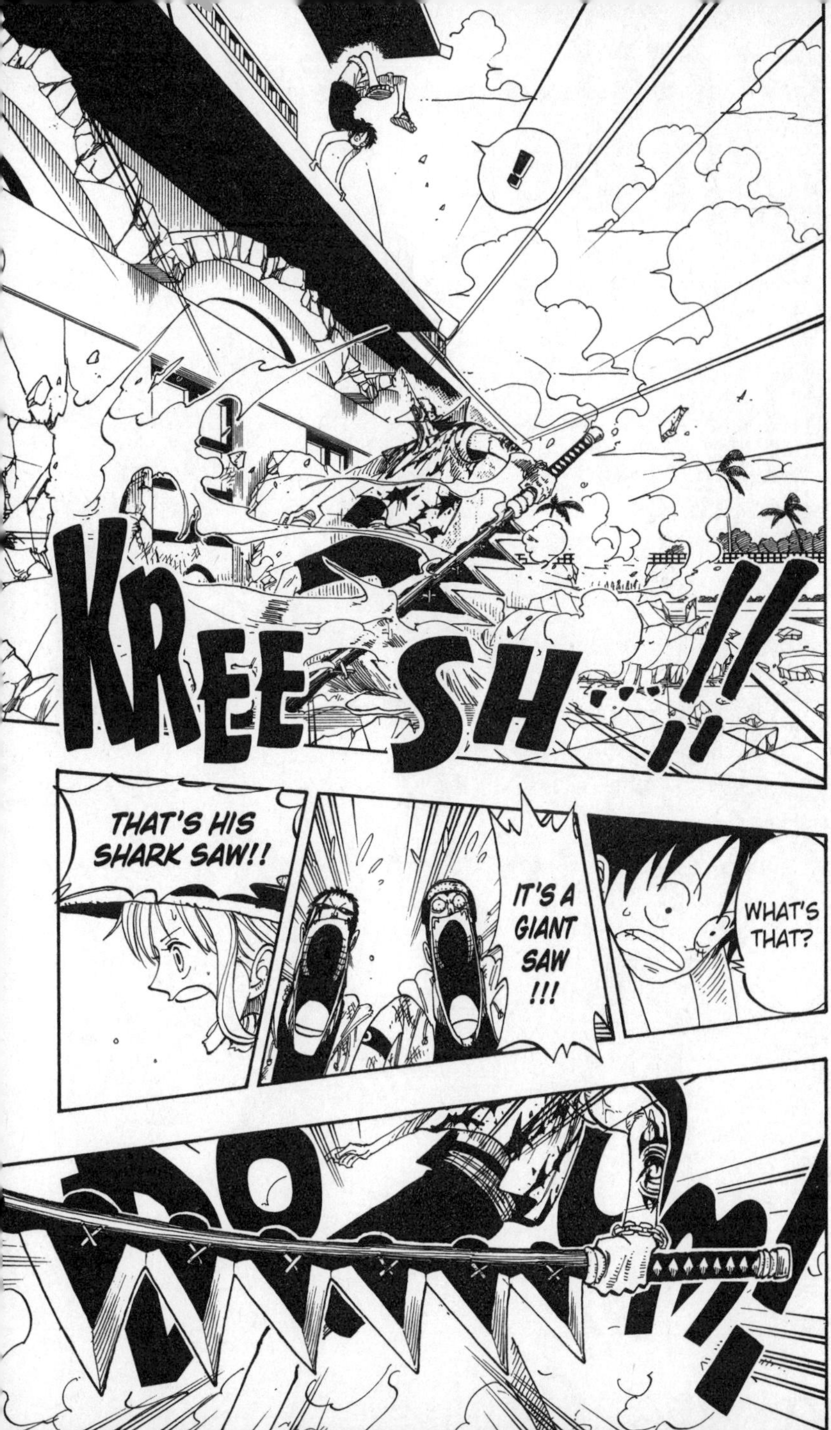
!
KREESH!!
WHAT'S THAT?
IT'S A GIANT SAW!!!
THAT'S HIS SHARK SAW!!

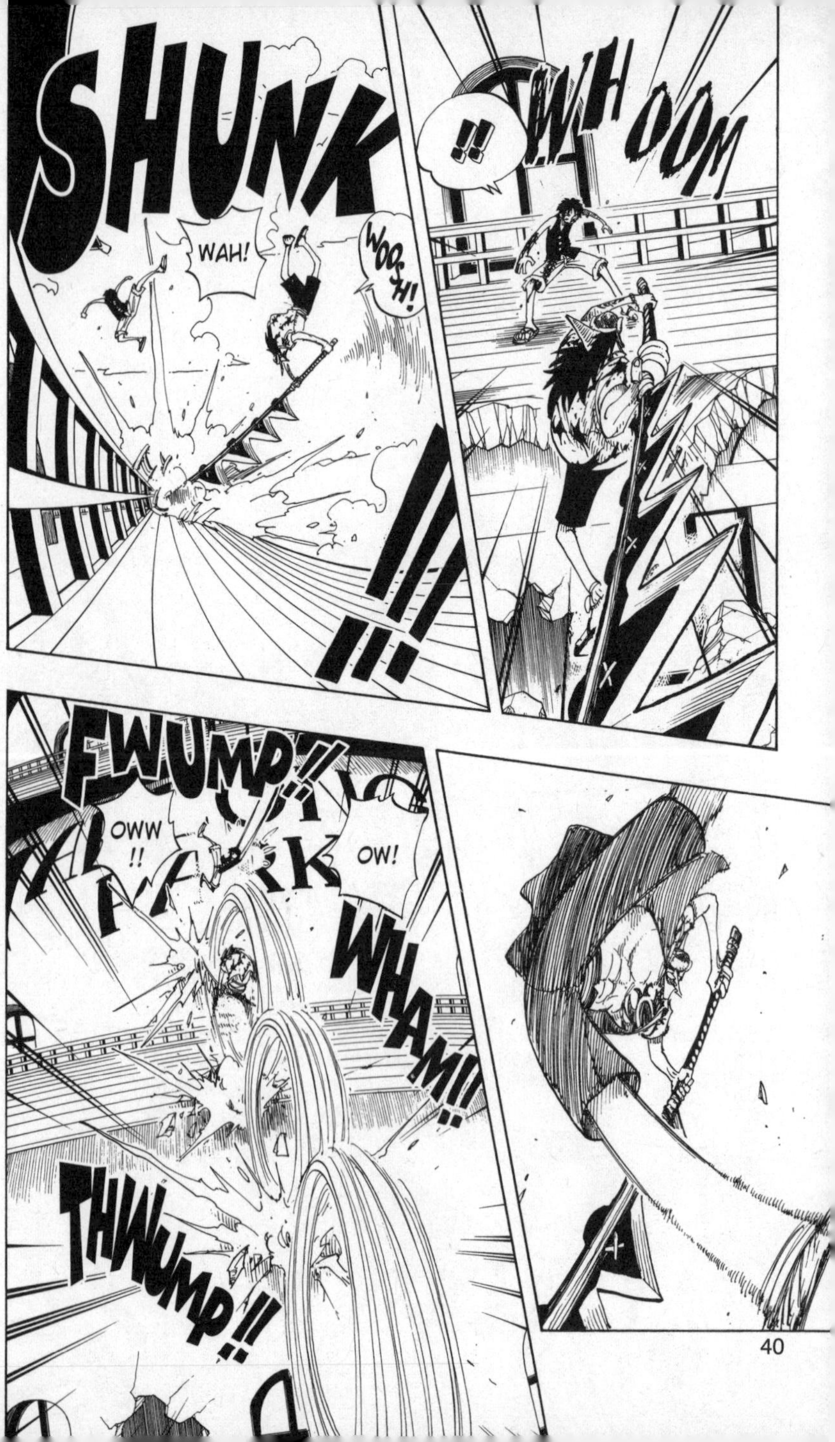
!!
TWHOOM
SHUNK
WOOSH!
WAH!
!!
!!
FWUMP!!
OW!
OWW!!
WHAM!!
THWUMP!!

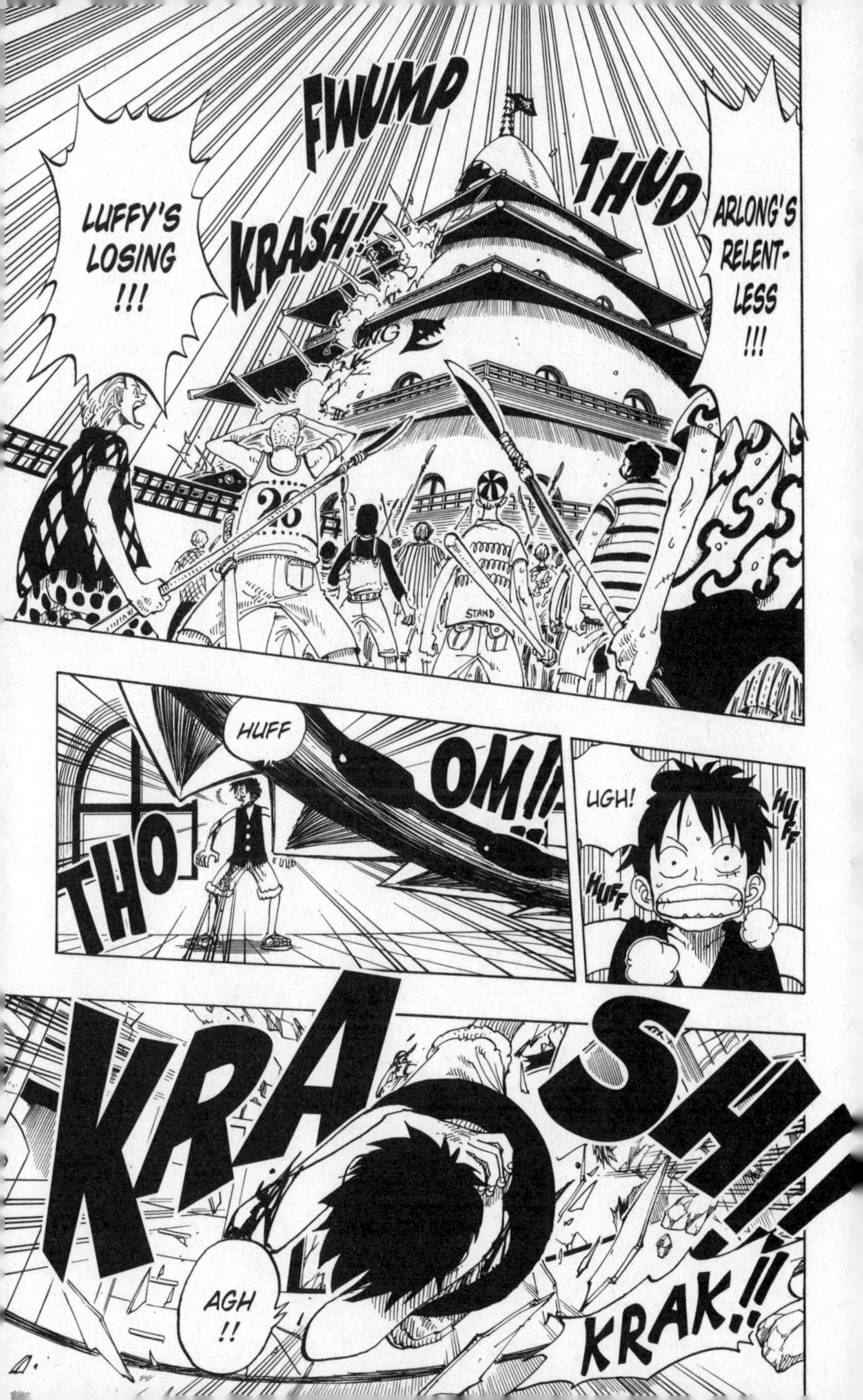
ARLONG'S RELENT-LESS !!!
THUD
FWUMP
KRASH!!
LUFFY'S LOSING !!!
UGH!
HUFF
HUFF
HUFF
OM!!
THO
KRASH!!
KRAK!!
AGH !!

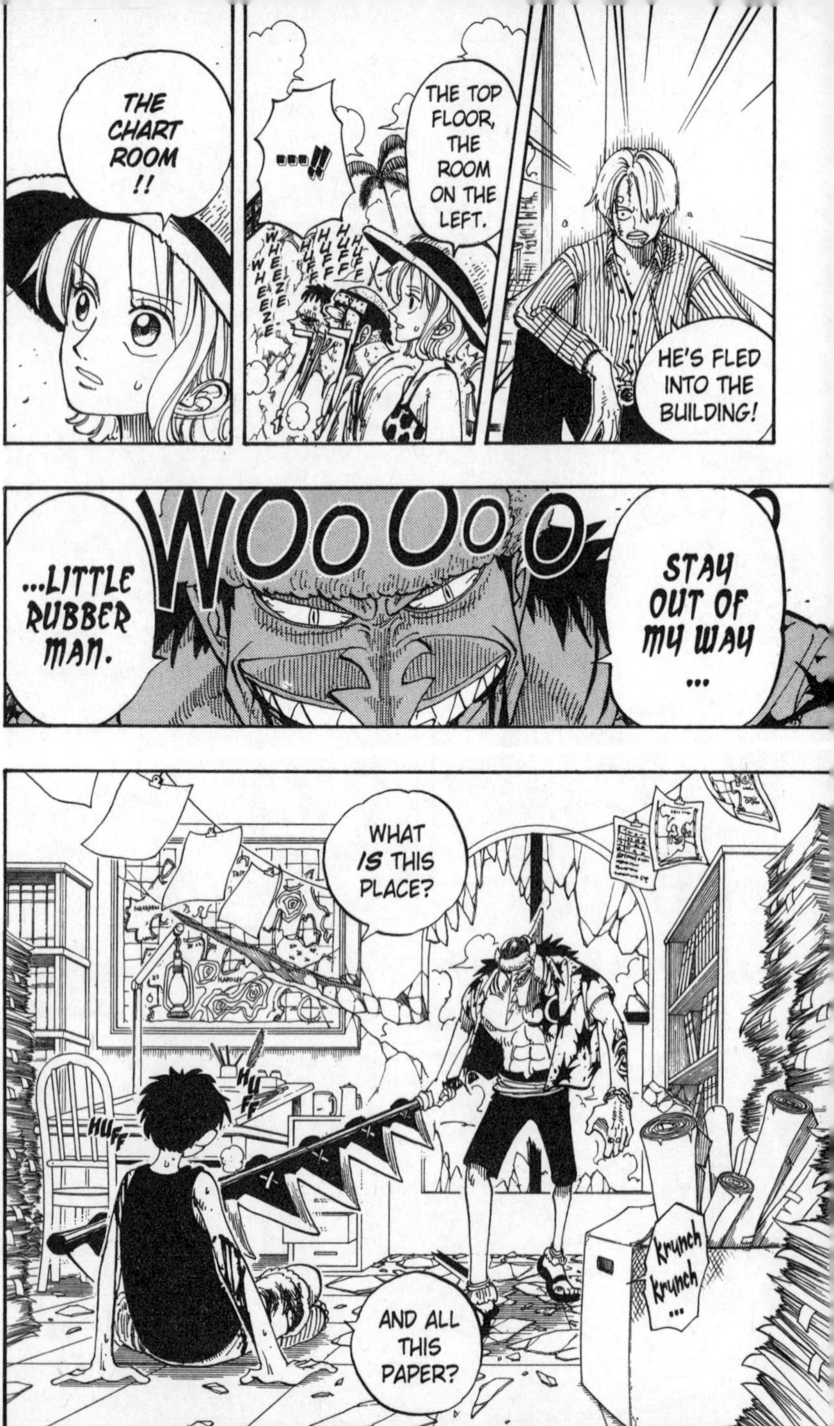
HE'S FLED INTO THE BUILDING!
THE TOP FLOOR, THE ROOM ON THE LEFT.
...!!
HUFF HUFF
WHEEZE WHEEZE
THE CHART ROOM !!
STAY OUT OF MY WAY ...
WOOOOO
...LITTLE RUBBER MAN.
WHAT IS THIS PLACE?
HUFF
HUFF
krunch krunch ...
AND ALL THIS PAPER?

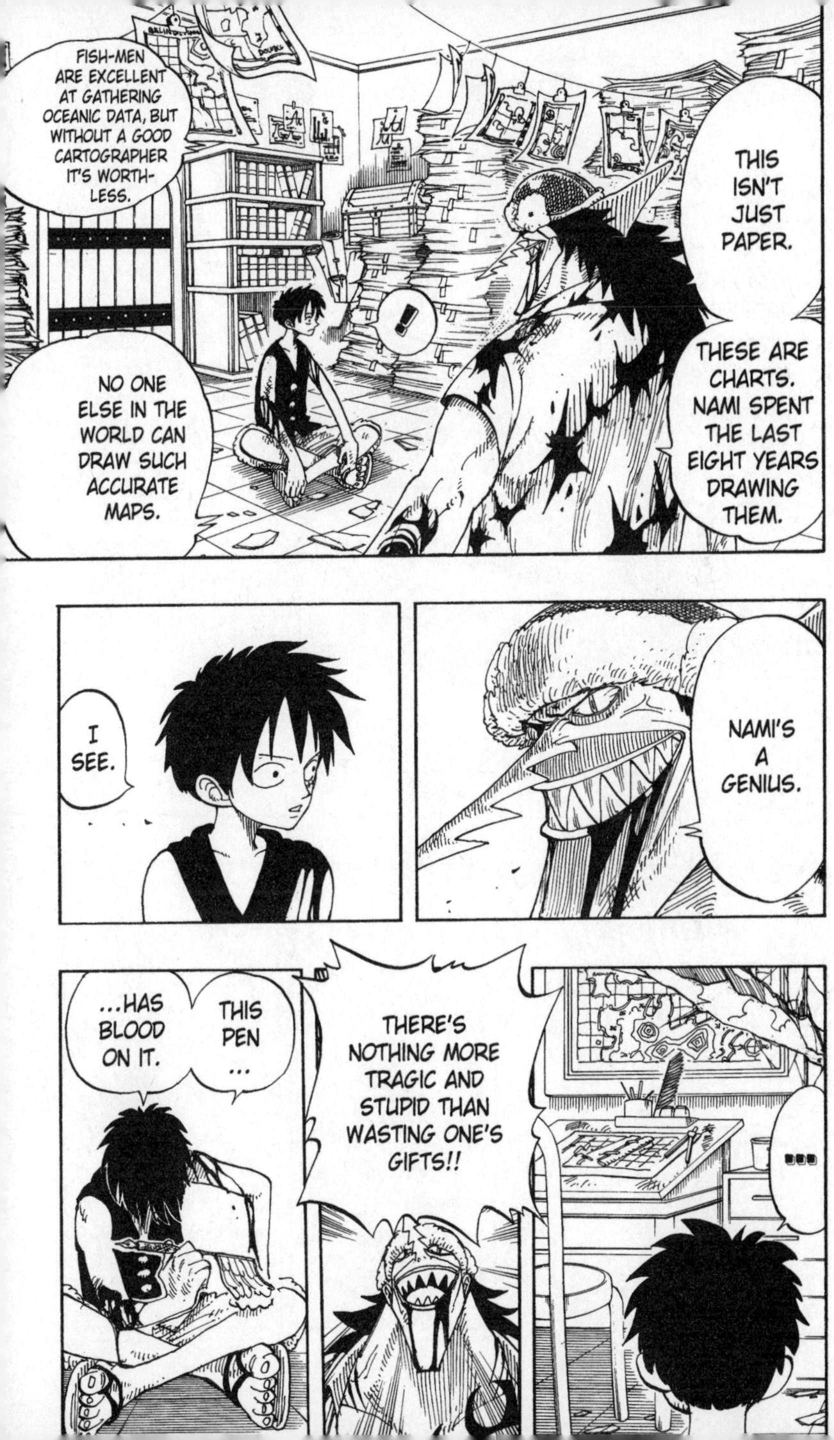

THIS ISN'T JUST PAPER.
THESE ARE CHARTS. NAMI SPENT THE LAST EIGHT YEARS DRAWING THEM.
!
FISH-MEN ARE EXCELLENT AT GATHERING OCEANIC DATA, BUT WITHOUT A GOOD CARTOGRAPHER IT'S WORTH-LESS.
NO ONE ELSE IN THE WORLD CAN DRAW SUCH ACCURATE MAPS.
NAMI'S A GENIUS.
I SEE.
...
THERE'S NOTHING MORE TRAGIC AND STUPID THAN WASTING ONE'S GIFTS!!
THIS PEN ...
...HAS BLOOD ON IT.

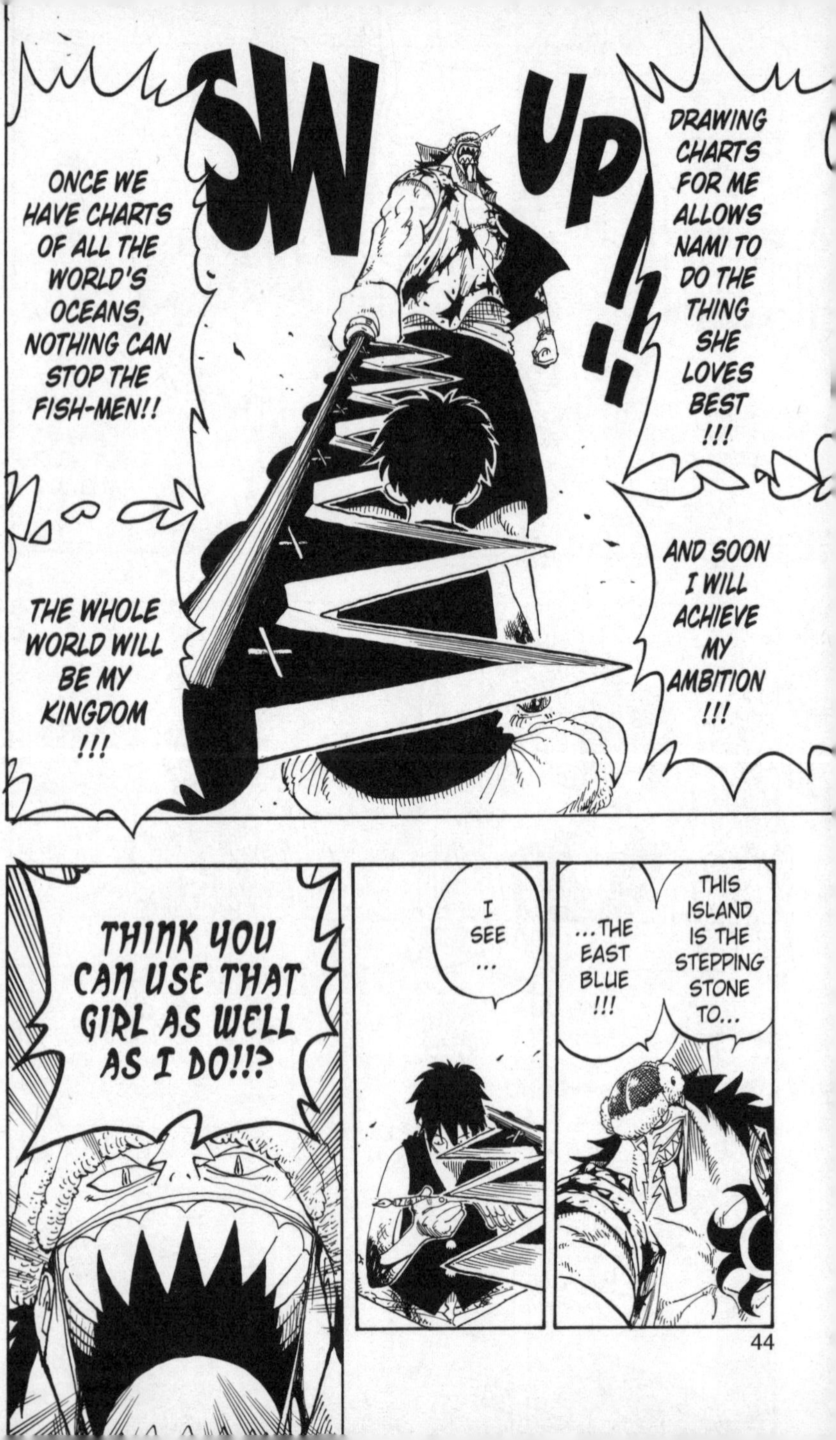
SWUP!!
DRAWING CHARTS FOR ME ALLOWS NAMI TO DO THE THING SHE LOVES BEST!!!
ONCE WE HAVE CHARTS OF ALL THE WORLD'S OCEANS, NOTHING CAN STOP THE FISH-MEN!!
AND SOON I WILL ACHIEVE MY AMBITION!!!
THE WHOLE WORLD WILL BE MY KINGDOM!!!
THIS ISLAND IS THE STEPPING STONE TO...
...THE EAST BLUE!!!
I SEE...
THINK YOU CAN USE THAT GIRL AS WELL AS I DO!!?

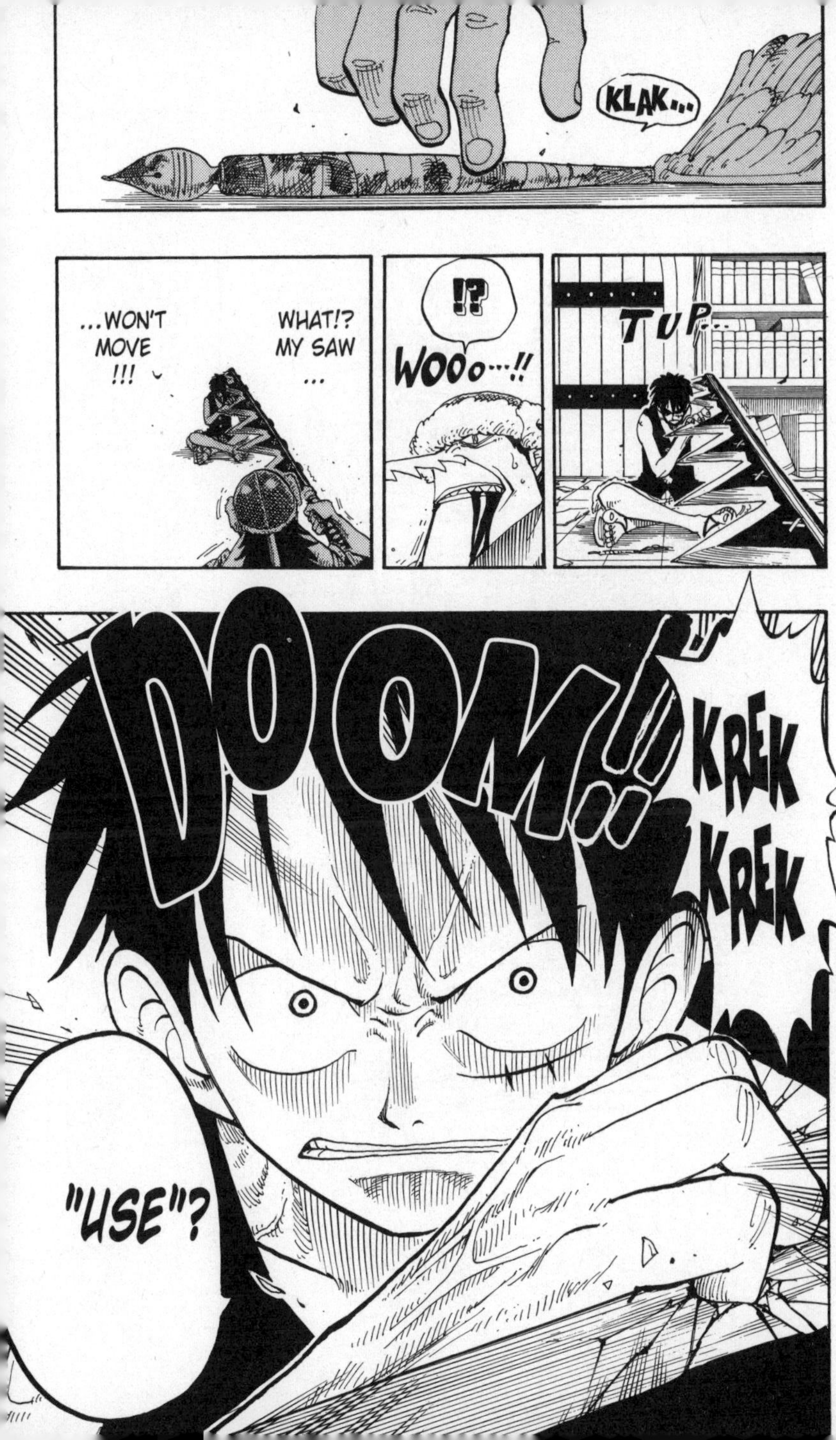
KLAK...
TUP...
!?
WOOo...!!
WHAT!? MY SAW ...
...WON'T MOVE !!!
DOOM!!
KREK KREK
"USE"?

1. Lounge

Conference Room, Galley, and Bridge

- Room for meetings and discussions
- The crew gathers here for meals and breaks.

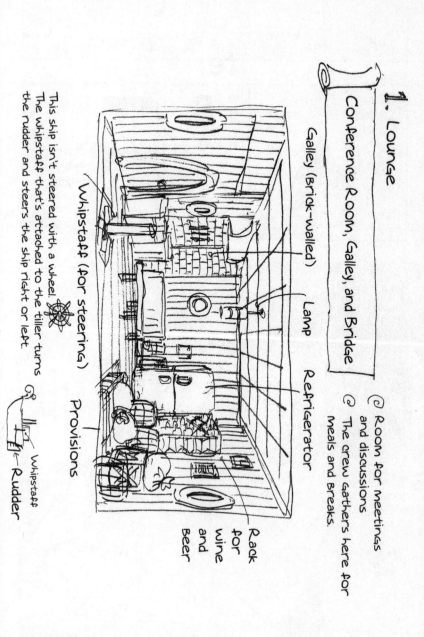

Galley (Brick-walled)

Lamp

Refrigerator

Rack for wine and Beer

Whipstaff (for steering)

Provisions

This ship isn't steered with a wheel. The whipstaff that's attached to the tiller turns the rudder and steers the ship right or left.

Whipstaff

Rudder

Chapter 93:
GOING DOWN

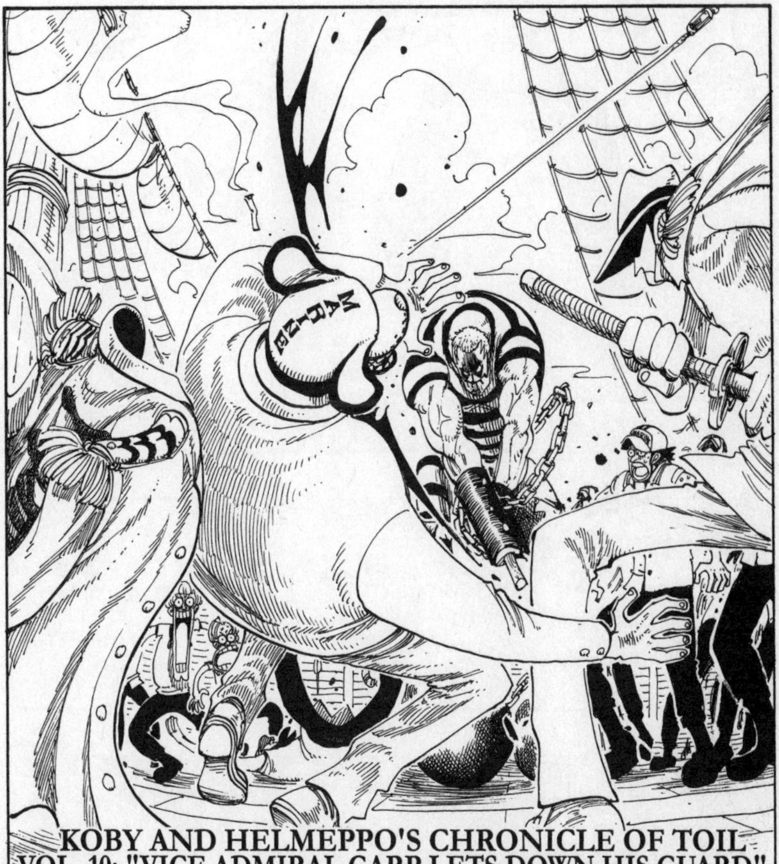
MARINE
KOBY AND HELMEPPO'S CHRONICLE OF TOIL
VOL. 10: "VICE ADMIRAL GARP LETS DOWN HIS GUARD"

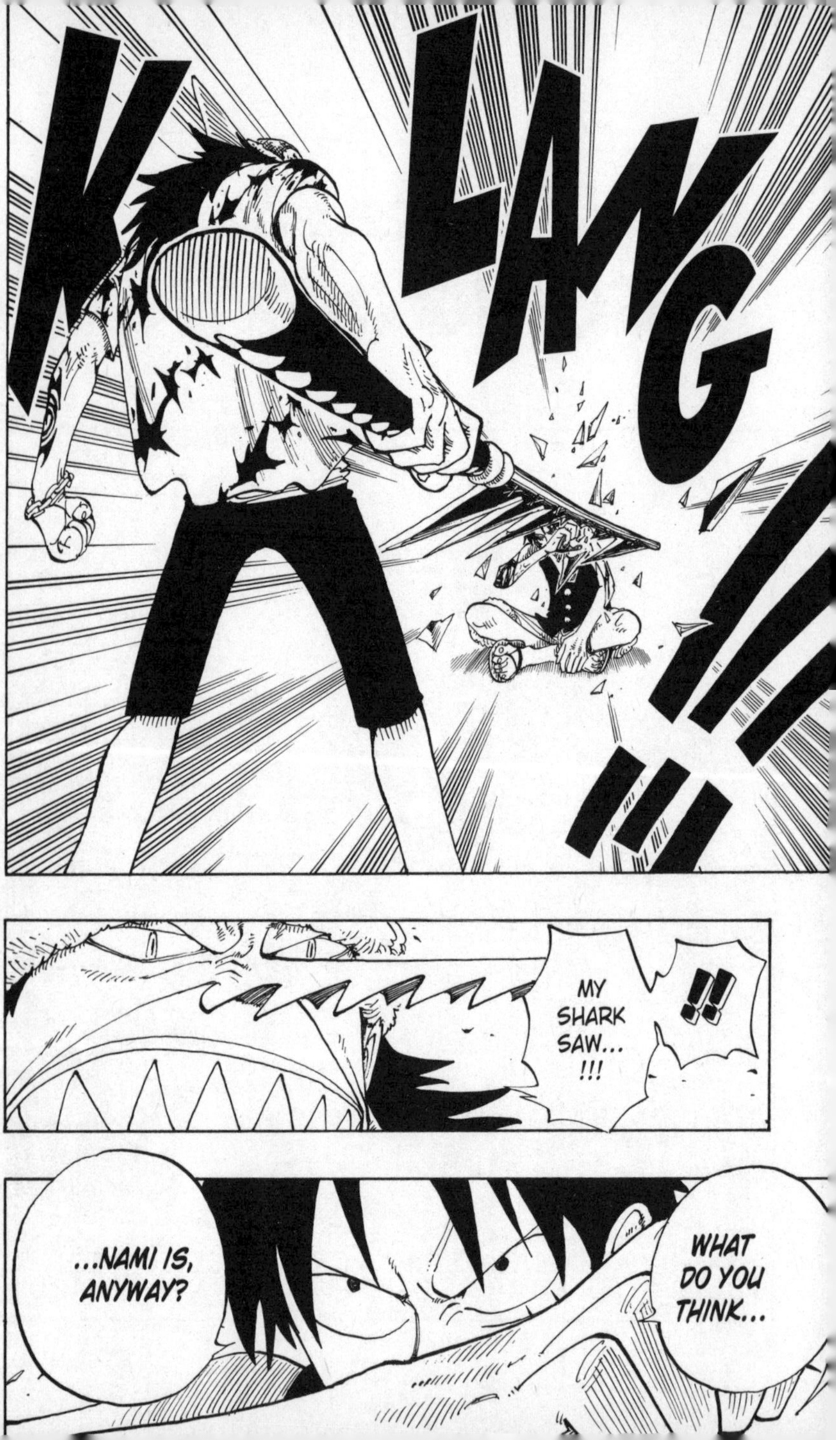
KLANG!!!!!!
!!!
MY SHARK SAW... !!!
!!
WHAT DO YOU THINK...
...NAMI IS, ANYWAY?

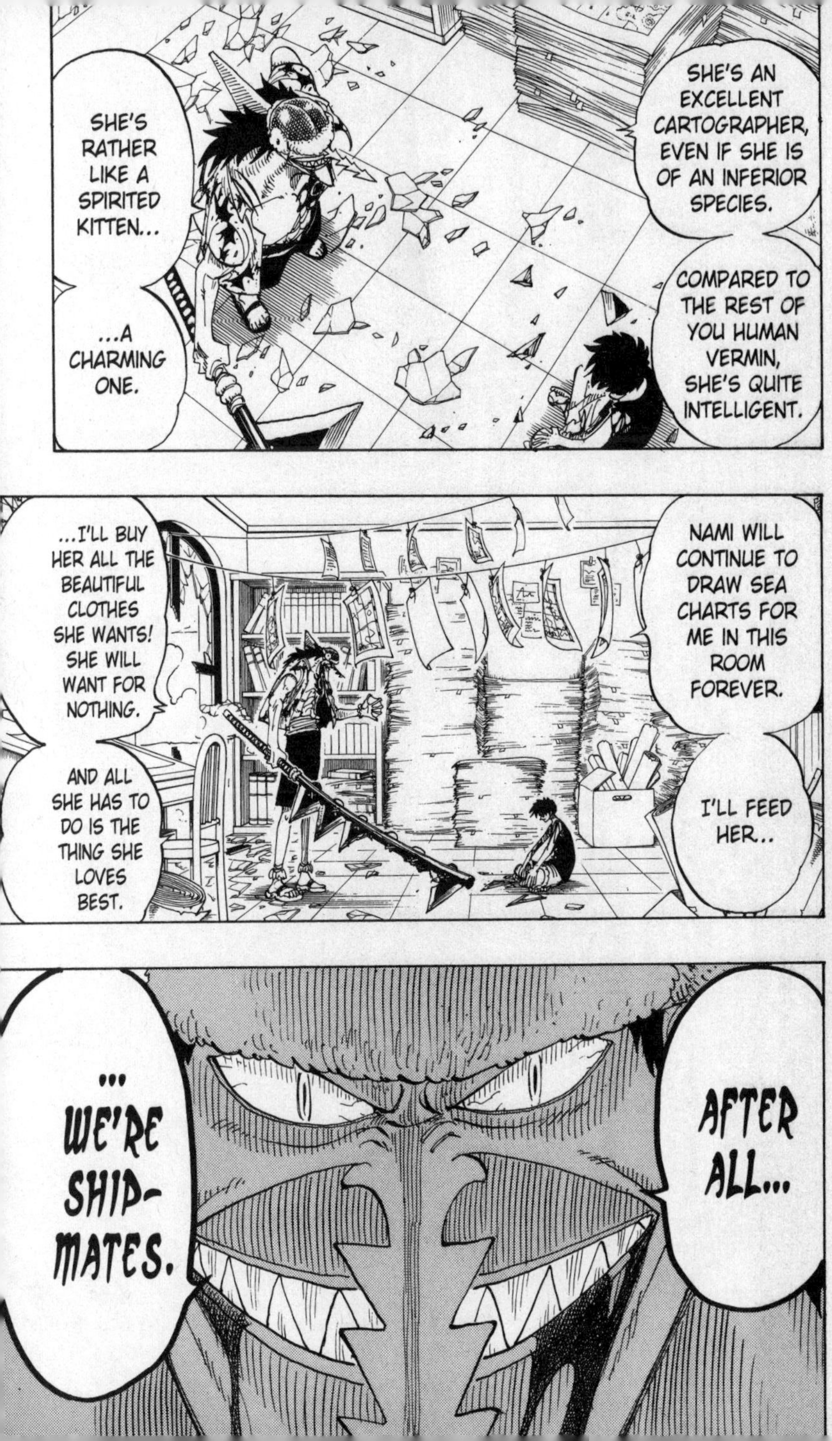
SHE'S AN EXCELLENT CARTOGRAPHER, EVEN IF SHE IS OF AN INFERIOR SPECIES.
COMPARED TO THE REST OF YOU HUMAN VERMIN, SHE'S QUITE INTELLIGENT.
SHE'S RATHER LIKE A SPIRITED KITTEN...
...A CHARMING ONE.
NAMI WILL CONTINUE TO DRAW SEA CHARTS FOR ME IN THIS ROOM FOREVER.
I'LL FEED HER...
...I'LL BUY HER ALL THE BEAUTIFUL CLOTHES SHE WANTS! SHE WILL WANT FOR NOTHING.
AND ALL SHE HAS TO DO IS THE THING SHE LOVES BEST.
AFTER ALL...
...WE'RE SHIP-MATES.

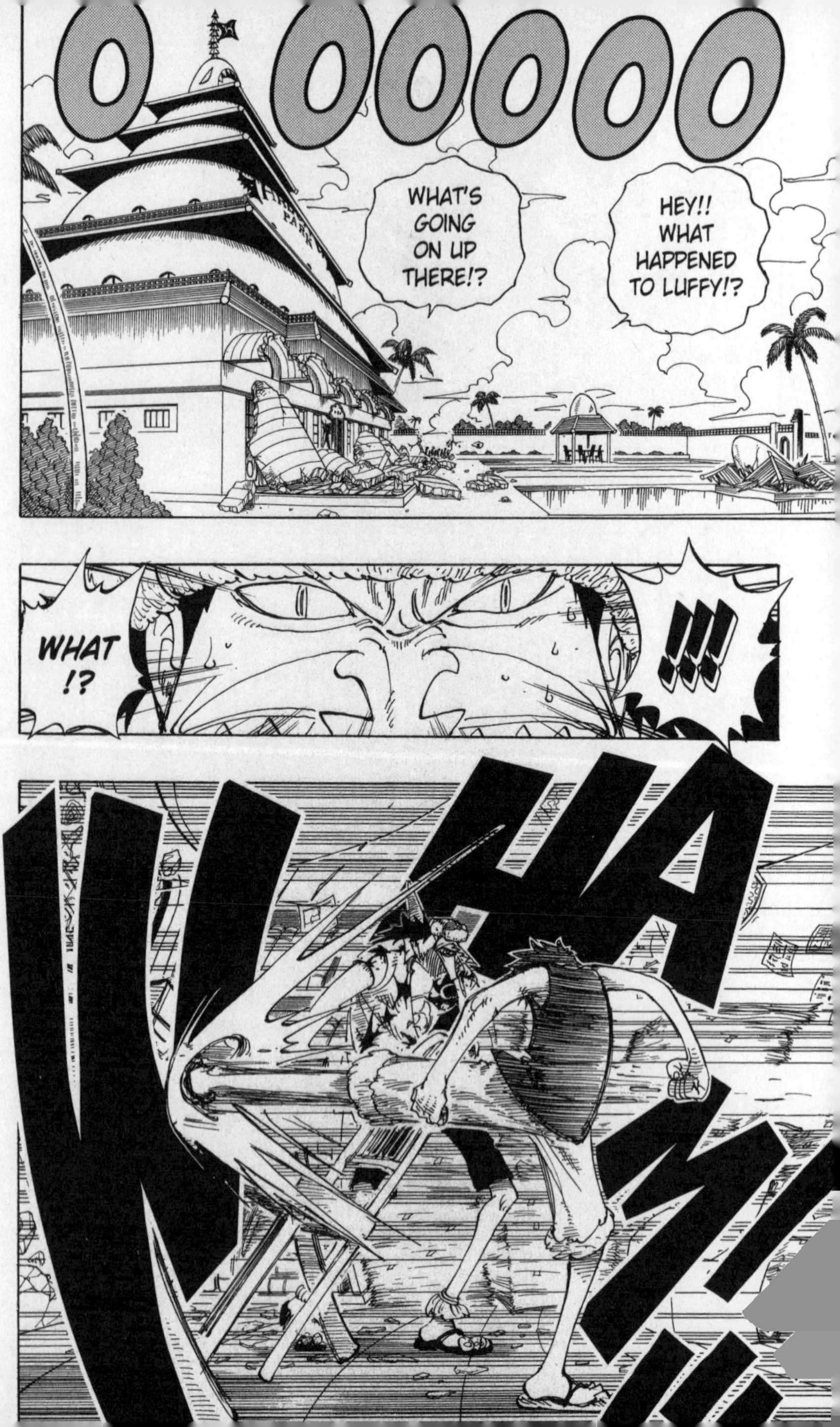
O OOOOO
HEY!! WHAT HAPPENED TO LUFFY!?
WHAT'S GOING ON UP THERE!?
!!!
WHAT !?

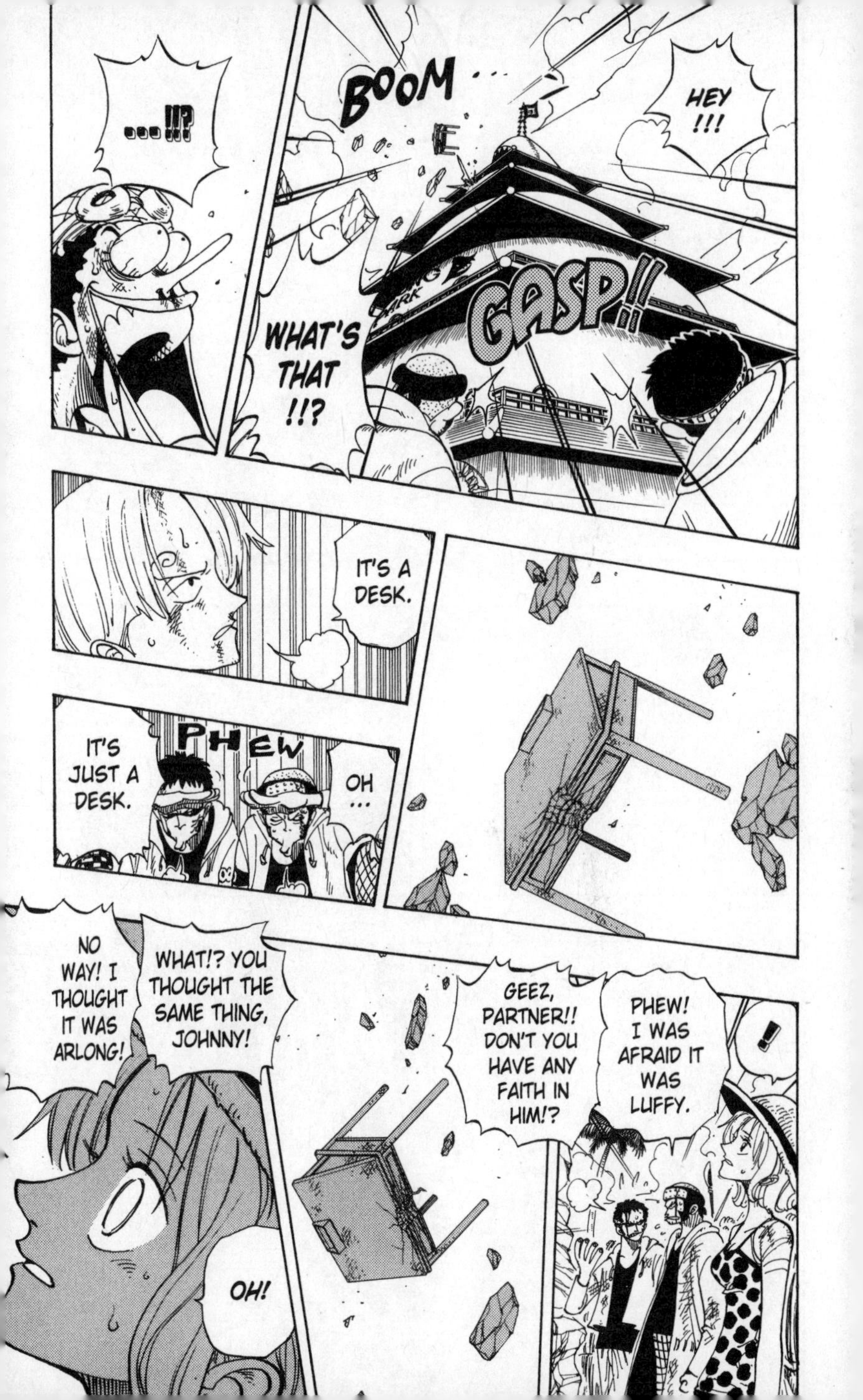
HEY !!!
BOOM
GASP!!
WHAT'S THAT !!?
...!!?
IT'S A DESK.
OH ...
PHEW
IT'S JUST A DESK.
!
PHEW! I WAS AFRAID IT WAS LUFFY.
GEEZ, PARTNER!! DON'T YOU HAVE ANY FAITH IN HIM!?
WHAT!? YOU THOUGHT THE SAME THING, JOHNNY!
NO WAY! I THOUGHT IT WAS ARLONG!
OH!

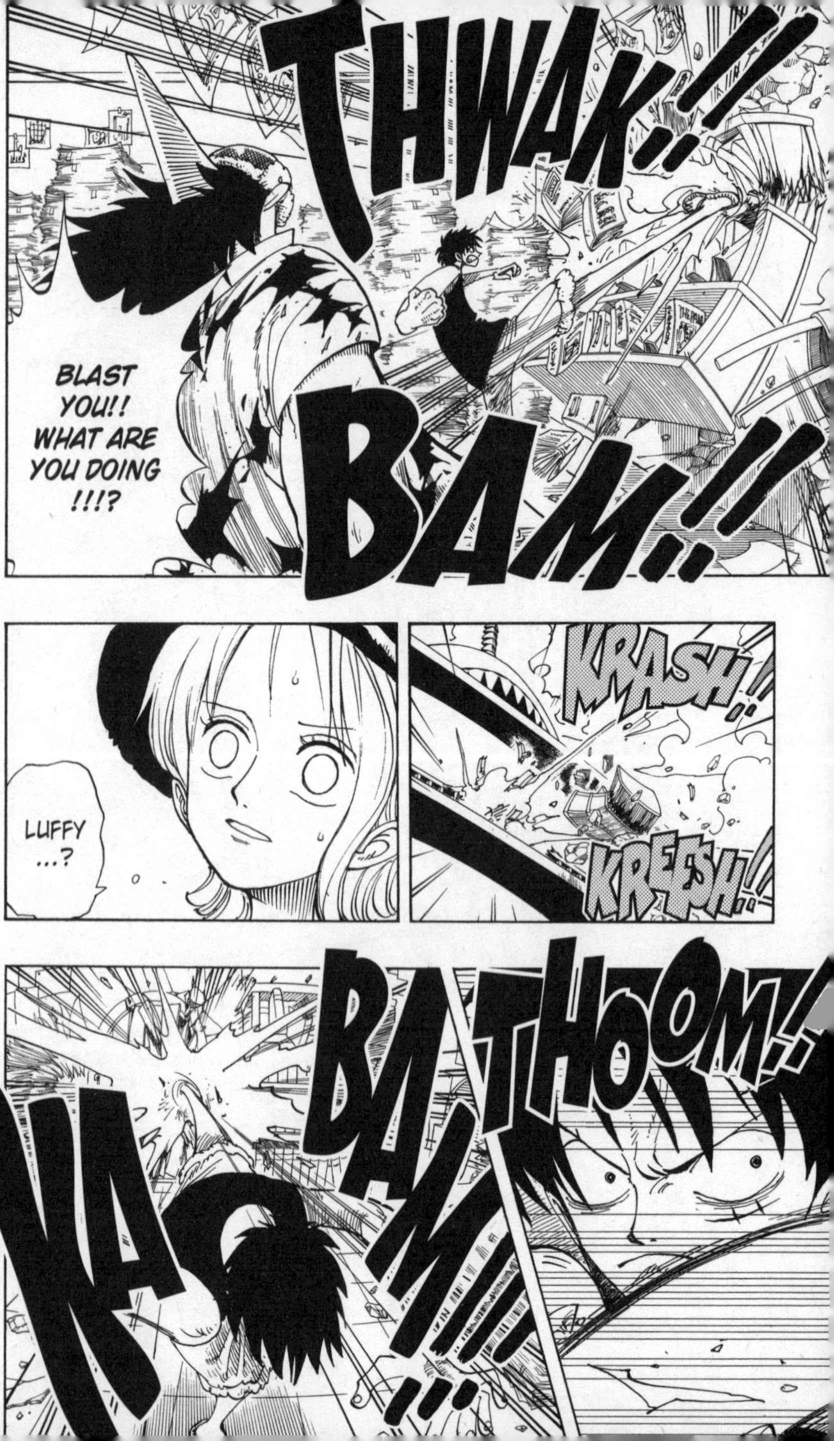
THWAK!!
BLAST YOU!! WHAT ARE YOU DOING!!!?
BAM!!
KRASH!!
KREESH!!
LUFFY ...?
BATHOOM!!
BAM!!!
KA

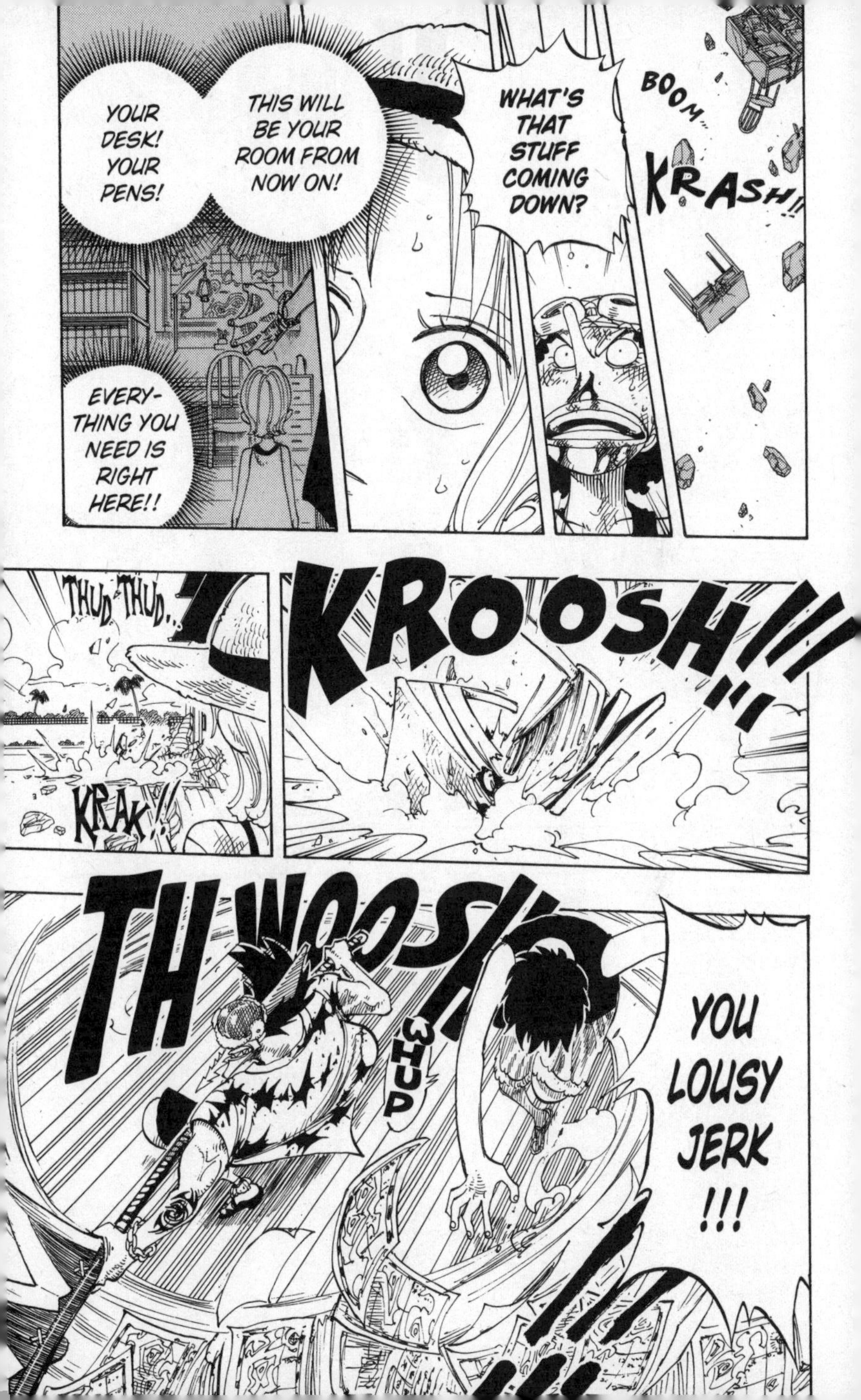
BOOM...
KRASH!!
WHAT'S THAT STUFF COMING DOWN?
THIS WILL BE YOUR ROOM FROM NOW ON!
YOUR DESK! YOUR PENS!
EVERY-THING YOU NEED IS RIGHT HERE!!
KROOSH!!!
THUD THUD...
KRAK!!
YOU LOUSY JERK!!!
THWOOSH
SHUP

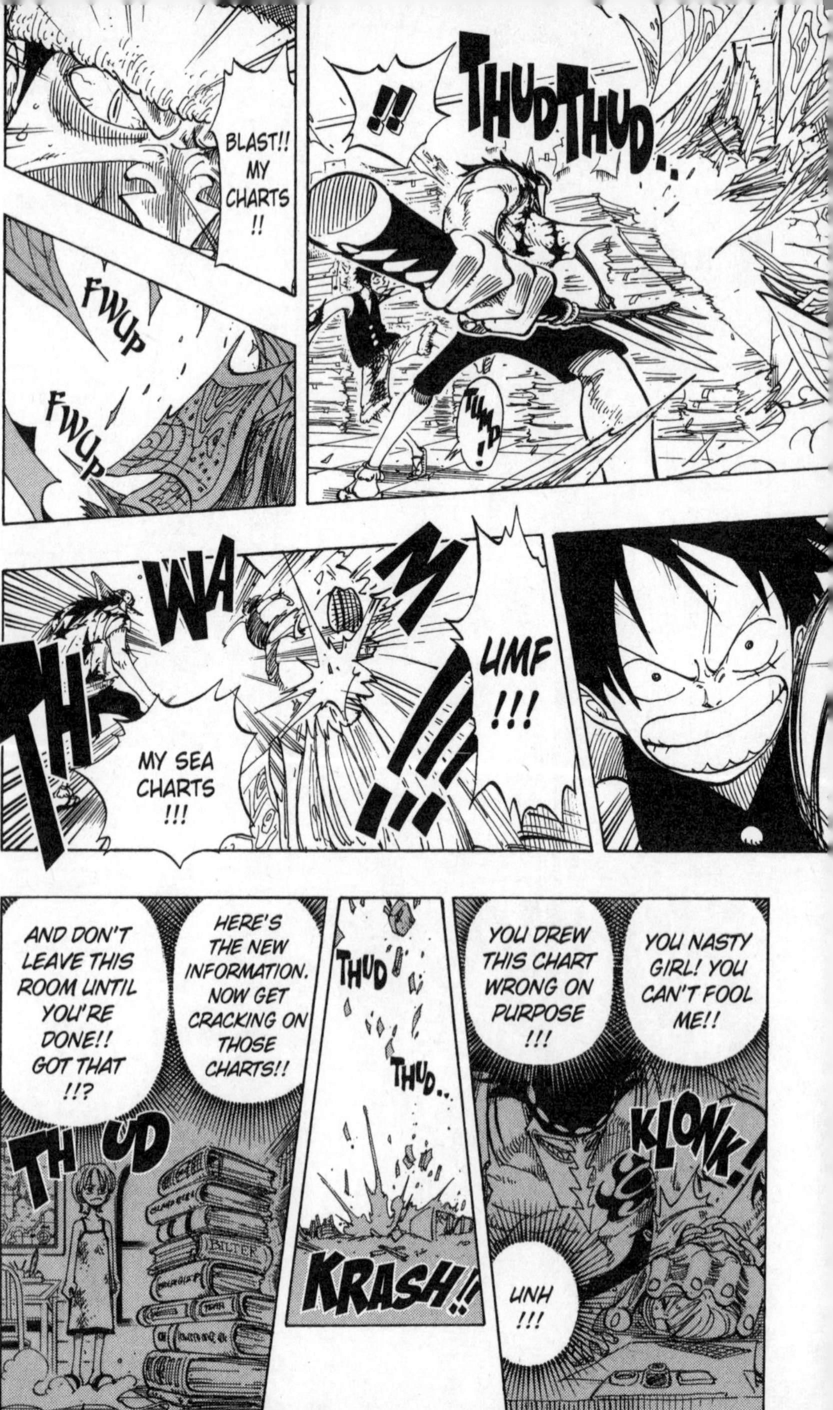
!!
THUD THUD...
TUMP!
BLAST!! MY CHARTS!!
FWUP
FWUP
THWAM!!!
UMF!!!
MY SEA CHARTS!!!
YOU NASTY GIRL! YOU CAN'T FOOL ME!!
YOU DREW THIS CHART WRONG ON PURPOSE!!!
KLONK!
UNH!!!
THUD
THUD...
KRASH!!
HERE'S THE NEW INFORMATION. NOW GET CRACKING ON THOSE CHARTS!!
AND DON'T LEAVE THIS ROOM UNTIL YOU'RE DONE!! GOT THAT!!?
THUD

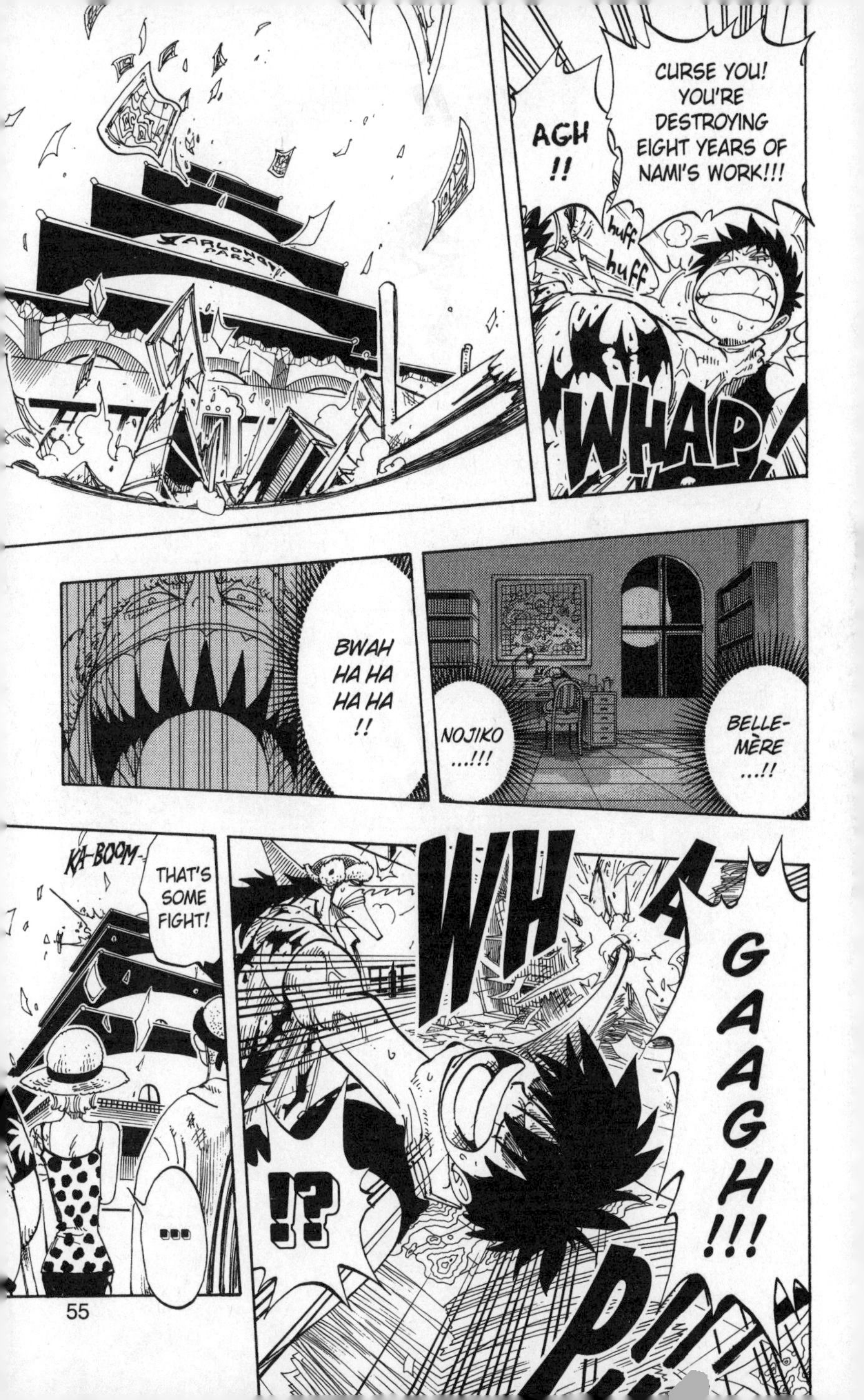
CURSE YOU! YOU'RE DESTROYING EIGHT YEARS OF NAMI'S WORK!!!
AGH !!
huff huff
WHAP!
BELLE-MÈRE ...!!
NOJIKO ...!!!
BWAH HA HA HA HA !!
WH A A GAAGH!!!
!?
P!!
KA-BOOM
THAT'S SOME FIGHT!
...

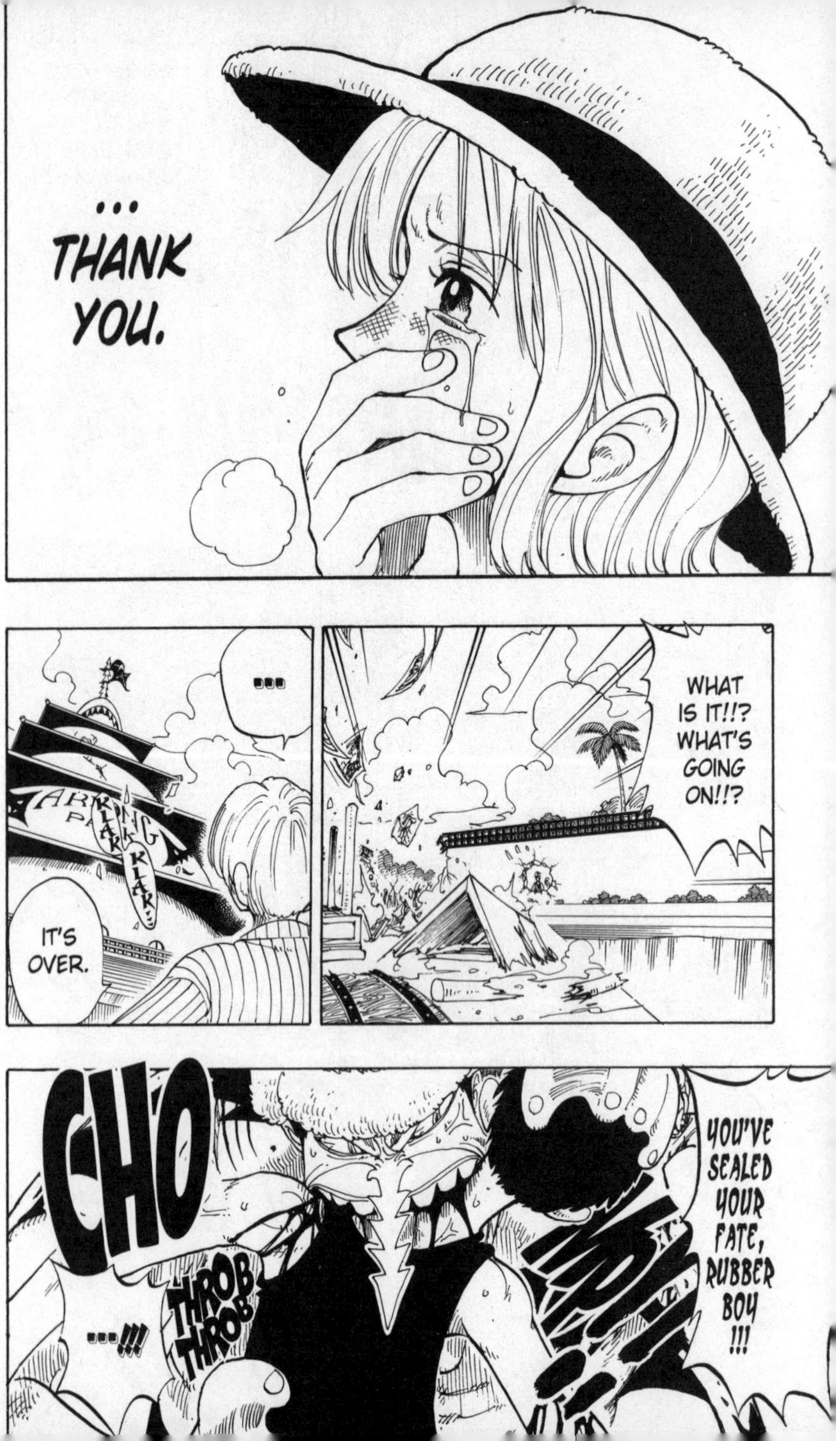

... THANK YOU.
WHAT IS IT!!? WHAT'S GOING ON!!?
...
KLAK KLAK KLAK
IT'S OVER.
YOU'VE SEALED YOUR FATE, RUBBER BOY!!!
CHO
THROB THROB
...!!!

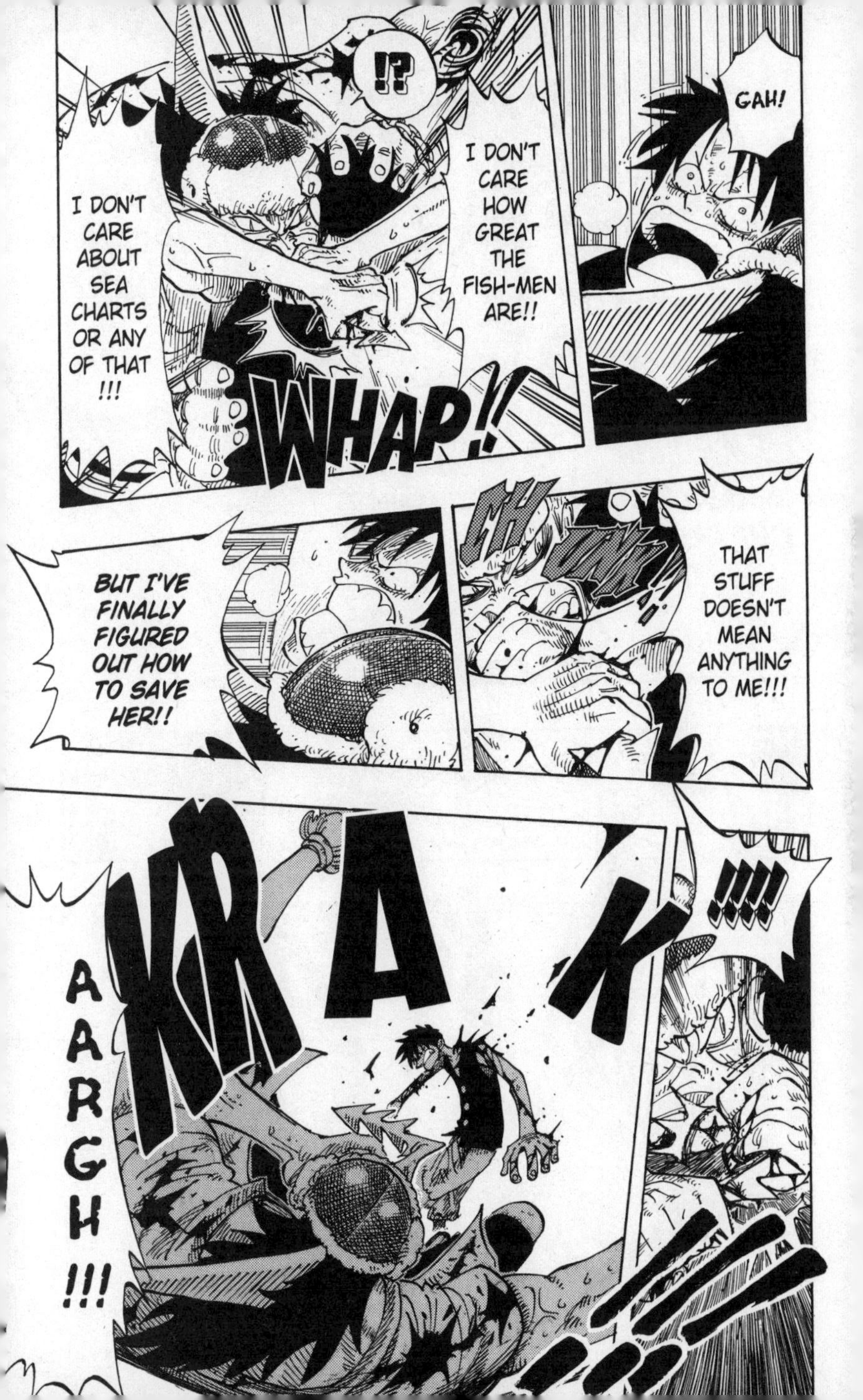
GAH!
!?
I DON'T CARE HOW GREAT THE FISH-MEN ARE!!
I DON'T CARE ABOUT SEA CHARTS OR ANY OF THAT!!!
WHAP!!
CHUNK!
THAT STUFF DOESN'T MEAN ANYTHING TO ME!!!
BUT I'VE FINALLY FIGURED OUT HOW TO SAVE HER!!
KRAK!!!!
AARGH!!!

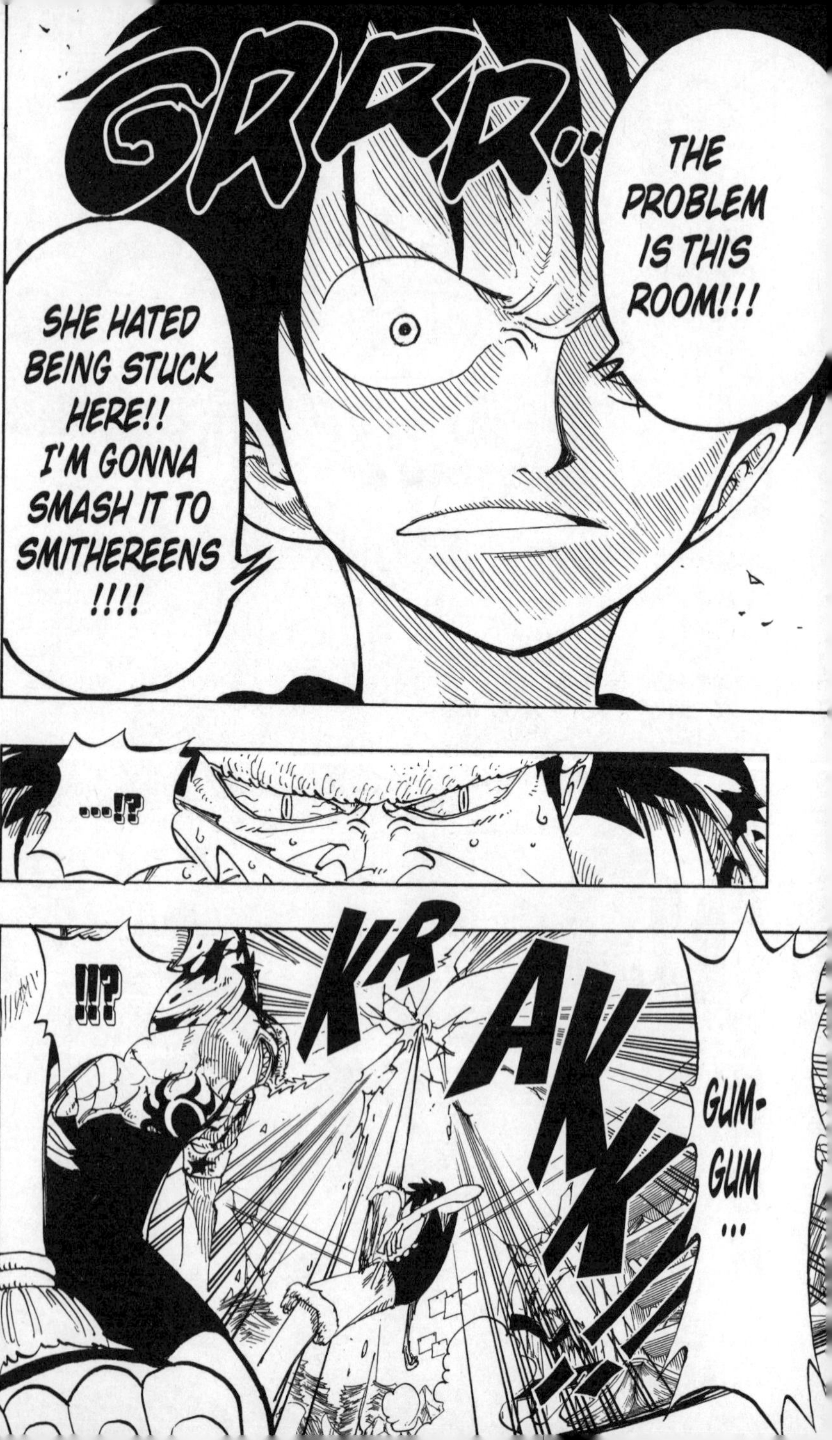
GRRR..
THE PROBLEM IS THIS ROOM!!!
SHE HATED BEING STUCK HERE!! I'M GONNA SMASH IT TO SMITHEREENS !!!!
...!?
GUM-GUM ...
KRAK
!!?

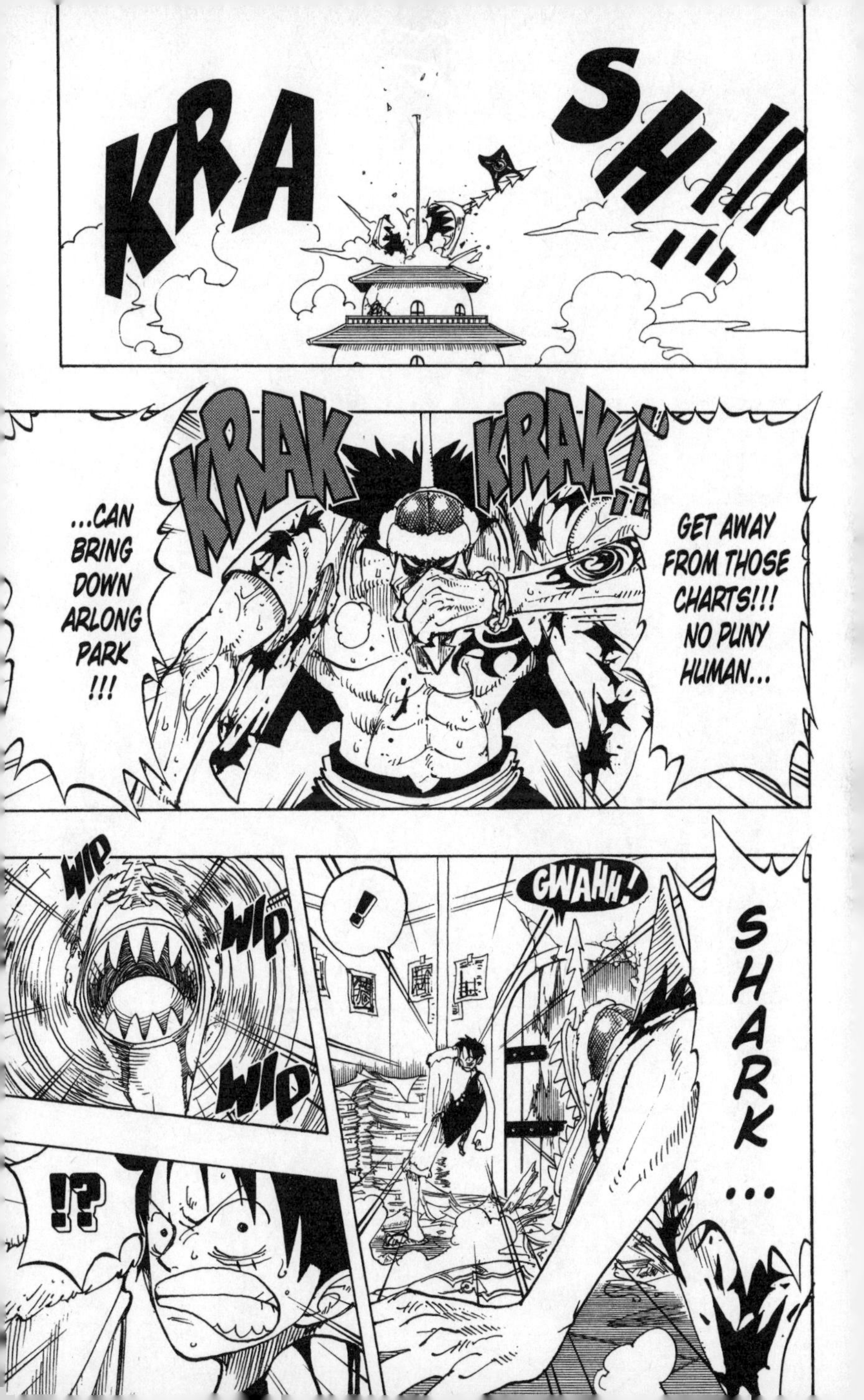
KRA
SH!!!
KRAK KRAK!!
GET AWAY FROM THOSE CHARTS!!! NO PUNY HUMAN...
...CAN BRING DOWN ARLONG PARK!!!
SHARK...
GWAHH!
!
WIP WIP WIP
!?

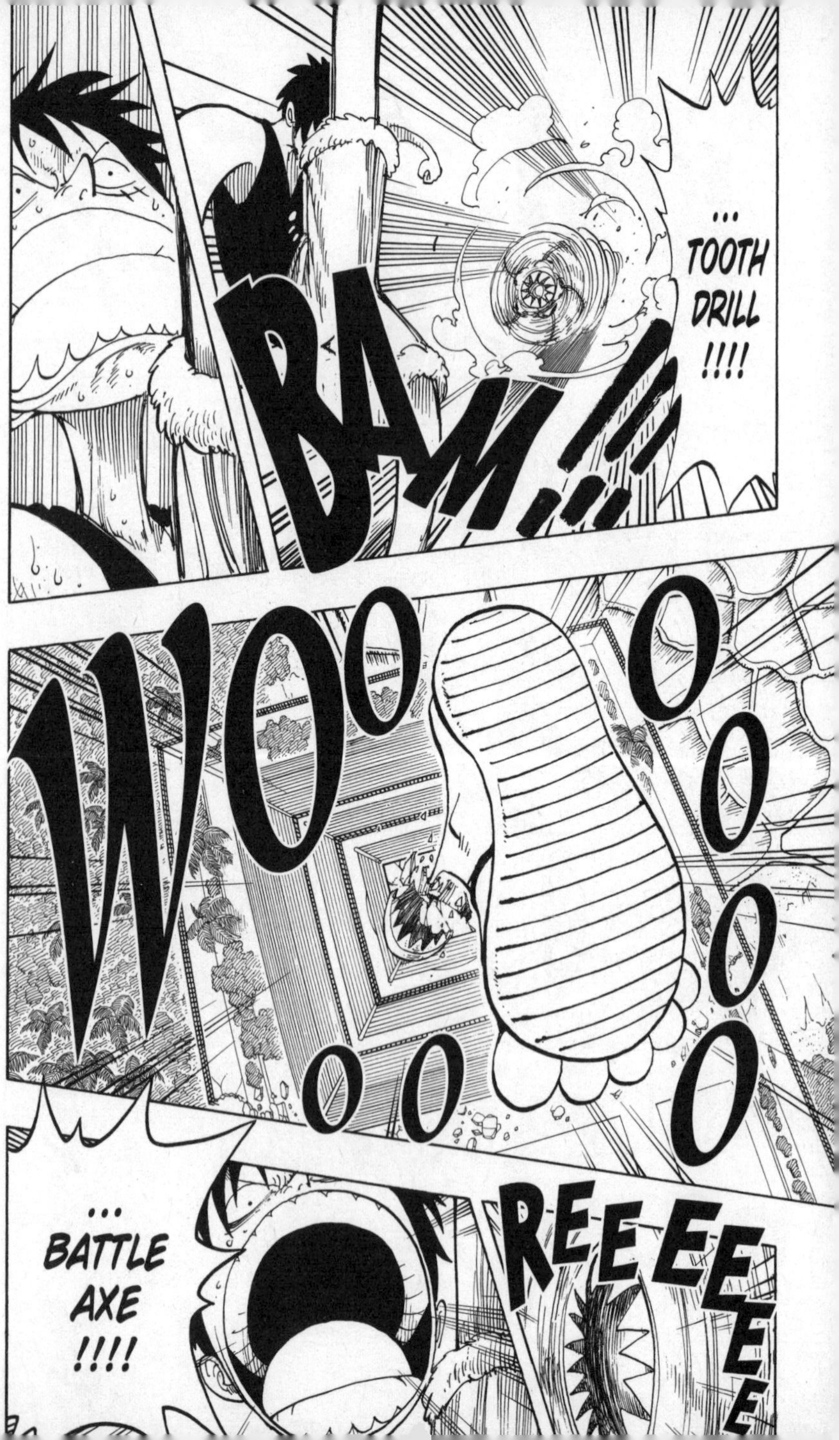

... TOOTH DRILL !!!!
BAM!!!
WOOOOOOOOOO
REEEEEEE
... BATTLE AXE !!!!

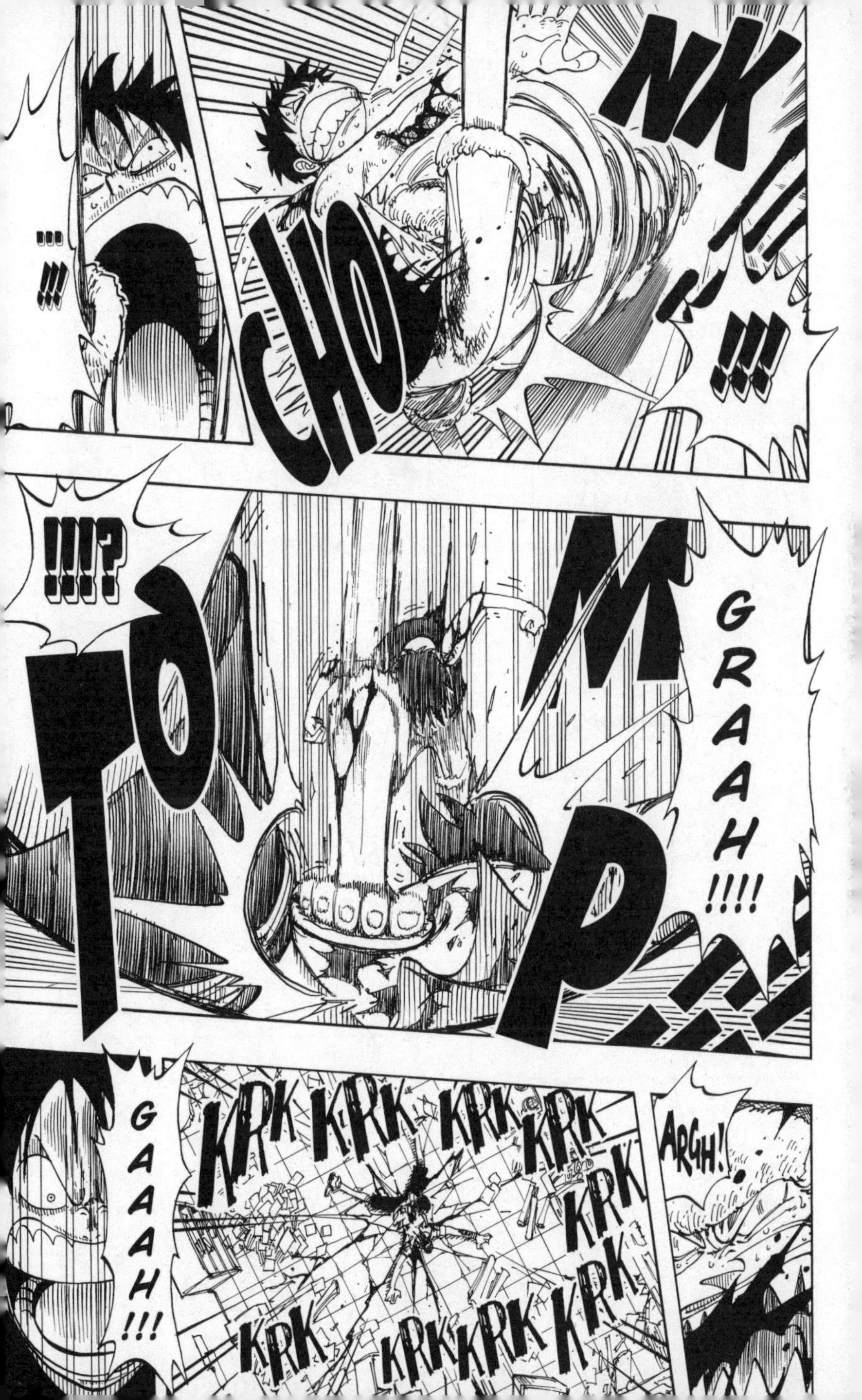

CHONK!!!
...!!!
GRAAH!!!!
TOMP!!
!!!?
ARGH!
KRK KRK KRK KRK
KRK KRK KRK
KRK KRK KRK KRK KRK
GAAAAH!!!

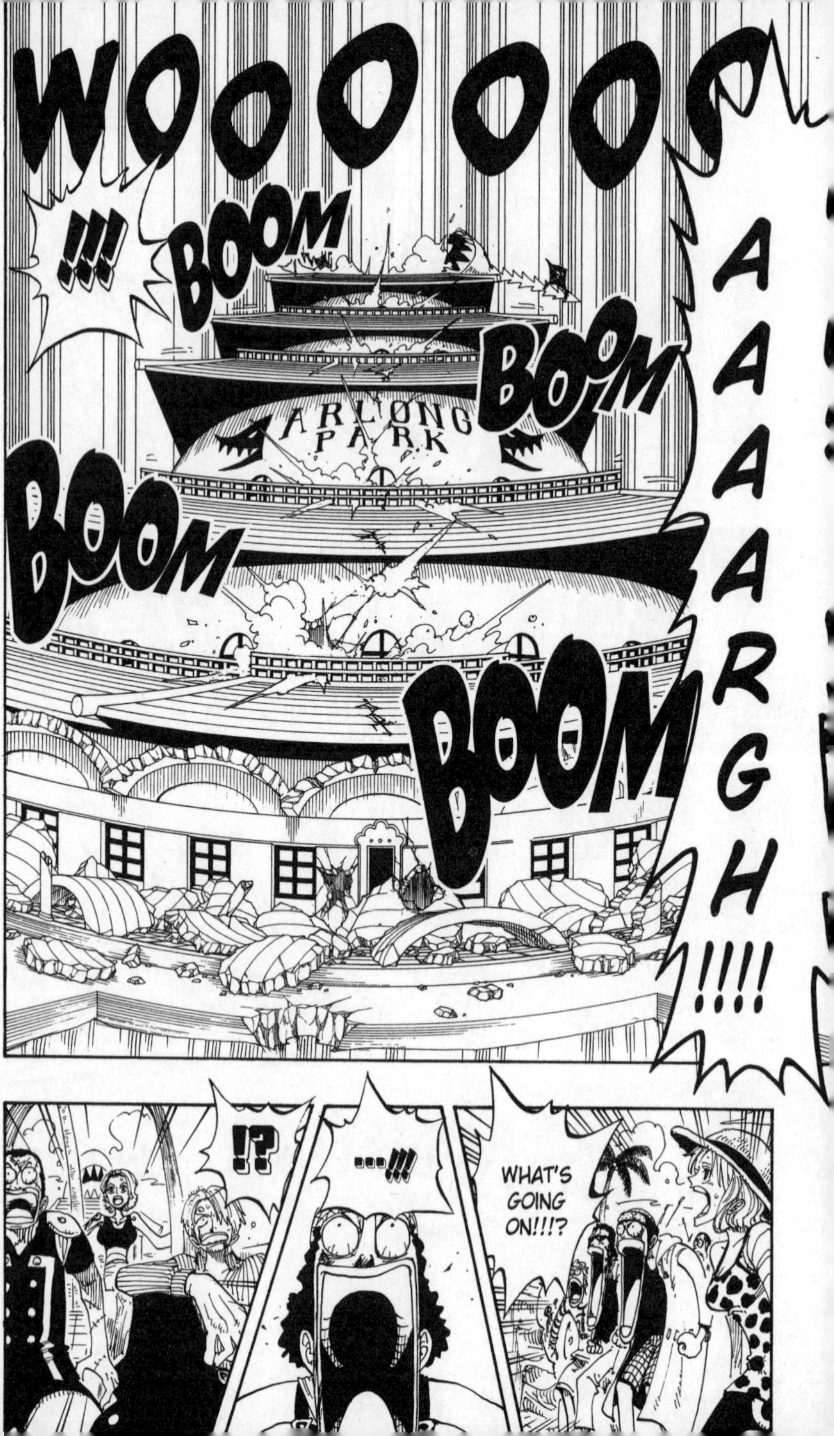
WOOOOOOOO
AAAARGH!!!!
!!!
BOOM
BOOM
ARLONG PARK
BOOM
BOOM
WHAT'S GOING ON!!!?
...!!!
!?

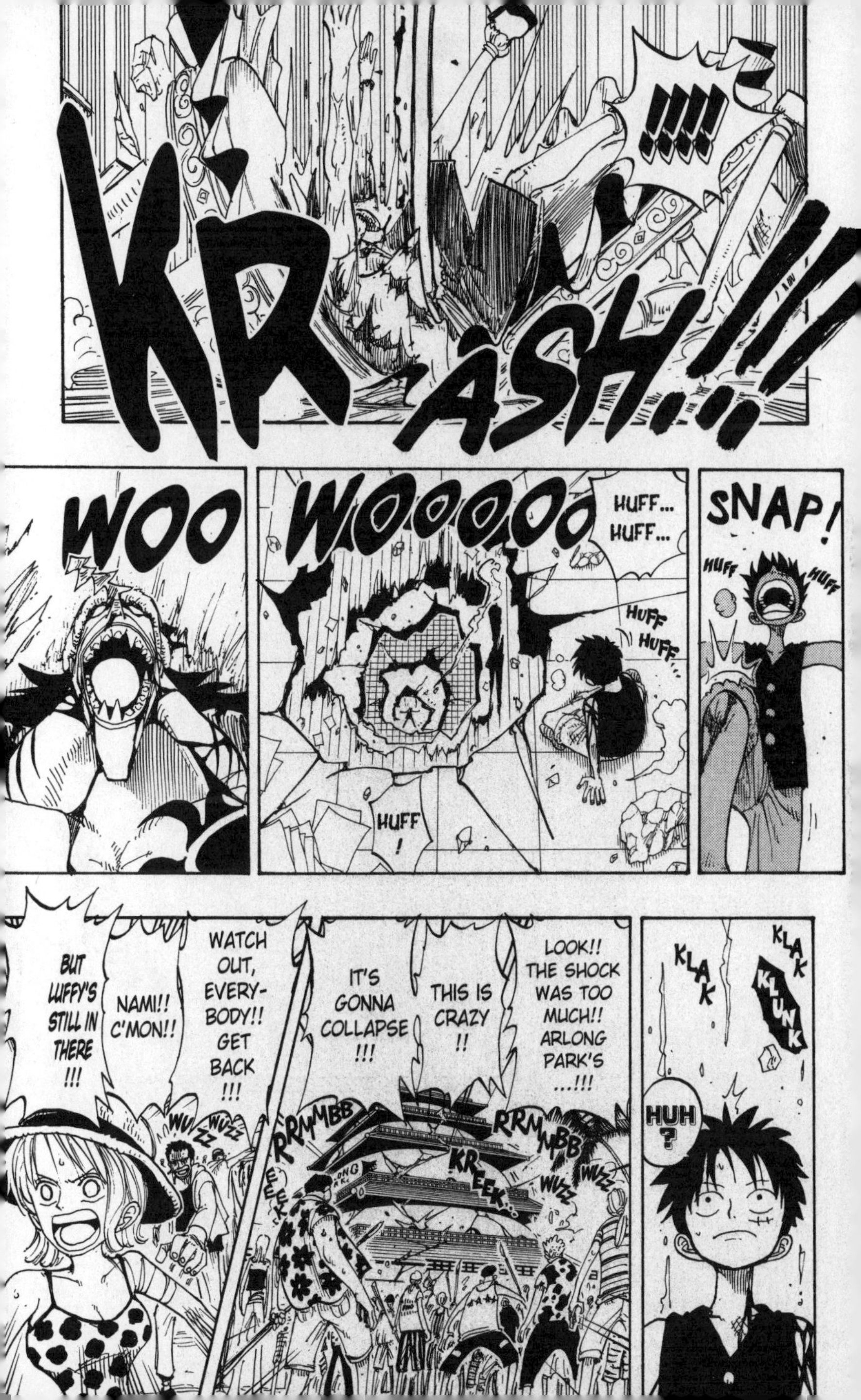
!!!!
KRASH!!!
SNAP!
HUFF HUFF
HUFF... HUFF...
HUFF HUFF...
WOOOOO
HUFF!
WOO
KLAK
KLAK
KLUNK
HUH?
LOOK!! THE SHOCK WAS TOO MUCH!! ARLONG PARK'S ...!!!
THIS IS CRAZY!!
IT'S GONNA COLLAPSE!!!
WATCH OUT, EVERY-BODY!! GET BACK!!!
NAMI!! C'MON!!
BUT LUFFY'S STILL IN THERE!!!
RRMMBB
RRMMBB
KREEK..
WUZZ
WUZZ
WUZZ WUZZ
EEEK

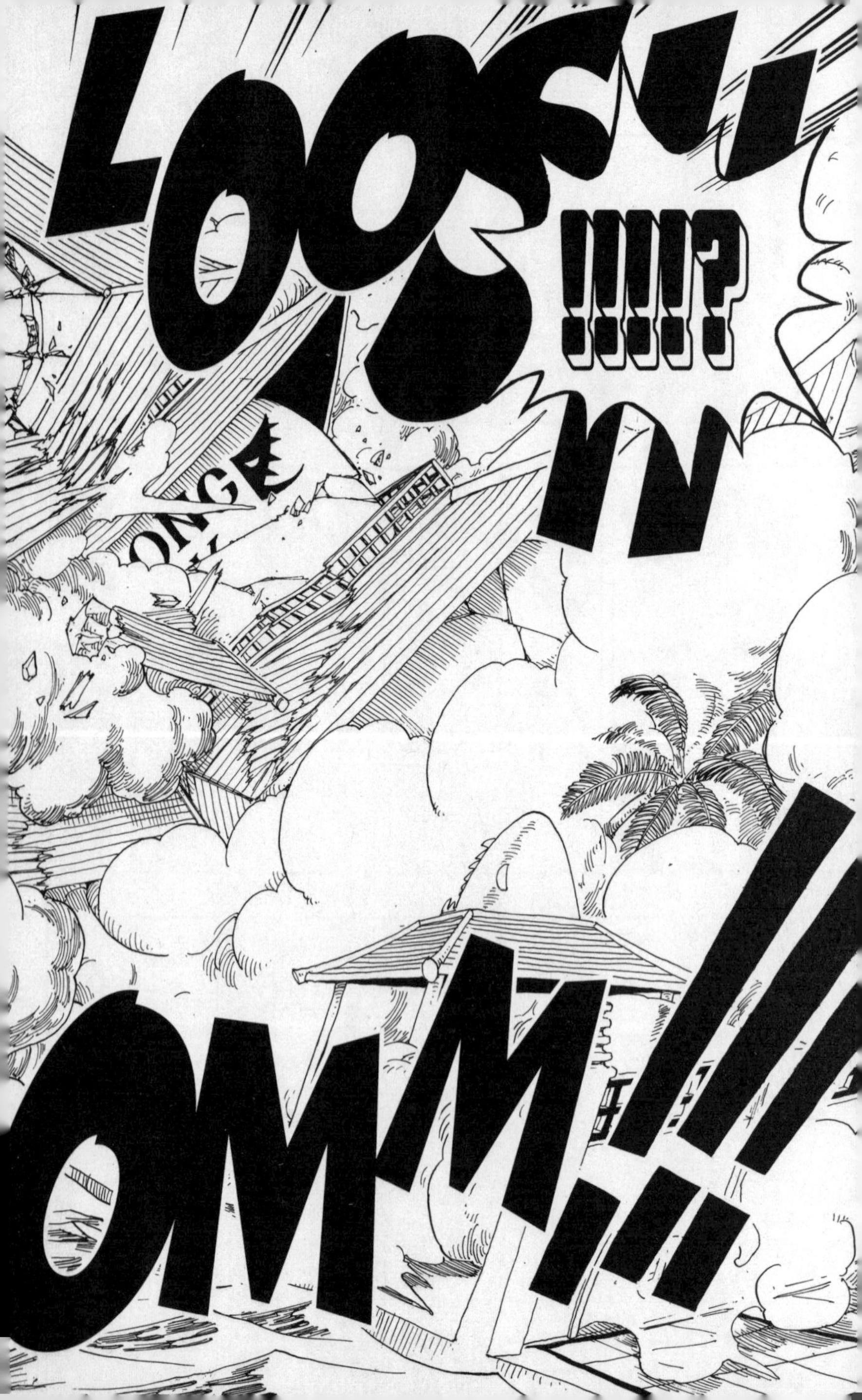

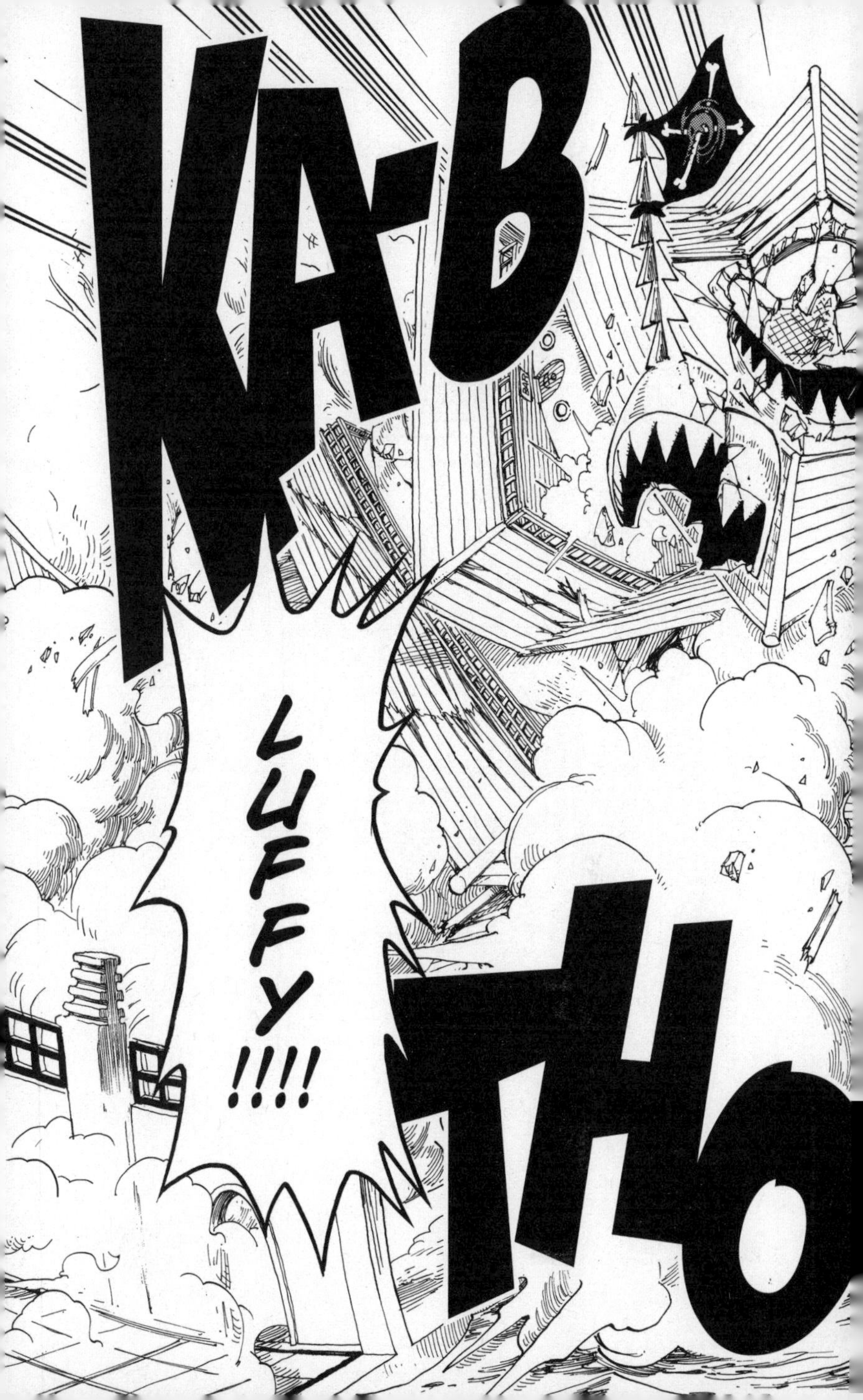
KA-B
LUFFY!!!!
THO

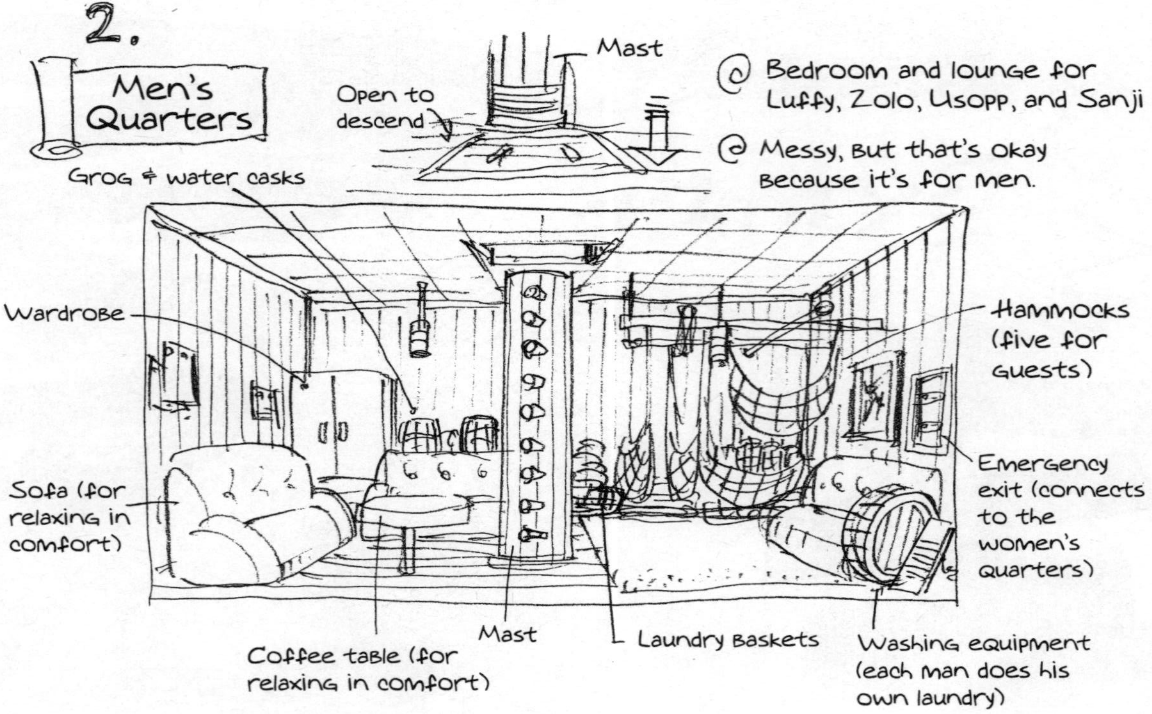
2.
Men's Quarters
Mast
Open to descend
@ Bedroom and lounge for Luffy, Zolo, Usopp, and Sanji
@ Messy, but that's okay because it's for men.
Grog & water casks
Wardrobe
Hammocks (five for guests)
Sofa (for relaxing in comfort)
Emergency exit (connects to the women's quarters)
Mast
Laundry baskets
Washing equipment (each man does his own laundry)
Coffee table (for relaxing in comfort)

Chapter 94:
THE OTHER VILLAIN

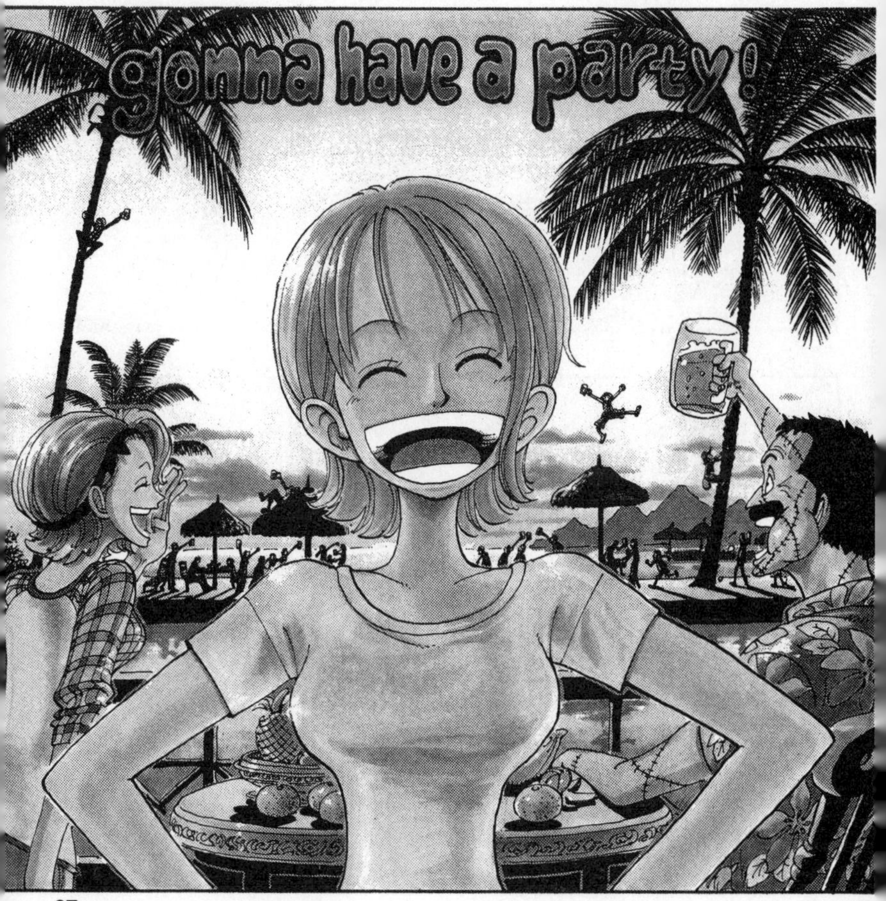
gonna have a party!

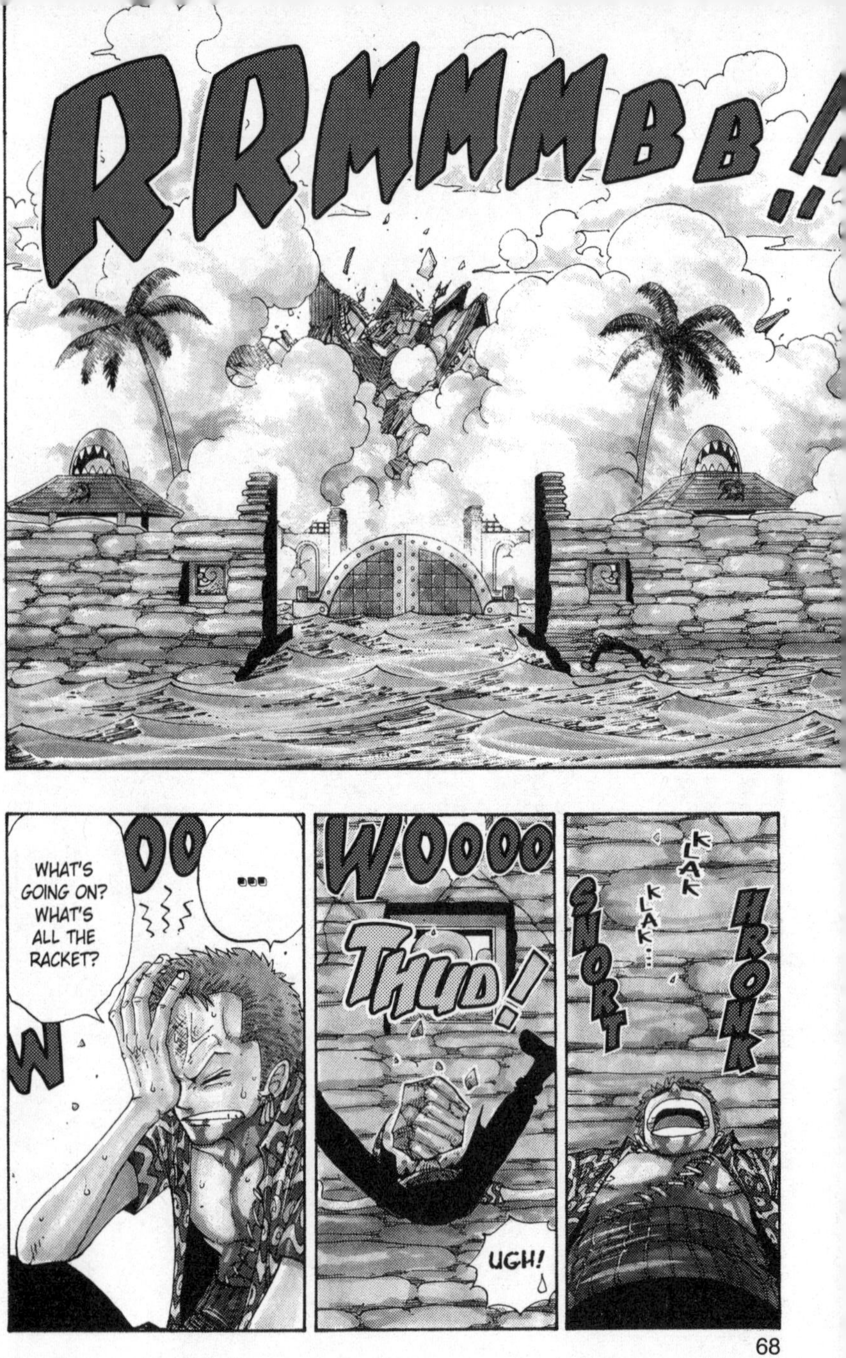
RRMMMBB!!
KLAK KLAK...
SNORT
HRONK
WOOOO
THUD!
UGH!
OO
...
WHAT'S GOING ON? WHAT'S ALL THE RACKET?
W

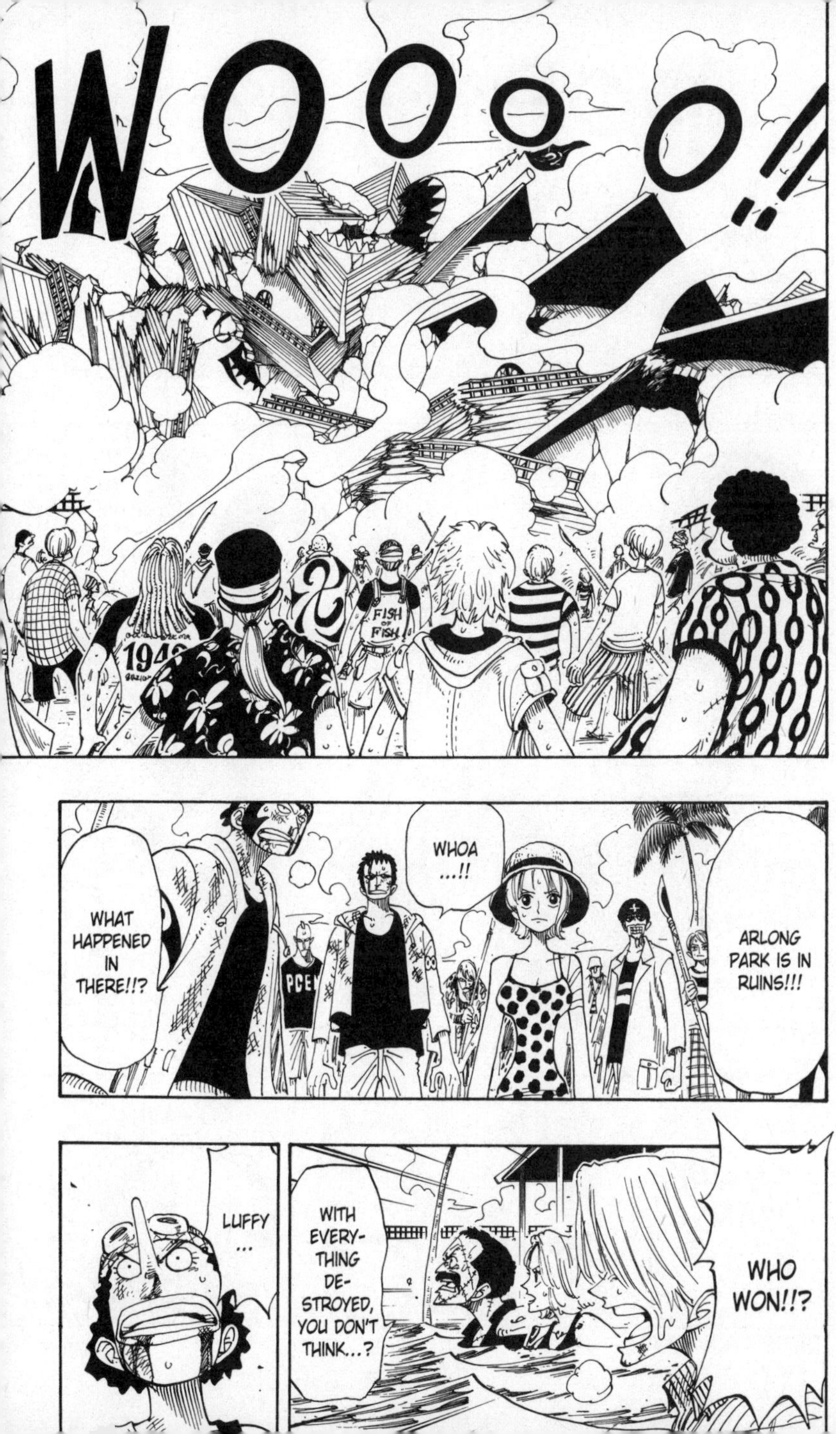
WOOOO!!
ARLONG PARK IS IN RUINS!!!
WHOA ...!!
WHAT HAPPENED IN THERE!!?
WHO WON!!?
WITH EVERY-THING DE-STROYED, YOU DON'T THINK...?
LUFFY ...

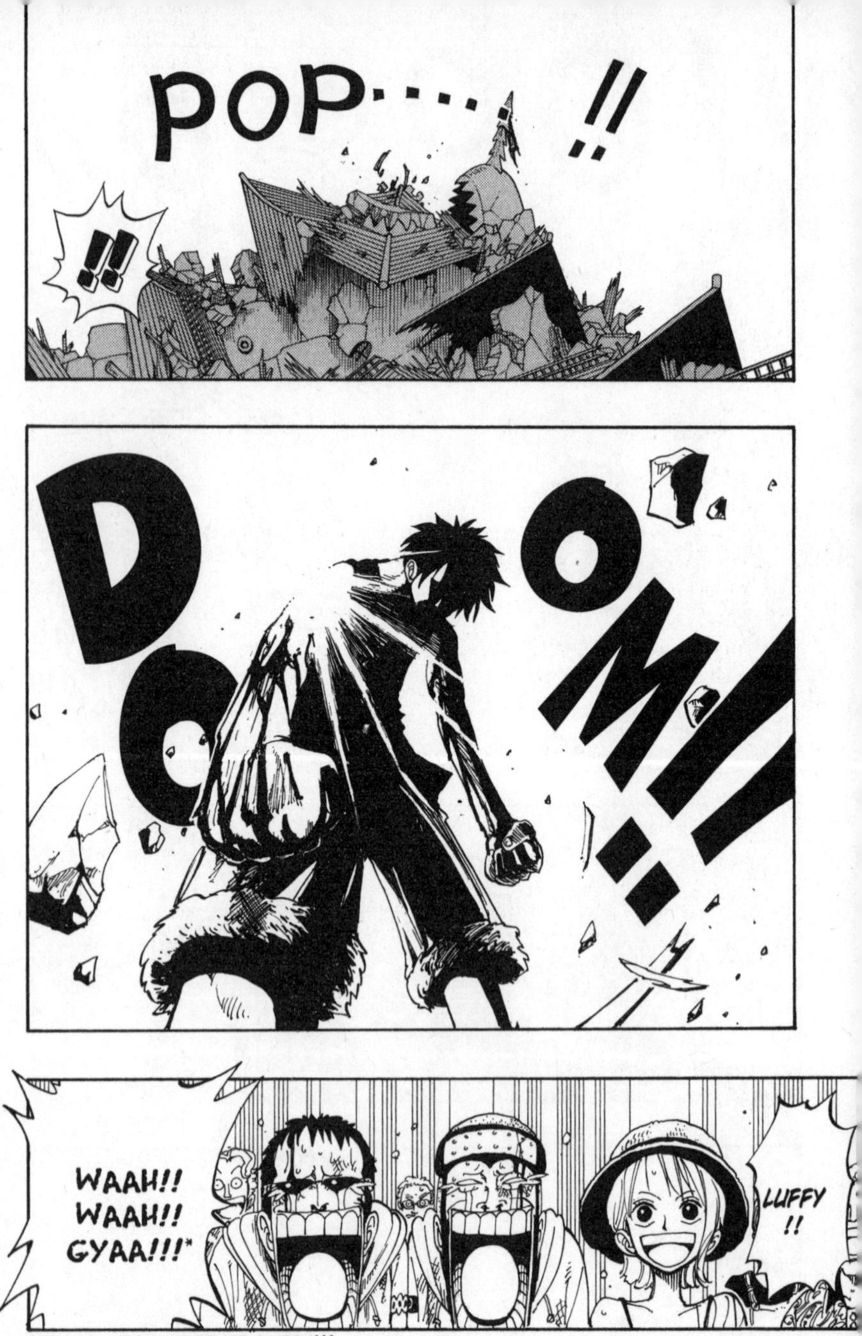
POP....!!
!!
DOOM!!
LUFFY!!
WAAH!! WAAH!! GYAA!!!*

*TRANSLATION: BROTHER LUFFY!!!

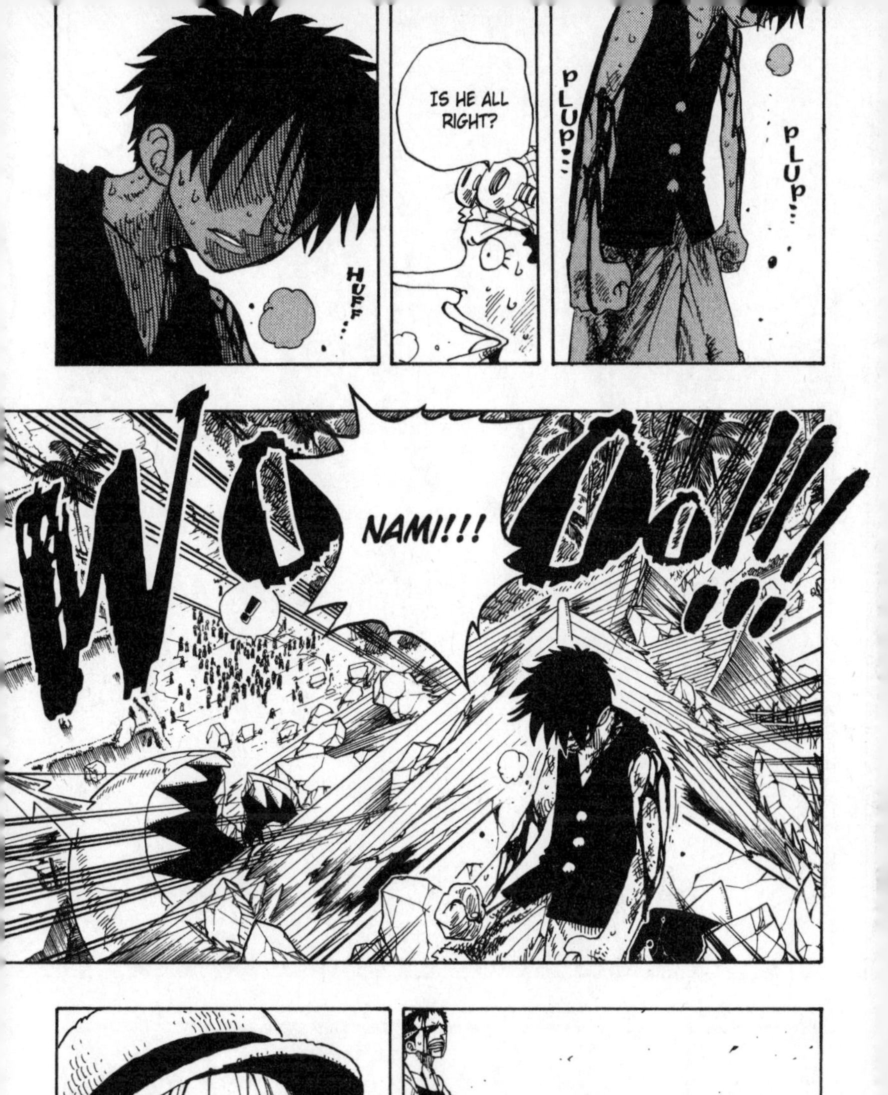
PLUP...
PLUP...
IS HE ALL RIGHT?
HUFF...
NAMI!!!
!
...?

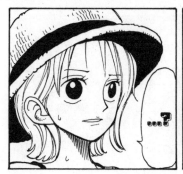

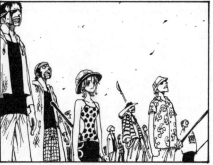

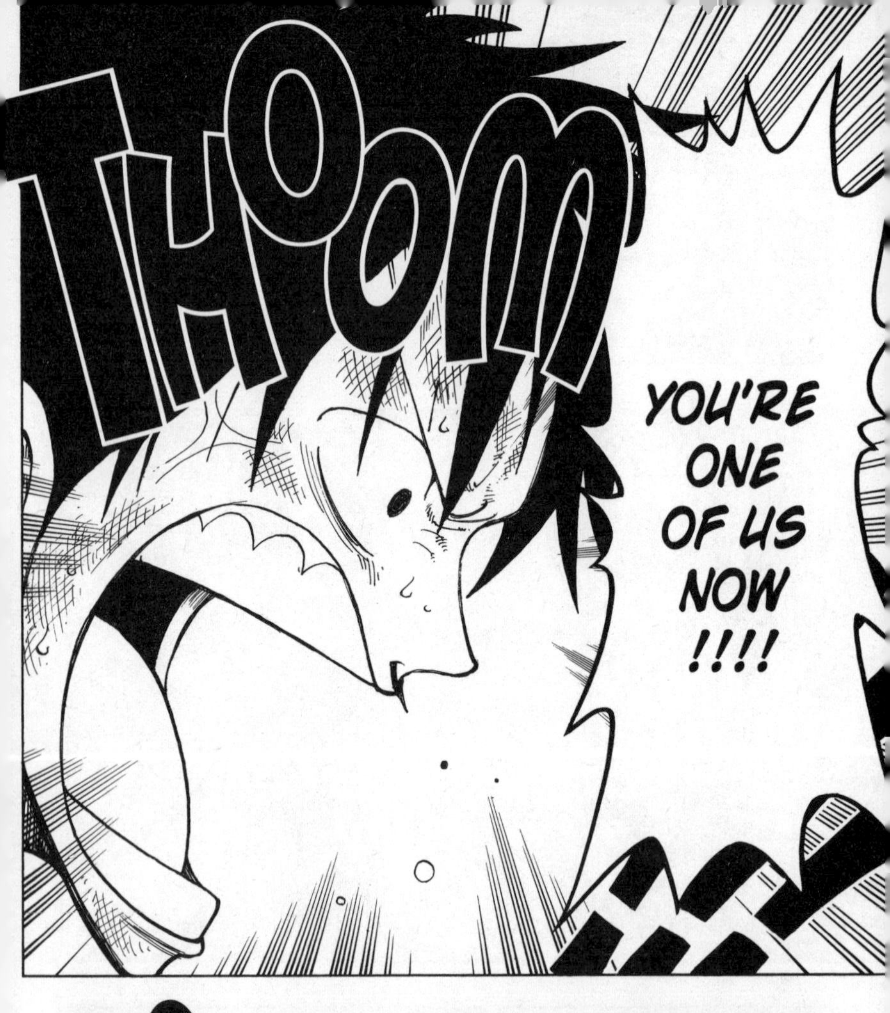
THOOM
YOU'RE ONE OF US NOW !!!!
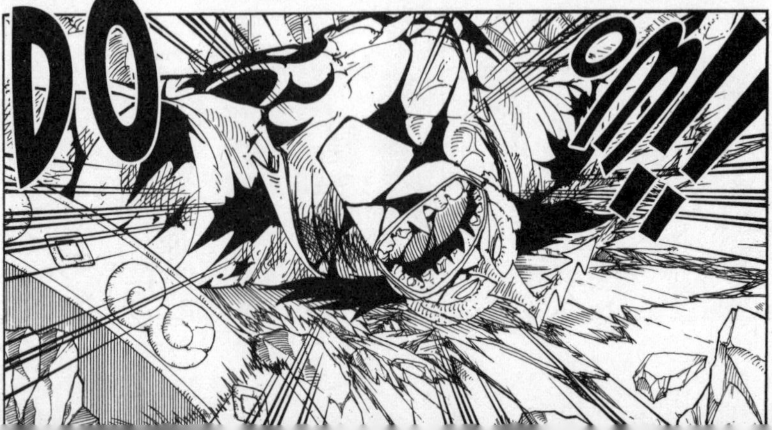
DOOM!!

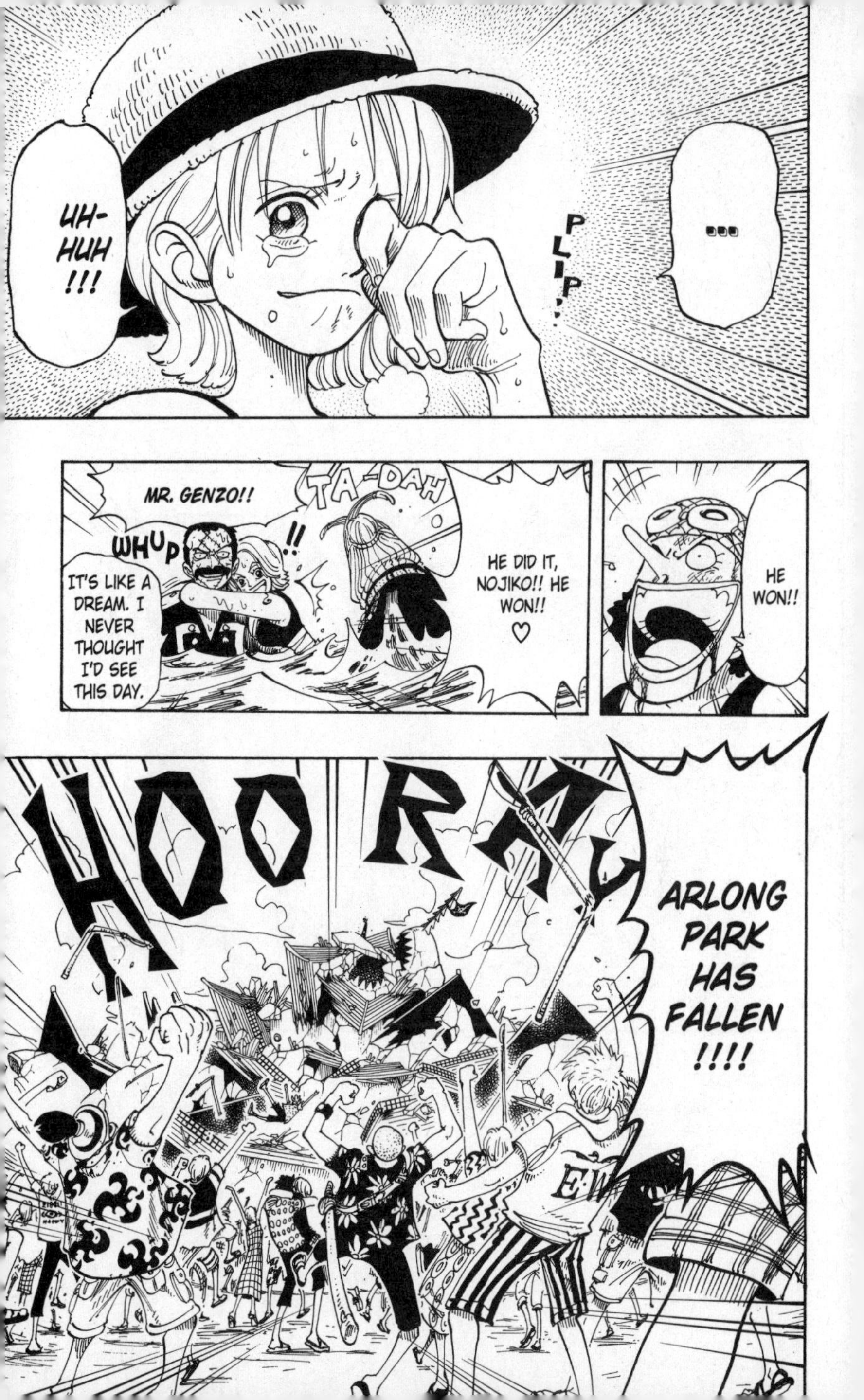
...
PLIP
UH-HUH!!!
HE WON!!
TA-DAH
HE DID IT, NOJIKO!! HE WON!! ♡
MR. GENZO!!
!!
WHUP
IT'S LIKE A DREAM. I NEVER THOUGHT I'D SEE THIS DAY.
ARLONG PARK HAS FALLEN!!!!
HOORAY

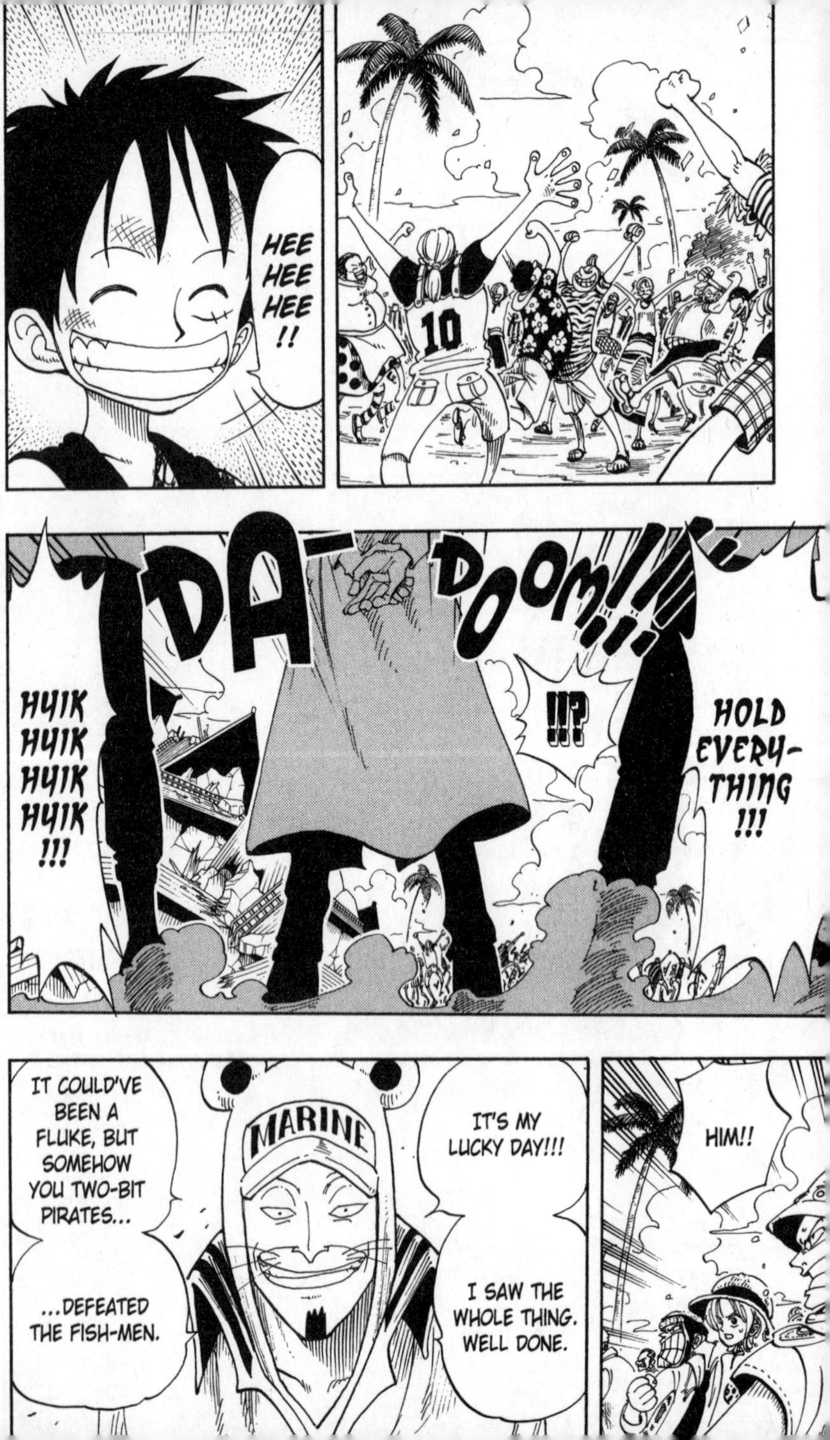
HEE HEE HEE !!
DA-DOOM!!!
HOLD EVERY-THING !!!
!!?
HYIK HYIK HYIK HYIK !!!
HIM!!
IT'S MY LUCKY DAY!!!
MARINE
IT COULD'VE BEEN A FLUKE, BUT SOMEHOW YOU TWO-BIT PIRATES...
I SAW THE WHOLE THING. WELL DONE.
...DEFEATED THE FISH-MEN.

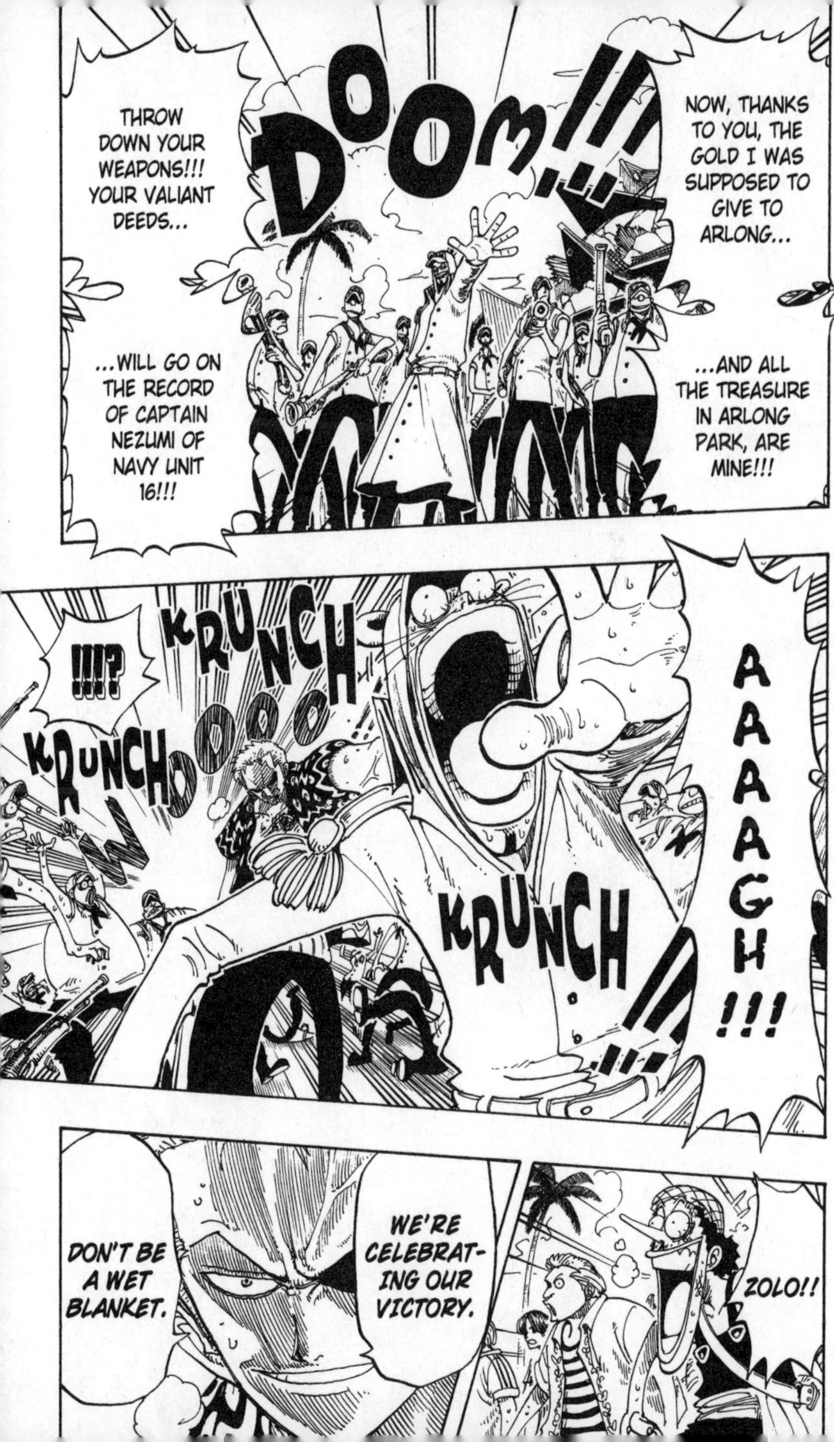
NOW, THANKS TO YOU, THE GOLD I WAS SUPPOSED TO GIVE TO ARLONG...
THROW DOWN YOUR WEAPONS!!! YOUR VALIANT DEEDS...
DOOM!!!
...AND ALL THE TREASURE IN ARLONG PARK, ARE MINE!!!
...WILL GO ON THE RECORD OF CAPTAIN NEZUMI OF NAVY UNIT 16!!!
AAAAAGH!!!
KRUNCH
!!!?
KRUNCH
KRUNCH
ZOLO!!
WE'RE CELEBRATING OUR VICTORY.
DON'T BE A WET BLANKET.

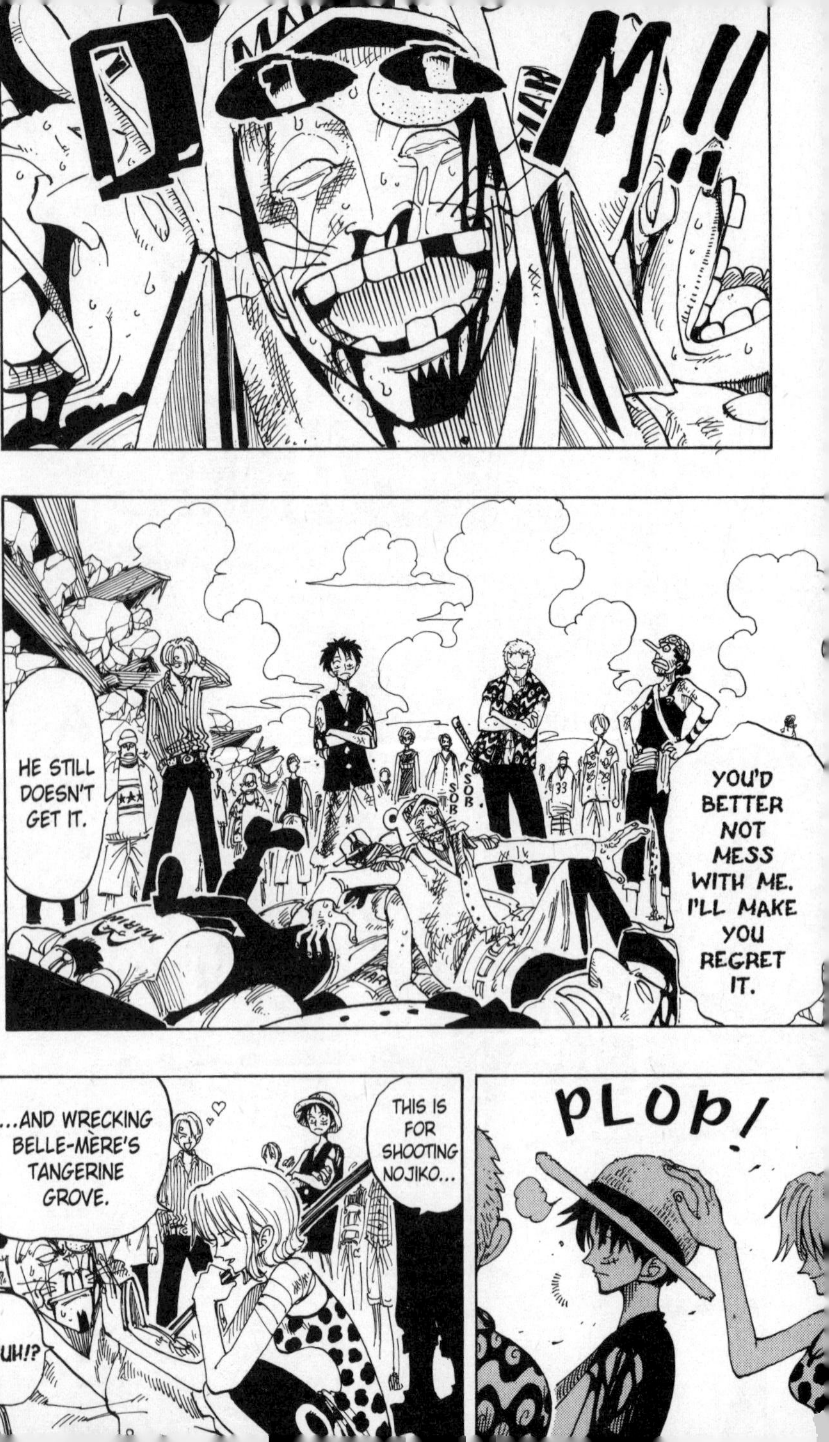
YOU'D BETTER NOT MESS WITH ME. I'LL MAKE YOU REGRET IT.
SOB SOB
HE STILL DOESN'T GET IT.
PLOP!
THIS IS FOR SHOOTING NOJIKO...
...AND WRECKING BELLE-MÈRE'S TANGERINE GROVE.
HUH!?

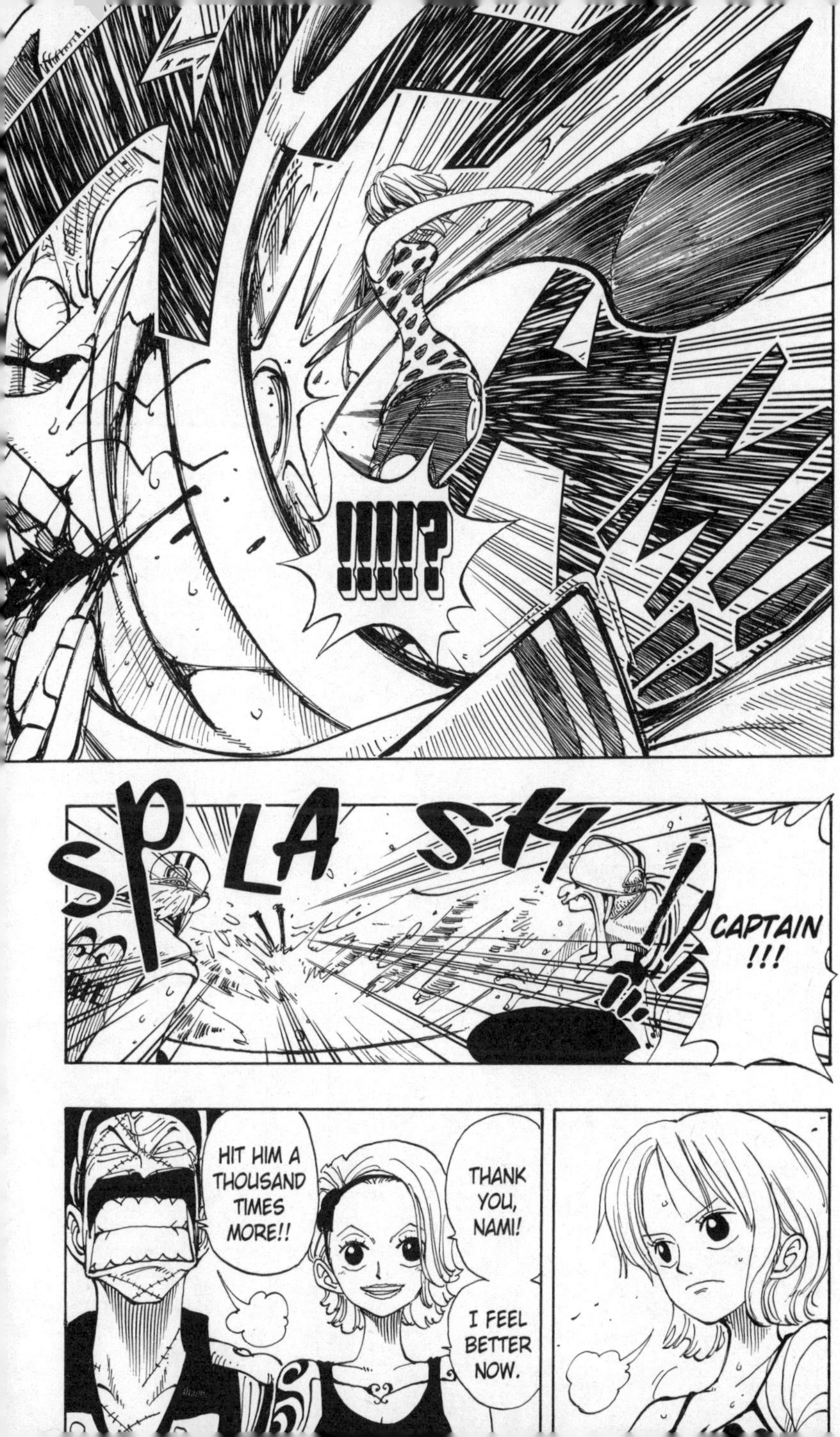
!!!!?
SPLASH!!!
CAPTAIN!!!
THANK YOU, NAMI!
I FEEL BETTER NOW.
HIT HIM A THOUSAND TIMES MORE!!

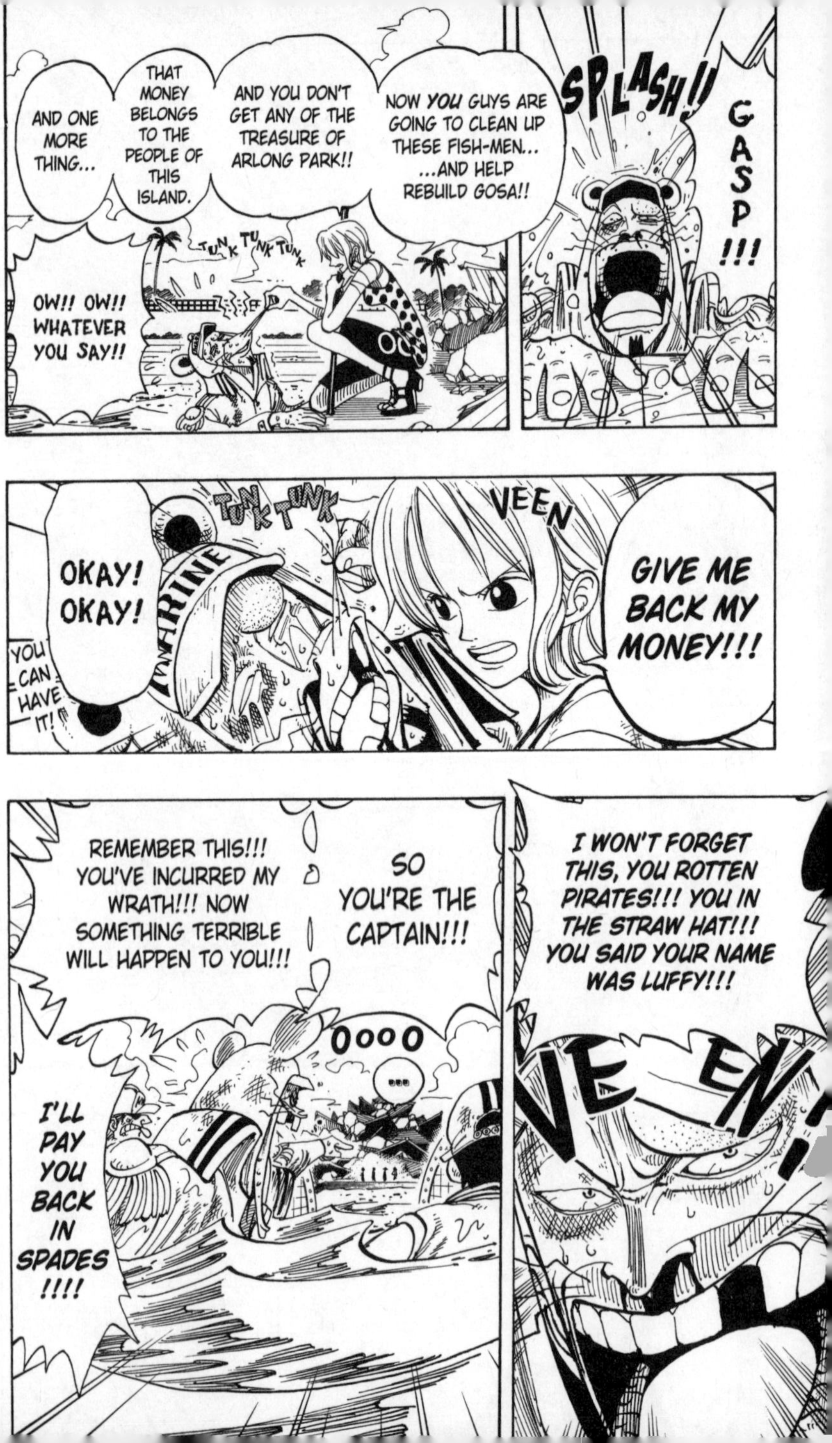
SPLASH!!
GASP!!!
NOW YOU GUYS ARE GOING TO CLEAN UP THESE FISH-MEN... ...AND HELP REBUILD GOSA!!
AND YOU DON'T GET ANY OF THE TREASURE OF ARLONG PARK!!
THAT MONEY BELONGS TO THE PEOPLE OF THIS ISLAND.
AND ONE MORE THING...
TUNK TUNK TUNK
OW!! OW!! WHATEVER YOU SAY!!
GIVE ME BACK MY MONEY!!!
VEEN
TUNK TUNK
OKAY! OKAY!
YOU CAN HAVE IT!
I WON'T FORGET THIS, YOU ROTTEN PIRATES!!! YOU IN THE STRAW HAT!!! YOU SAID YOUR NAME WAS LUFFY!!!
VEEN
SO YOU'RE THE CAPTAIN!!!
REMEMBER THIS!!! YOU'VE INCURRED MY WRATH!!! NOW SOMETHING TERRIBLE WILL HAPPEN TO YOU!!!
OOOO
I'LL PAY YOU BACK IN SPADES!!!!

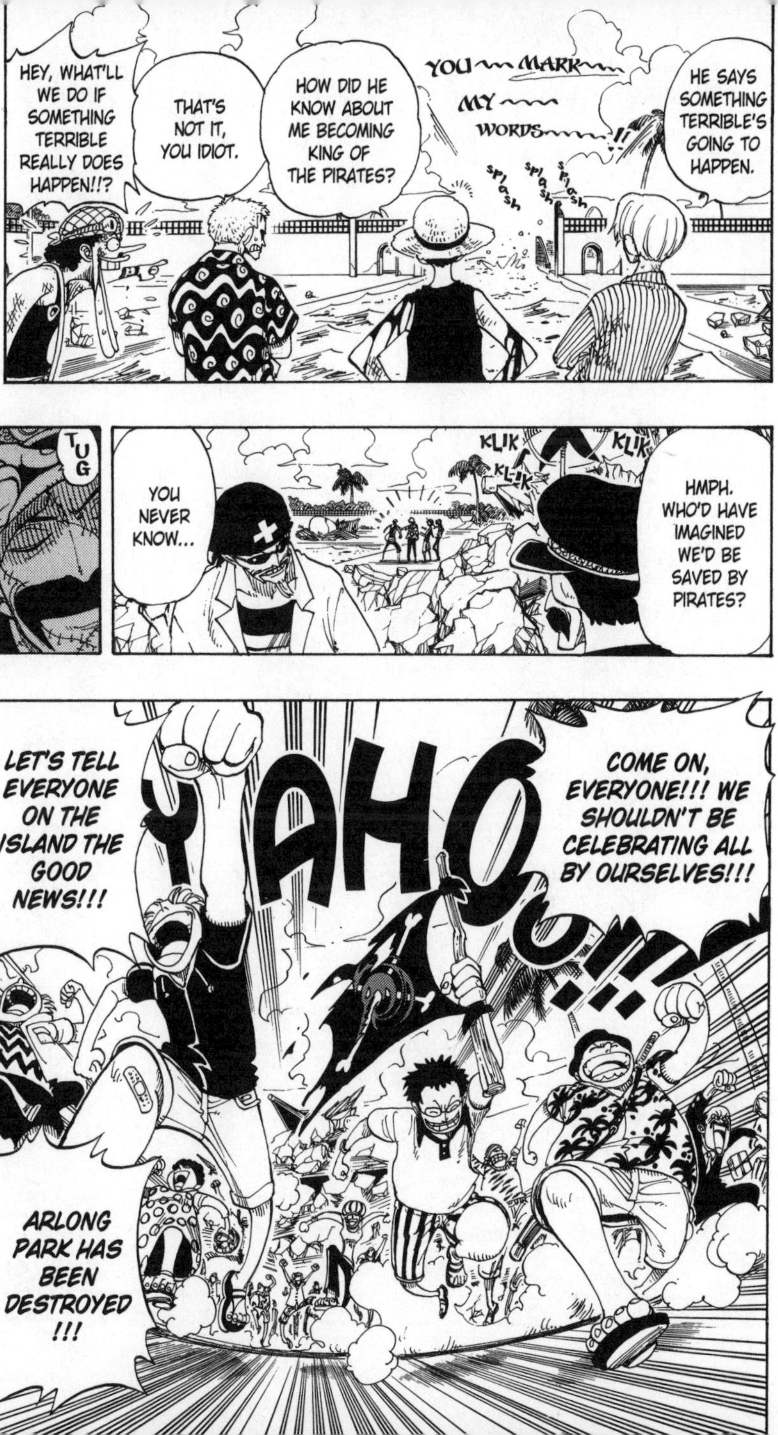
YOU MARK MY WORDS!!
splash splash splash
HE SAYS SOMETHING TERRIBLE'S GOING TO HAPPEN.
HOW DID HE KNOW ABOUT ME BECOMING KING OF THE PIRATES?
THAT'S NOT IT, YOU IDIOT.
HEY, WHAT'LL WE DO IF SOMETHING TERRIBLE REALLY DOES HAPPEN!!?
KLIK KLIK KLIK
HMPH. WHO'D HAVE IMAGINED WE'D BE SAVED BY PIRATES?
YOU NEVER KNOW...
TUG
COME ON, EVERYONE!!! WE SHOULDN'T BE CELEBRATING ALL BY OURSELVES!!!
YAHOO!!!
LET'S TELL EVERYONE ON THE ISLAND THE GOOD NEWS!!!
ARLONG PARK HAS BEEN DESTROYED!!!

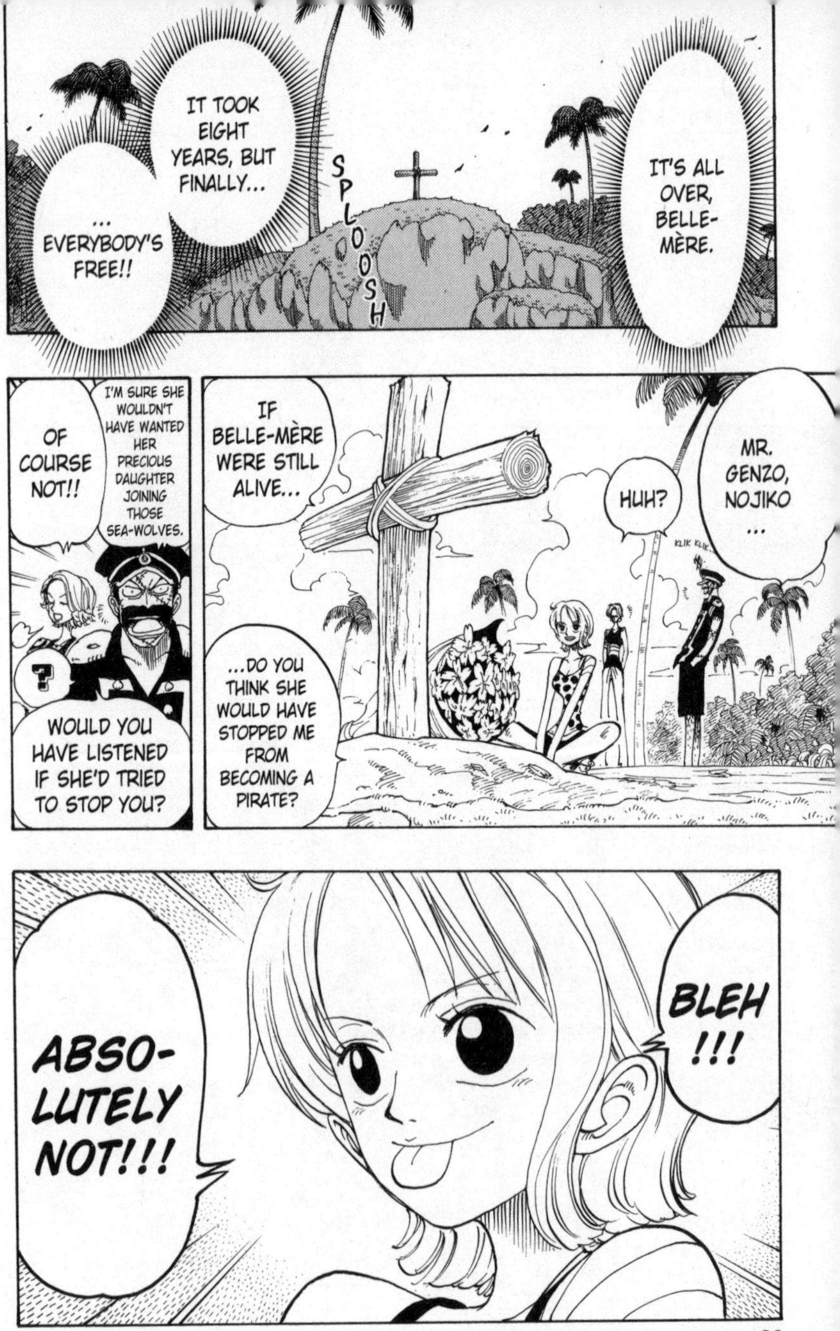
IT'S ALL OVER, BELLE-MÈRE.
SPLOOSH
IT TOOK EIGHT YEARS, BUT FINALLY...
... EVERYBODY'S FREE!!
MR. GENZO, NOJIKO ...
HUH?
KLIK KLIK
IF BELLE-MÈRE WERE STILL ALIVE...
...DO YOU THINK SHE WOULD HAVE STOPPED ME FROM BECOMING A PIRATE?
I'M SURE SHE WOULDN'T HAVE WANTED HER PRECIOUS DAUGHTER JOINING THOSE SEA-WOLVES.
OF COURSE NOT!!
?
WOULD YOU HAVE LISTENED IF SHE'D TRIED TO STOP YOU?
BLEH !!!
ABSO-LUTELY NOT!!!

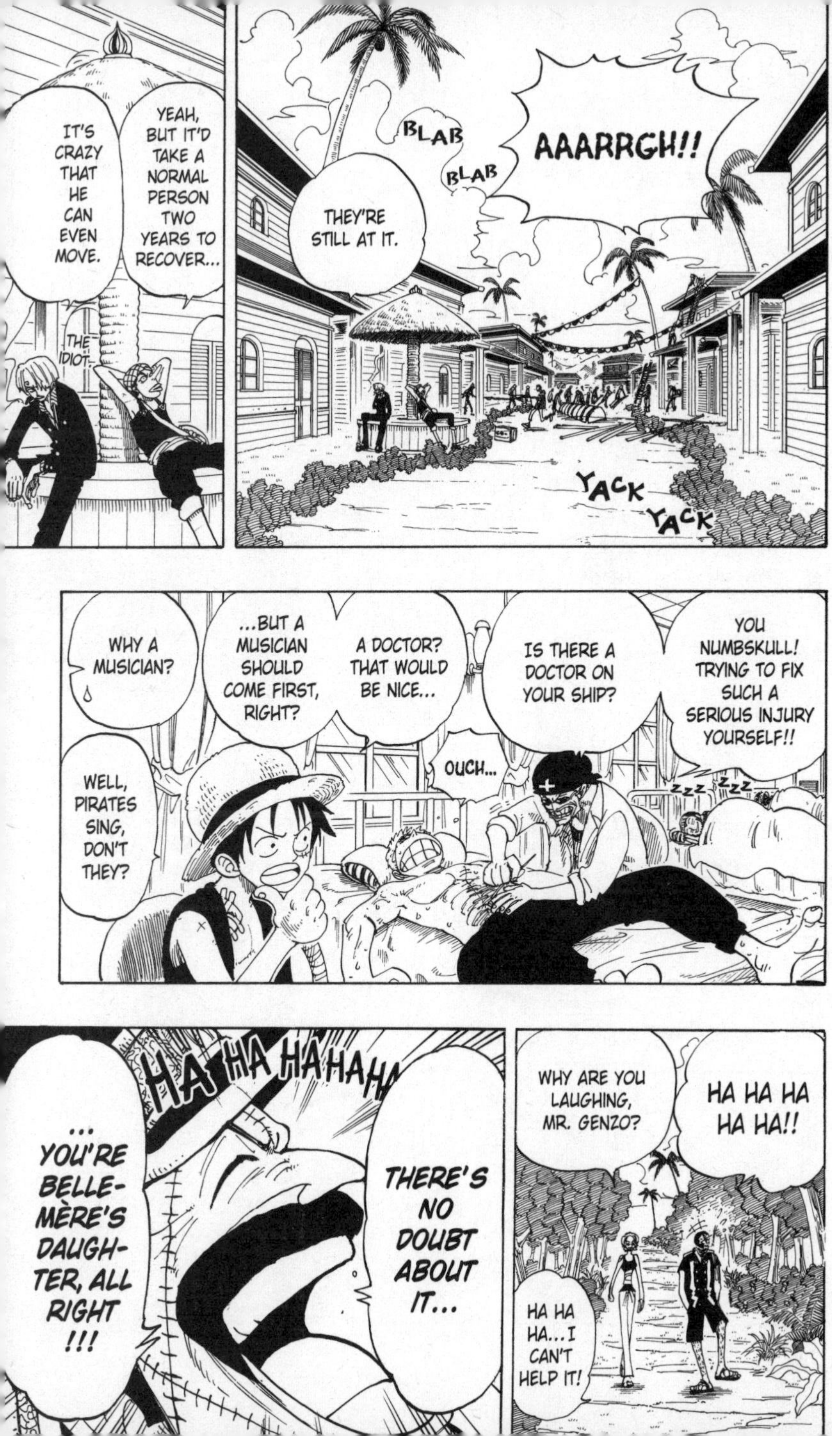
AAARRGH!!
BLAB
BLAB
THEY'RE STILL AT IT.
YACK
YACK
YEAH, BUT IT'D TAKE A NORMAL PERSON TWO YEARS TO RECOVER...
IT'S CRAZY THAT HE CAN EVEN MOVE.
THE IDIOT...
YOU NUMBSKULL! TRYING TO FIX SUCH A SERIOUS INJURY YOURSELF!!
IS THERE A DOCTOR ON YOUR SHIP?
A DOCTOR? THAT WOULD BE NICE...
...BUT A MUSICIAN SHOULD COME FIRST, RIGHT?
WHY A MUSICIAN?
ZZZ
ZZZ
OUCH...
WELL, PIRATES SING, DON'T THEY?
HA HA HA HA HA!!
WHY ARE YOU LAUGHING, MR. GENZO?
HA HA HA... I CAN'T HELP IT!
HA HA HAHAHA
THERE'S NO DOUBT ABOUT IT...
...YOU'RE BELLE-MÈRE'S DAUGHTER, ALL RIGHT!!!

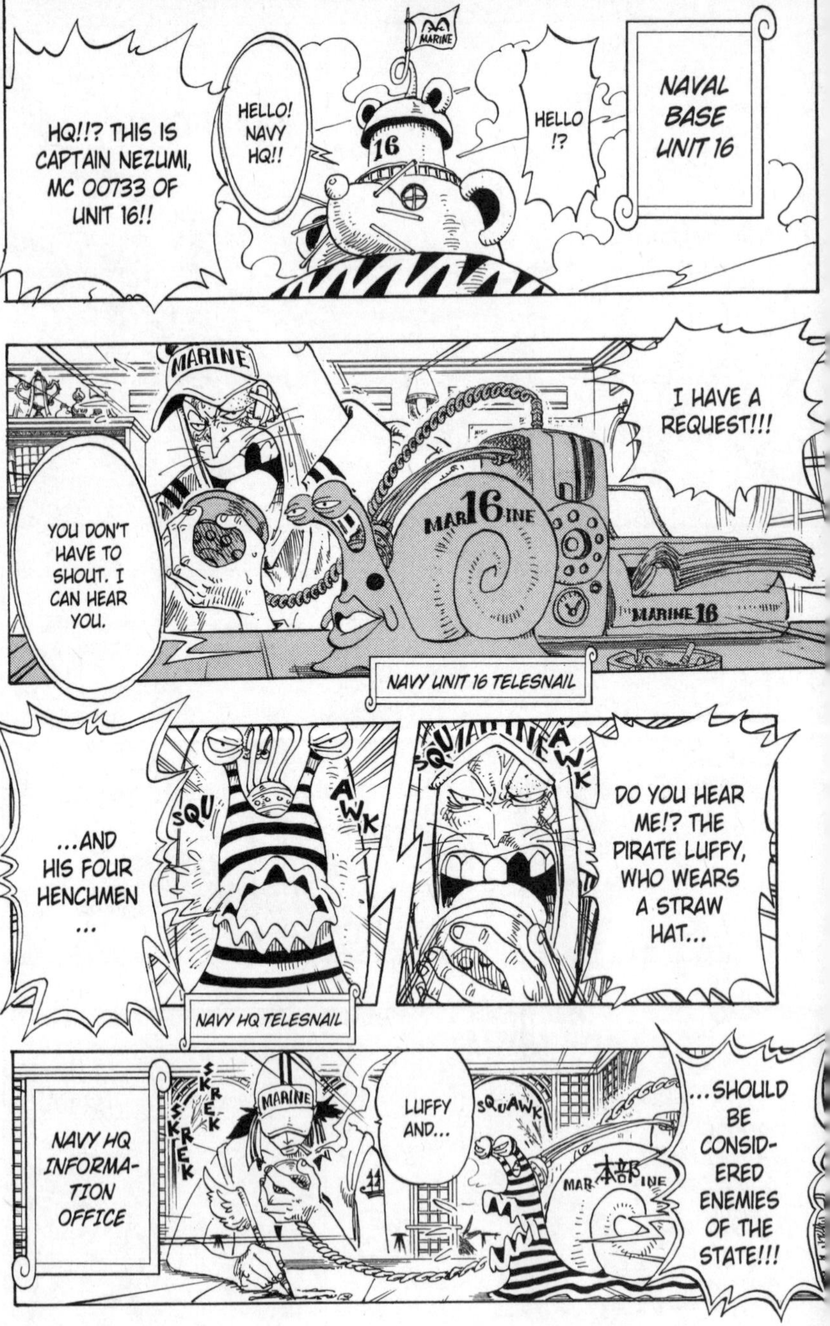
NAVAL BASE UNIT 16
HELLO !?
HELLO! NAVY HQ!!
HQ!!? THIS IS CAPTAIN NEZUMI, MC 00733 OF UNIT 16!!
I HAVE A REQUEST!!!
YOU DON'T HAVE TO SHOUT. I CAN HEAR YOU.
NAVY UNIT 16 TELESNAIL
SQUAWK
DO YOU HEAR ME!? THE PIRATE LUFFY, WHO WEARS A STRAW HAT...
SQUAWK
...AND HIS FOUR HENCHMEN ...
NAVY HQ TELESNAIL
...SHOULD BE CONSID-ERED ENEMIES OF THE STATE!!!
SQUAWK
LUFFY AND...
SKREK SKREK
NAVY HQ INFORMA-TION OFFICE

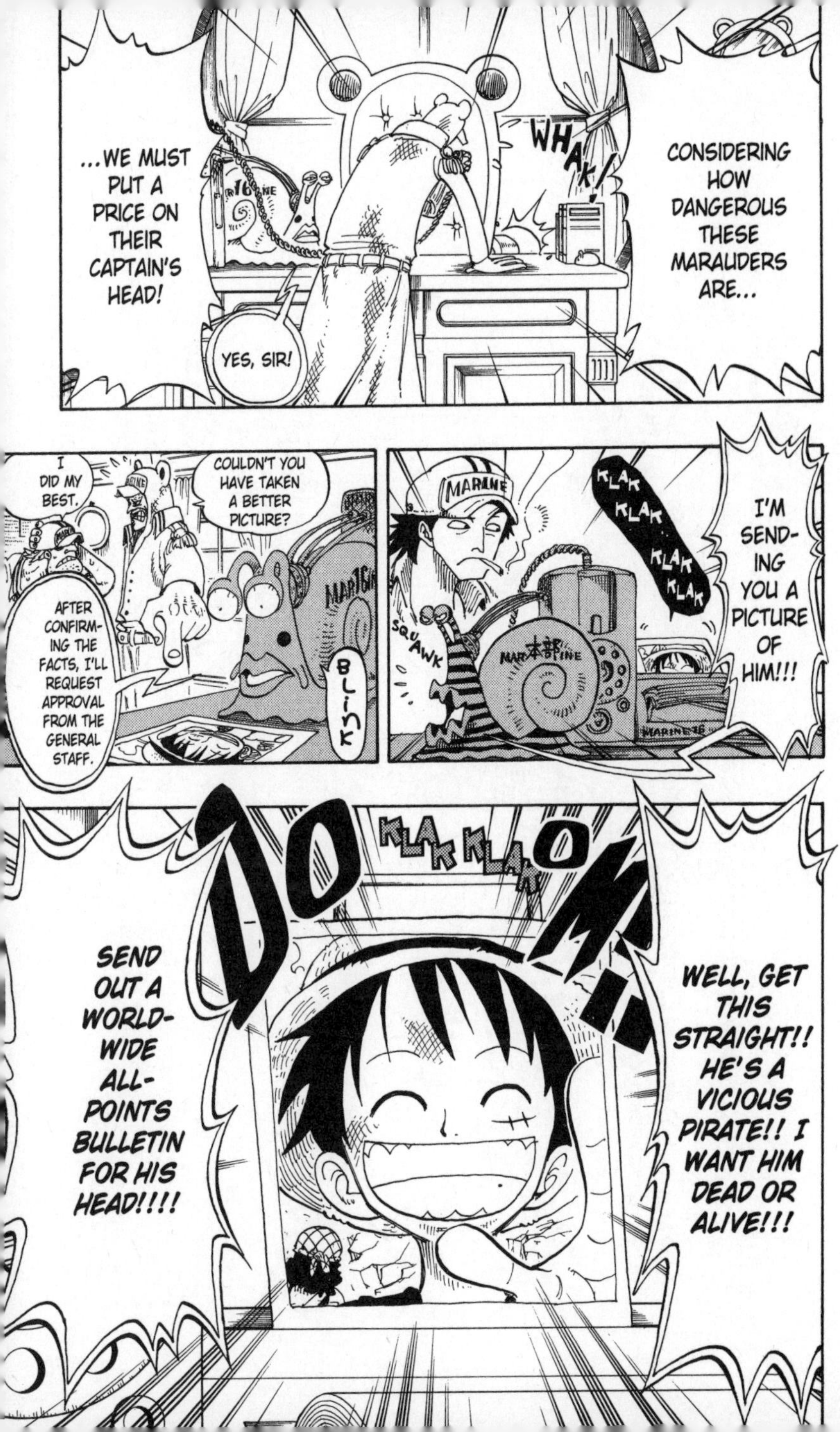
CONSIDERING HOW DANGEROUS THESE MARAUDERS ARE...
WHAK!
...WE MUST PUT A PRICE ON THEIR CAPTAIN'S HEAD!
YES, SIR!
I'M SENDING YOU A PICTURE OF HIM!!!
KLAK KLAK KLAK KLAK
SQUAWK
COULDN'T YOU HAVE TAKEN A BETTER PICTURE?
I DID MY BEST.
AFTER CONFIRMING THE FACTS, I'LL REQUEST APPROVAL FROM THE GENERAL STAFF.
BLINK
WELL, GET THIS STRAIGHT!! HE'S A VICIOUS PIRATE!! I WANT HIM DEAD OR ALIVE!!!
DOOM!!
KLAK KLAK
SEND OUT A WORLD-WIDE ALL-POINTS BULLETIN FOR HIS HEAD!!!!

3.

Storeroom & Battery Deck

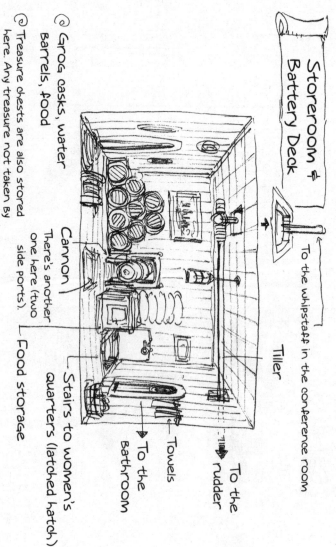

To the whipstaff in the conference room
Tiller
To the rudder
Towels
To the Bathroom
Cannon
There's another one here (two side ports).
Stairs to women's quarters (latched hatch)
Food storage

@ Grog casks, water barrels, food

@ Treasure chests are also stored here. Any treasure not taken by Nami to her room is kept here.

Chapter 95: SPIN, PINWHEEL

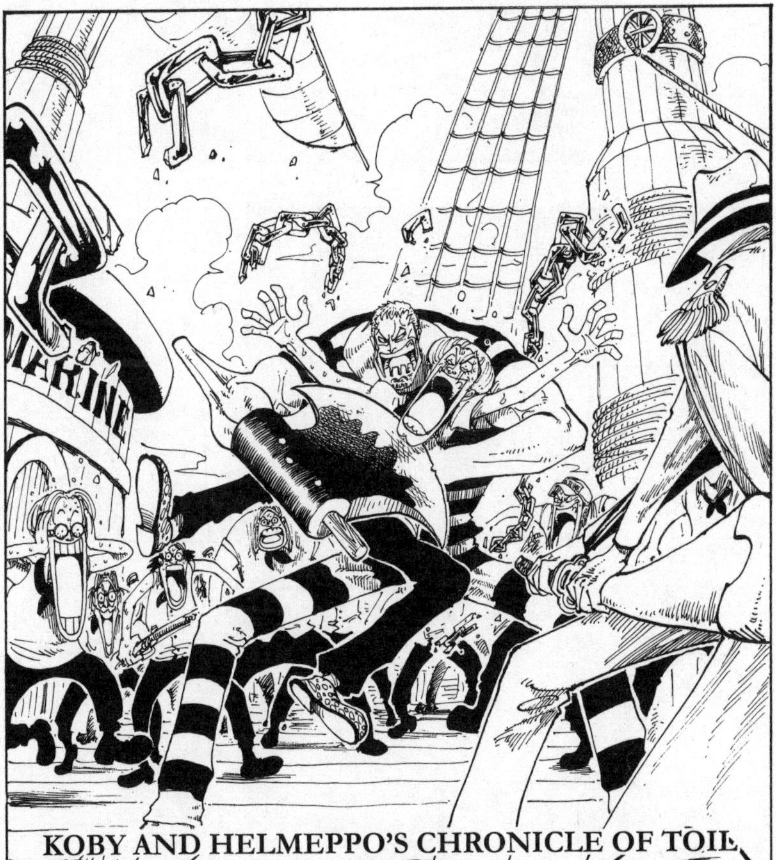
MARINE
KOBY AND HELMEPPO'S CHRONICLE OF TOIL
VOL. 11: "THE IMPROBABLE HOSTAGE"

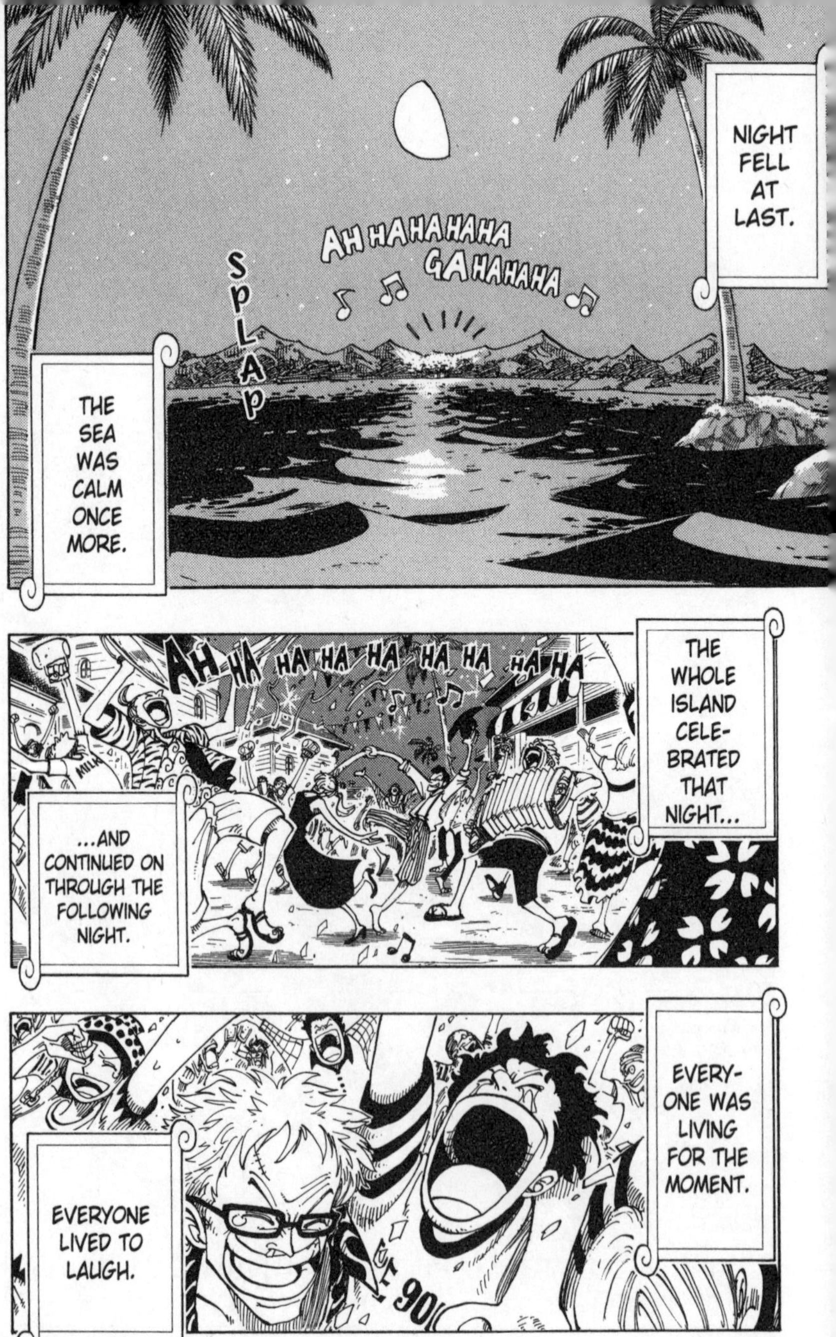
NIGHT FELL AT LAST.
AH HAHAHAHA GAHAHAHA
SPLAP
THE SEA WAS CALM ONCE MORE.
THE WHOLE ISLAND CELE-BRATED THAT NIGHT...
AH HA HA HA HA HA HA HA HA
...AND CONTINUED ON THROUGH THE FOLLOWING NIGHT.
EVERY-ONE WAS LIVING FOR THE MOMENT.
EVERYONE LIVED TO LAUGH.

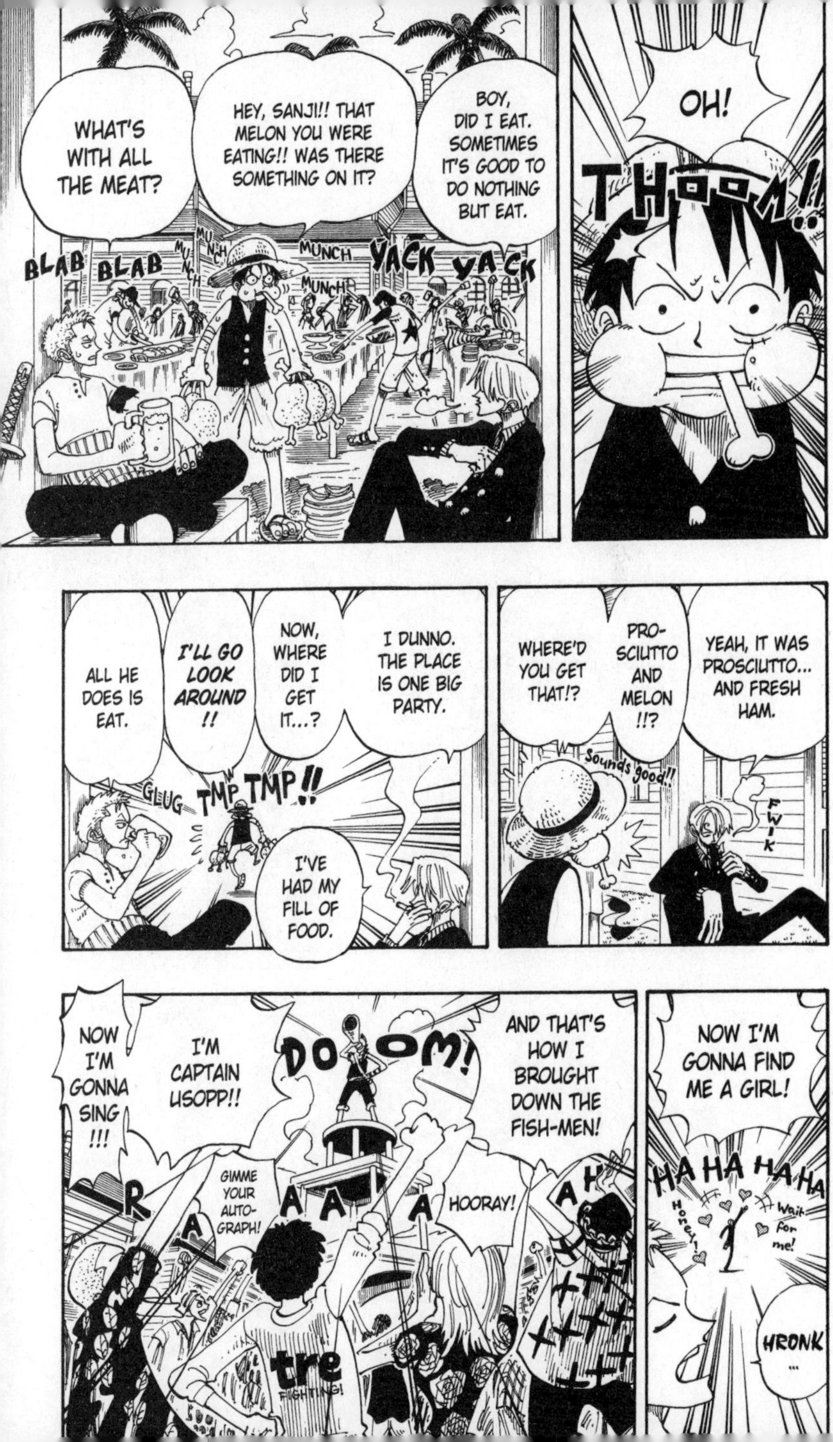
OH!
THOOOM!!
BOY, DID I EAT. SOMETIMES IT'S GOOD TO DO NOTHING BUT EAT.
YACK YACK
HEY, SANJI!! THAT MELON YOU WERE EATING!! WAS THERE SOMETHING ON IT?
MUNCH
MUNCH
MUNCH MUNCH
WHAT'S WITH ALL THE MEAT?
BLAB BLAB
YEAH, IT WAS PROSCIUTTO... AND FRESH HAM.
PRO-SCIUTTO AND MELON!!?
WHERE'D YOU GET THAT!?
Sounds good!!
FWIK
I DUNNO. THE PLACE IS ONE BIG PARTY.
NOW, WHERE DID I GET IT...?
I'LL GO LOOK AROUND!!
ALL HE DOES IS EAT.
TMP TMP!!
GLUG
I'VE HAD MY FILL OF FOOD.
NOW I'M GONNA FIND ME A GIRL!
HAHA HAHA
Wait for me!
Honey!!
HRONK...
AND THAT'S HOW I BROUGHT DOWN THE FISH-MEN!
DOOM!
I'M CAPTAIN USOPP!!
NOW I'M GONNA SING!!!
AH
HOORAY!
A
A A
GIMME YOUR AUTO-GRAPH!
R A
tre
FIGHTING!

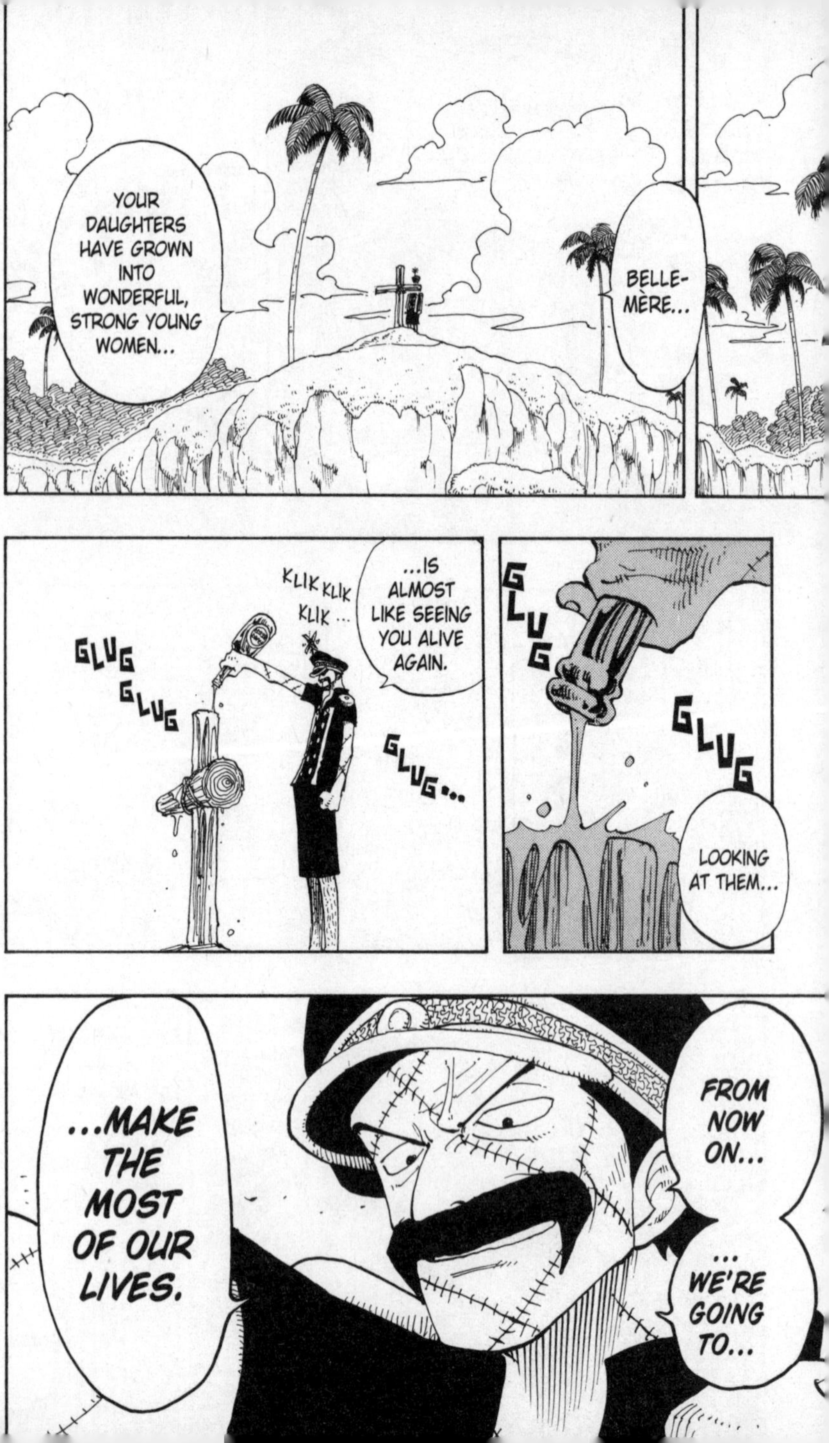
BELLE-MÈRE...
YOUR DAUGHTERS HAVE GROWN INTO WONDERFUL, STRONG YOUNG WOMEN...
GLUG
GLUG
LOOKING AT THEM...
...IS ALMOST LIKE SEEING YOU ALIVE AGAIN.
KLIK KLIK KLIK...
GLUG GLUG
GLUG...
FROM NOW ON...
...WE'RE GOING TO...
...MAKE THE MOST OF OUR LIVES.

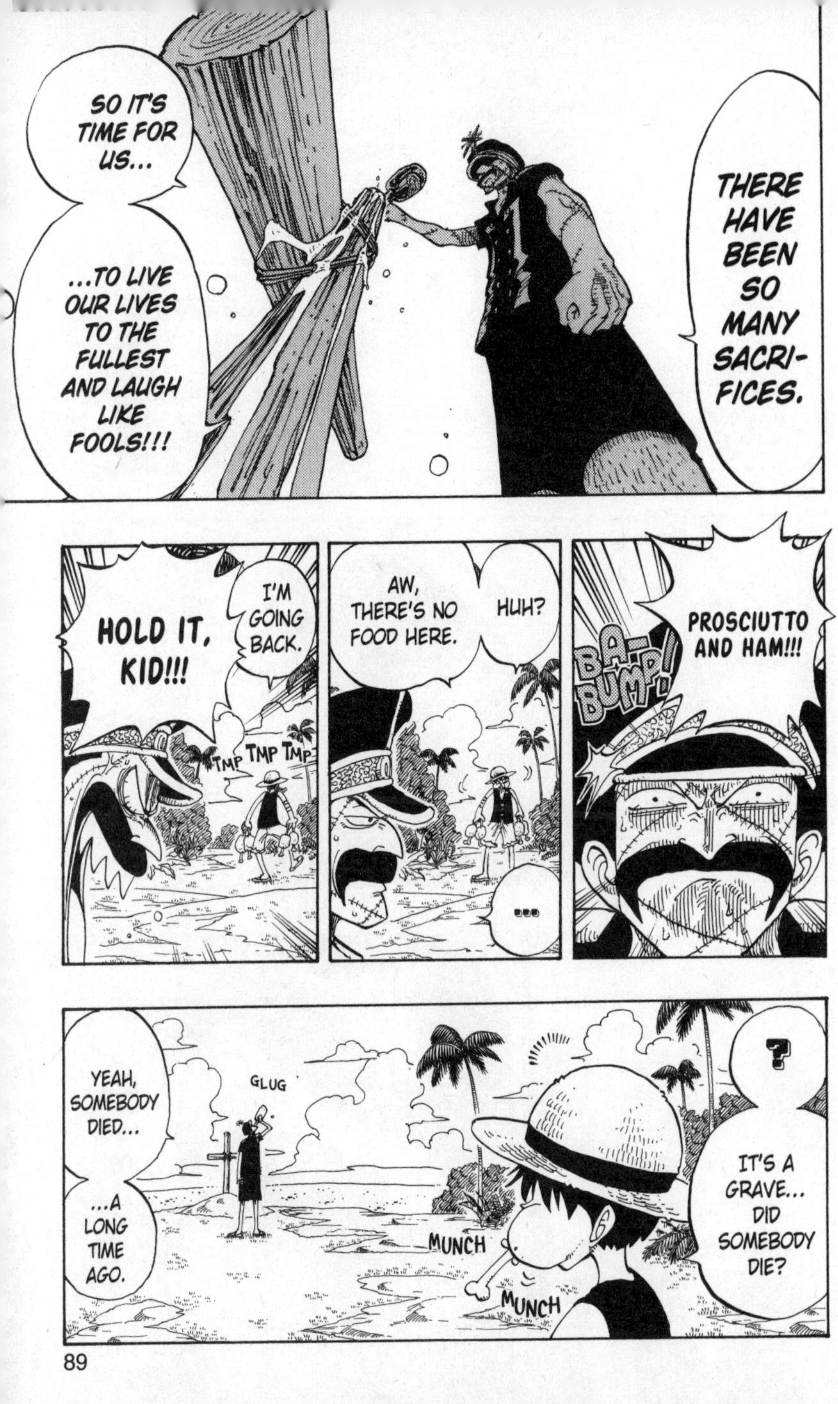
THERE HAVE BEEN SO MANY SACRIFICES.
SO IT'S TIME FOR US...
...TO LIVE OUR LIVES TO THE FULLEST AND LAUGH LIKE FOOLS!!!
BA-BUMP!
PROSCIUTTO AND HAM!!!
HUH?
AW, THERE'S NO FOOD HERE.
...
I'M GOING BACK.
HOLD IT, KID!!!
TMP TMP TMP
?
IT'S A GRAVE... DID SOMEBODY DIE?
MUNCH
MUNCH
GLUG
YEAH, SOMEBODY DIED...
...A LONG TIME AGO.

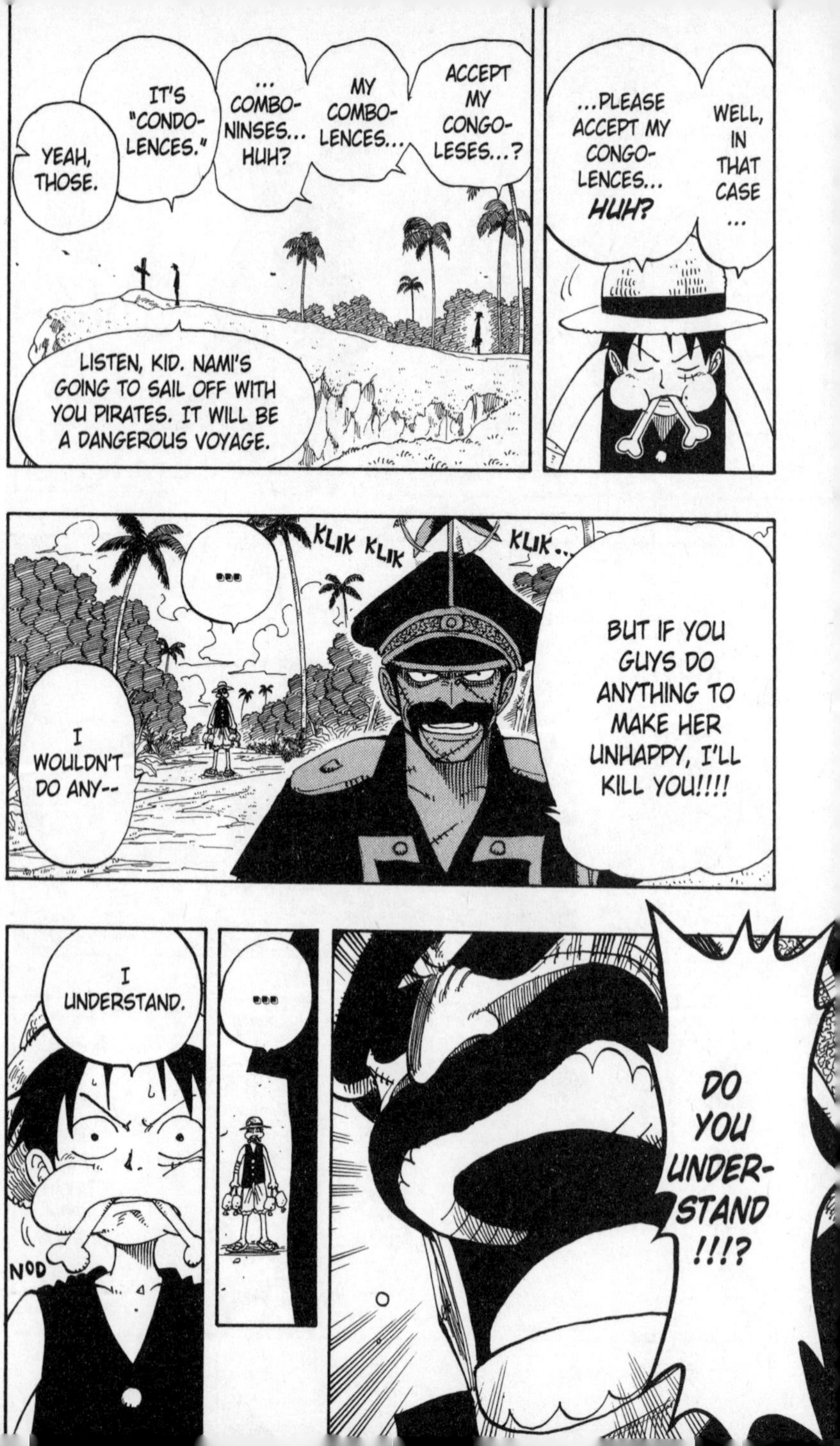
WELL, IN THAT CASE ...
...PLEASE ACCEPT MY CONGO-LENCES... HUH?
ACCEPT MY CONGO-LESES...?
MY COMBO-LENCES...
... COMBO-NINSES... HUH?
IT'S "CONDO-LENCES."
YEAH, THOSE.
LISTEN, KID. NAMI'S GOING TO SAIL OFF WITH YOU PIRATES. IT WILL BE A DANGEROUS VOYAGE.
KLIK...
KLIK KLIK
BUT IF YOU GUYS DO ANYTHING TO MAKE HER UNHAPPY, I'LL KILL YOU!!!!
...
I WOULDN'T DO ANY--
DO YOU UNDER-STAND!!!?
...
I UNDERSTAND.
NOD

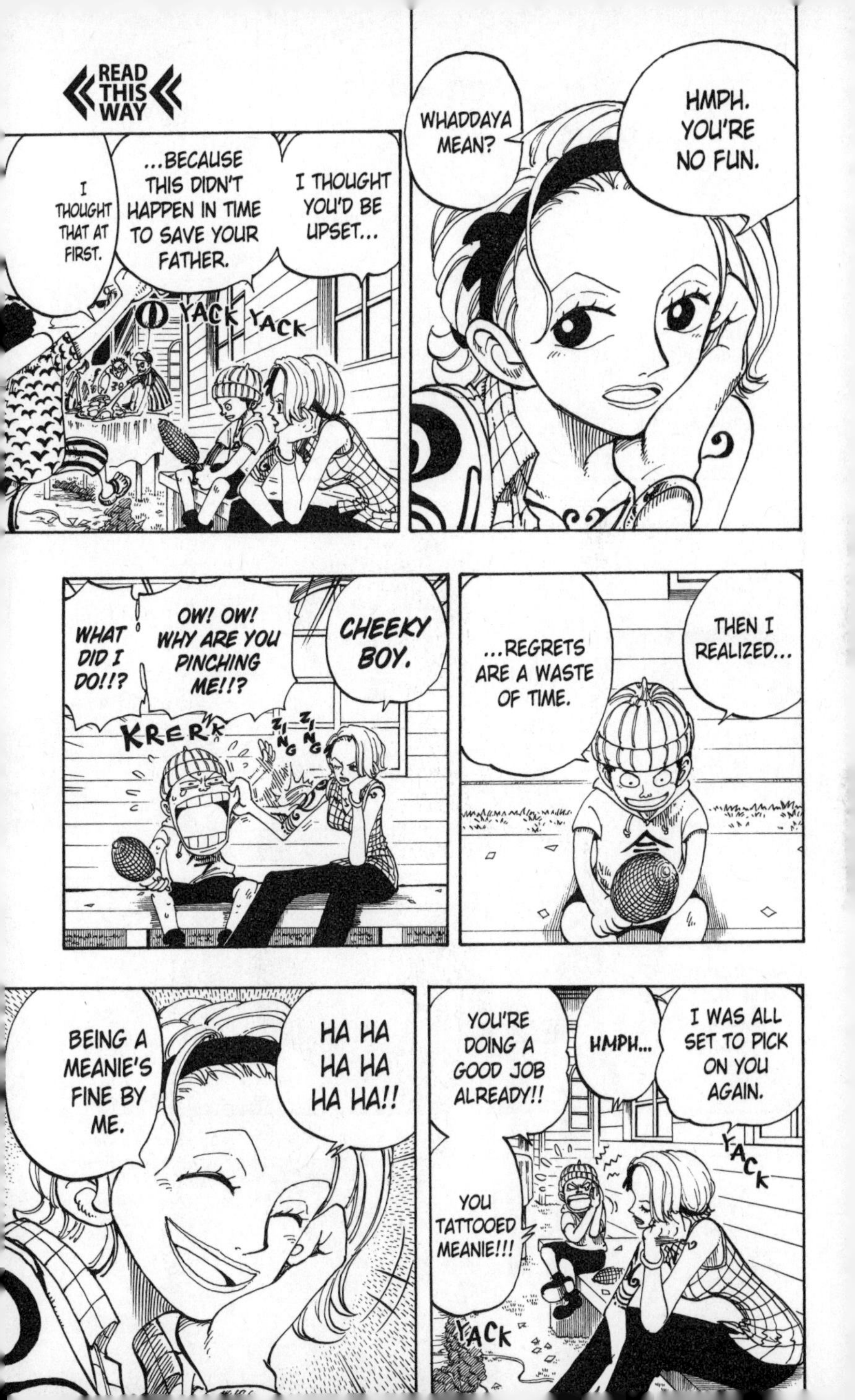
READ THIS WAY
HMPH. YOU'RE NO FUN.
WHADDAYA MEAN?
I THOUGHT YOU'D BE UPSET...
...BECAUSE THIS DIDN'T HAPPEN IN TIME TO SAVE YOUR FATHER.
I THOUGHT THAT AT FIRST.
YACK YACK
THEN I REALIZED...
...REGRETS ARE A WASTE OF TIME.
CHEEKY BOY.
OW! OW! WHY ARE YOU PINCHING ME!!?
WHAT DID I DO!!?
ZING ZING
KRERK
I WAS ALL SET TO PICK ON YOU AGAIN.
HMPH...
YOU'RE DOING A GOOD JOB ALREADY!!
YACK
YOU TATTOOED MEANIE!!!
YACK
HA HA HA HA HA HA!!
BEING A MEANIE'S FINE BY ME.

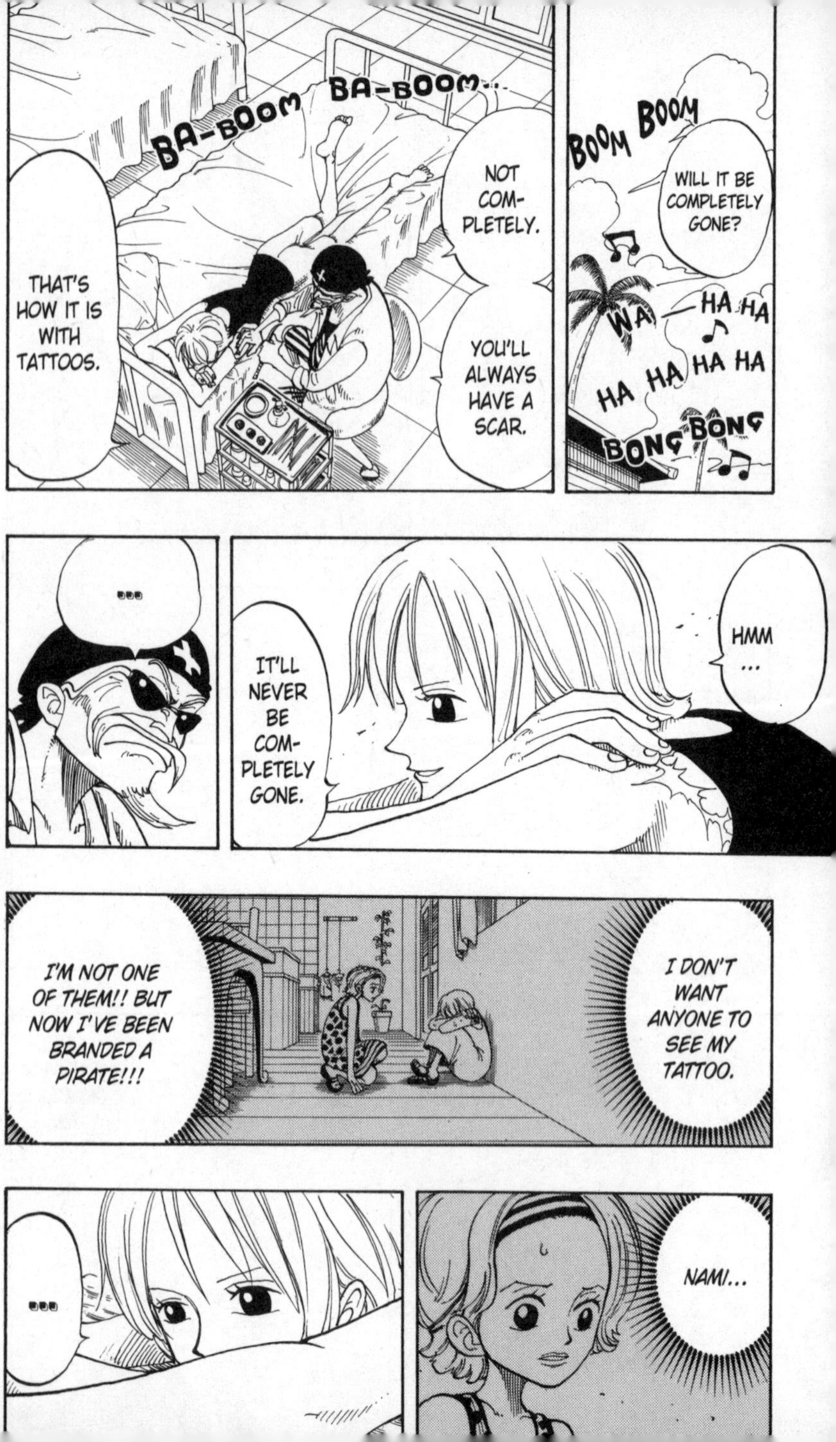
BOOM BOOM
WILL IT BE COMPLETELY GONE?
WA—HA HA
HA HA HA HA
BONG BONG
BA-BOOM BA-BOOM...
NOT COM-PLETELY.
YOU'LL ALWAYS HAVE A SCAR.
THAT'S HOW IT IS WITH TATTOOS.
HMM ...
IT'LL NEVER BE COM-PLETELY GONE.
...
I DON'T WANT ANYONE TO SEE MY TATTOO.
I'M NOT ONE OF THEM!! BUT NOW I'VE BEEN BRANDED A PIRATE!!!
NAMI...
...

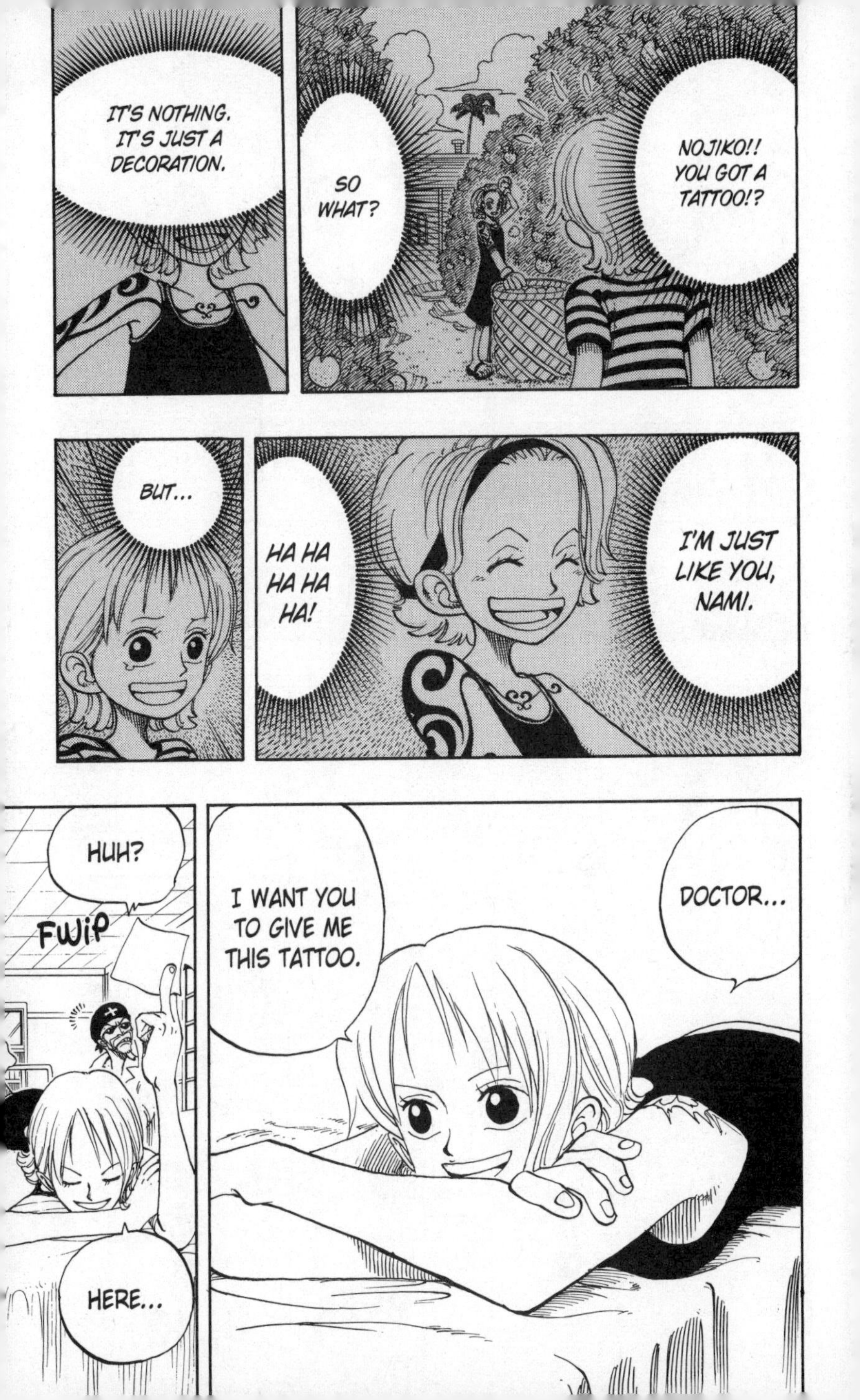
NOJIKO!! YOU GOT A TATTOO!?
SO WHAT?
IT'S NOTHING. IT'S JUST A DECORATION.
I'M JUST LIKE YOU, NAMI.
HA HA HA HA HA!
BUT...
DOCTOR...
I WANT YOU TO GIVE ME THIS TATTOO.
HUH?
FWIP
HERE...

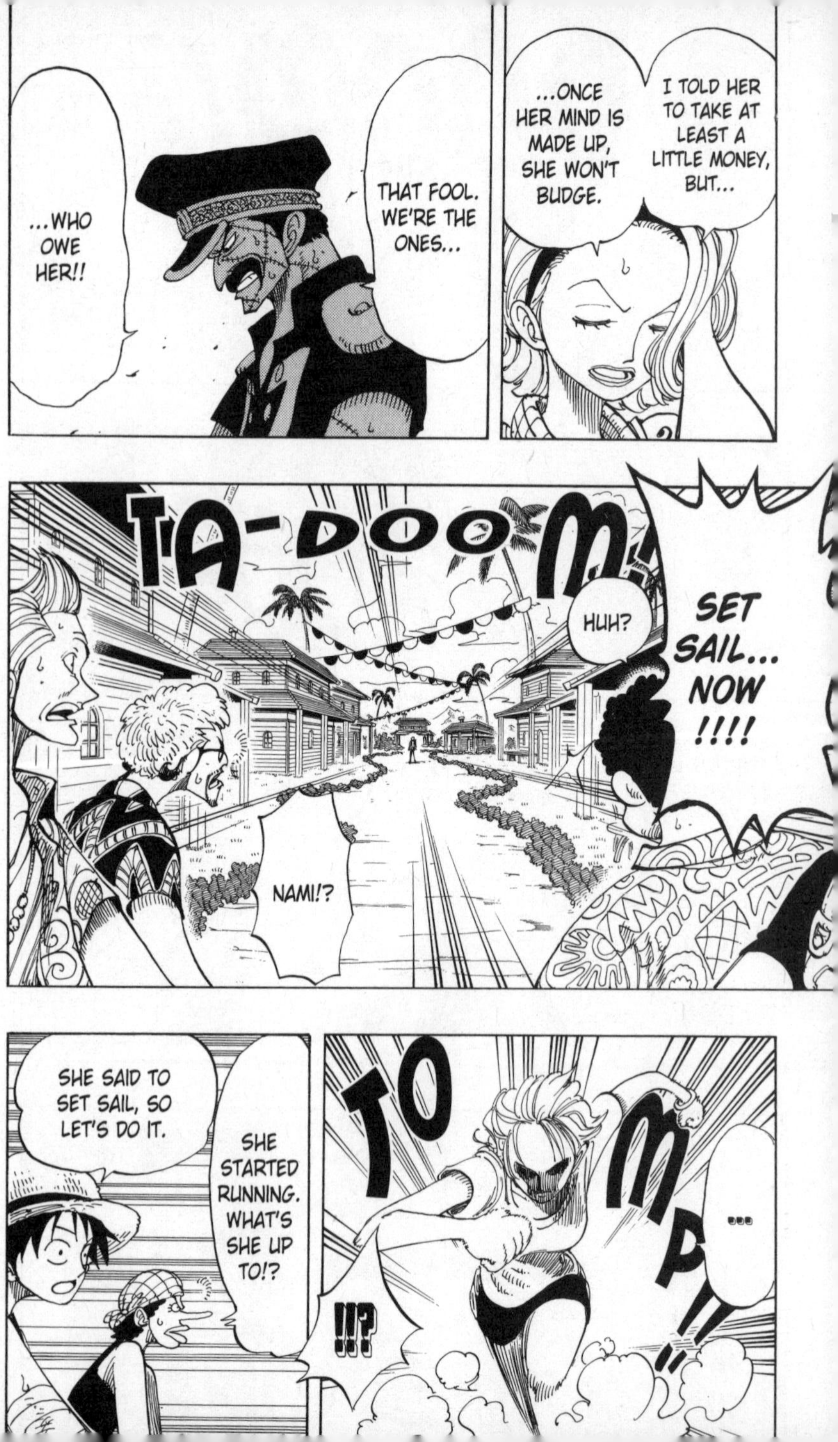
I TOLD HER TO TAKE AT LEAST A LITTLE MONEY, BUT...
...ONCE HER MIND IS MADE UP, SHE WON'T BUDGE.
THAT FOOL. WE'RE THE ONES...
...WHO OWE HER!!
TA-DOOM
SET SAIL... NOW !!!!
HUH?
NAMI!?
TOMP!!
...
!!?
SHE STARTED RUNNING. WHAT'S SHE UP TO!?
SHE SAID TO SET SAIL, SO LET'S DO IT.

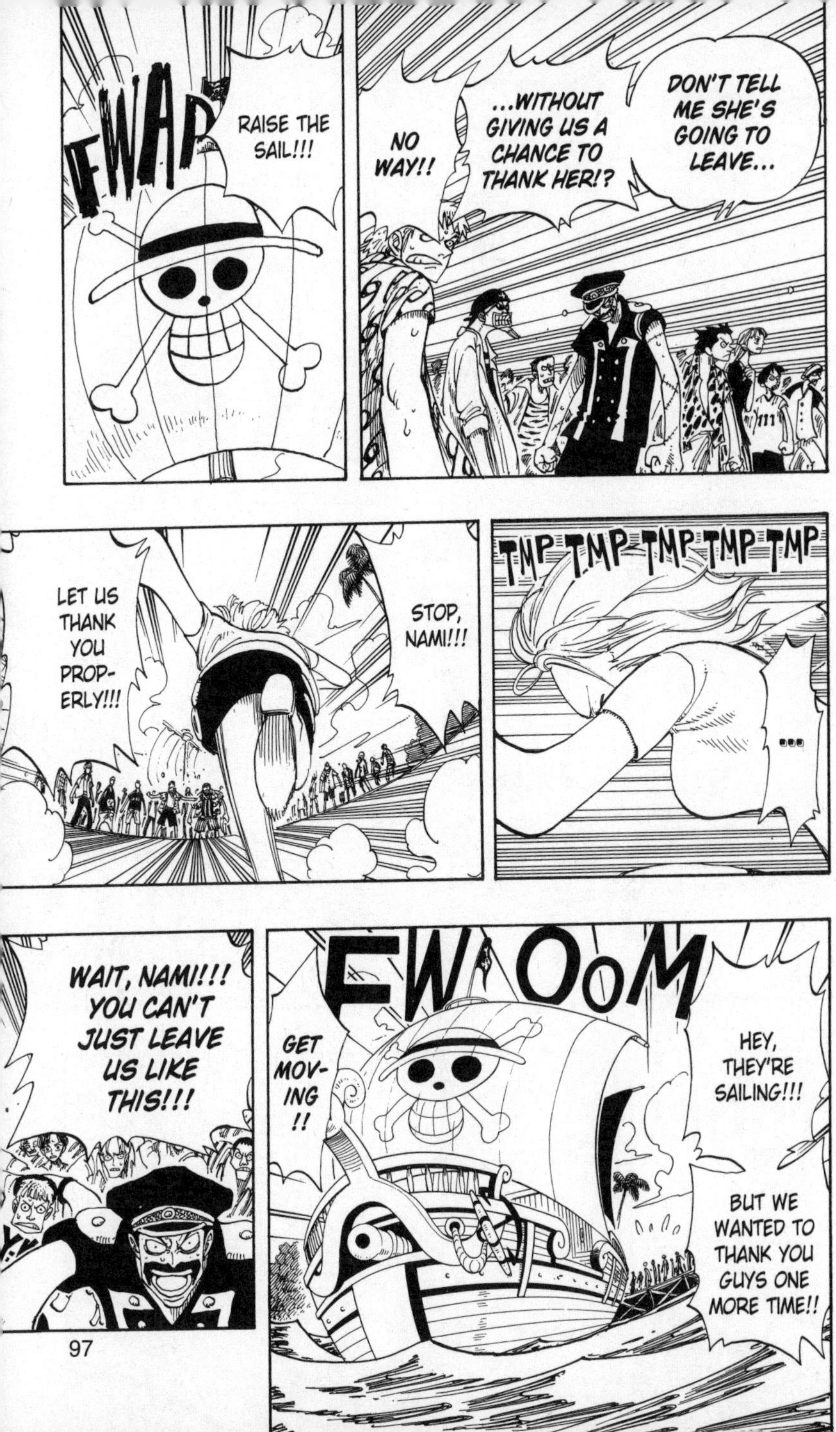
DON'T TELL ME SHE'S GOING TO LEAVE...
...WITHOUT GIVING US A CHANCE TO THANK HER!?
NO WAY!!
FWAP
RAISE THE SAIL!!!
TMP TMP TMP TMP TMP
...
STOP, NAMI!!!
LET US THANK YOU PROP-ERLY!!!
FWOOM
HEY, THEY'RE SAILING!!!
BUT WE WANTED TO THANK YOU GUYS ONE MORE TIME!!
GET MOV-ING!!
WAIT, NAMI!!! YOU CAN'T JUST LEAVE US LIKE THIS!!!

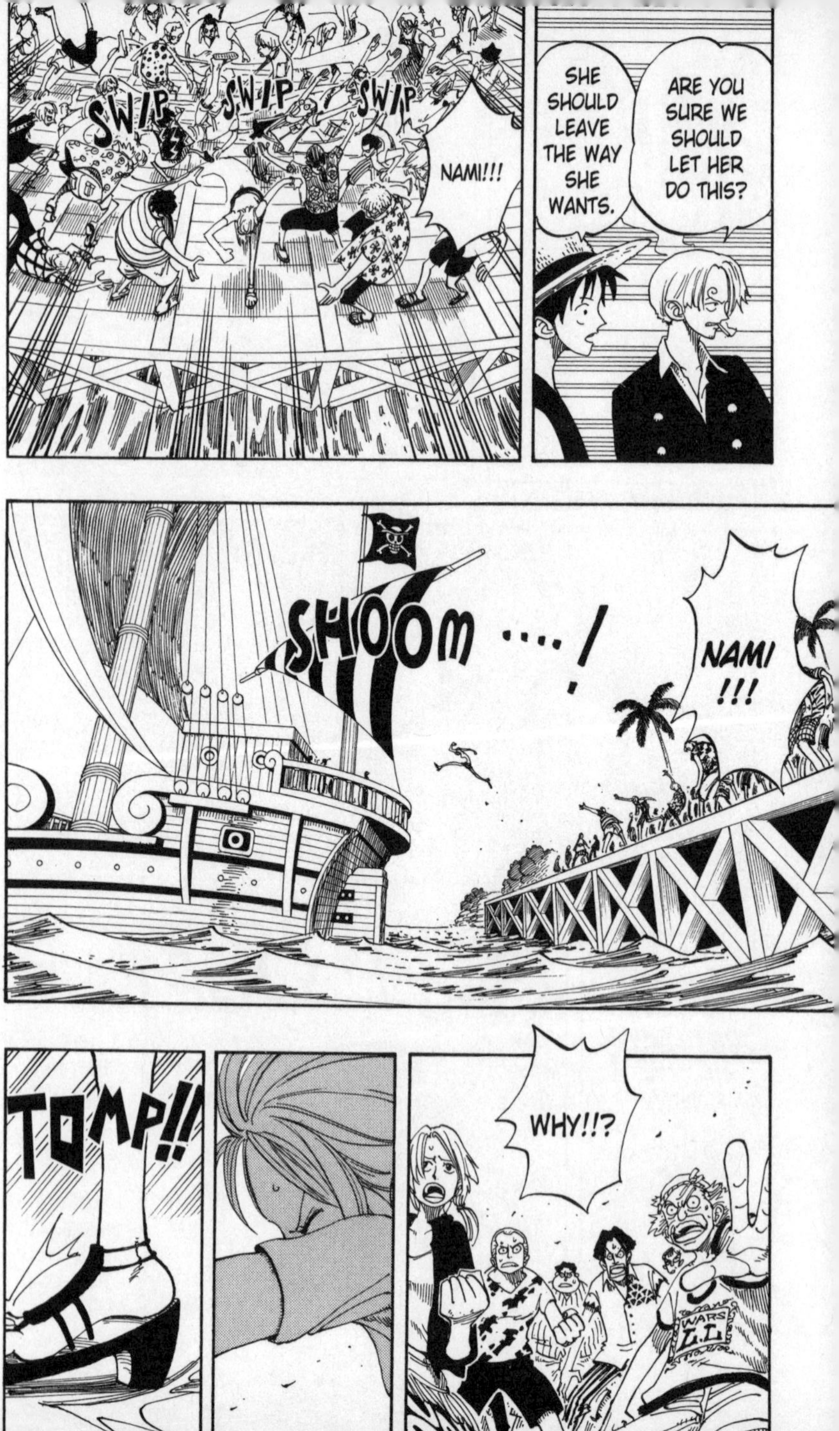
ARE YOU SURE WE SHOULD LET HER DO THIS?
SHE SHOULD LEAVE THE WAY SHE WANTS.
NAMI!!!
SWIP SWIP SWIP
NAMI !!!
SHOOM ....!
WHY!!?
TOMP!!

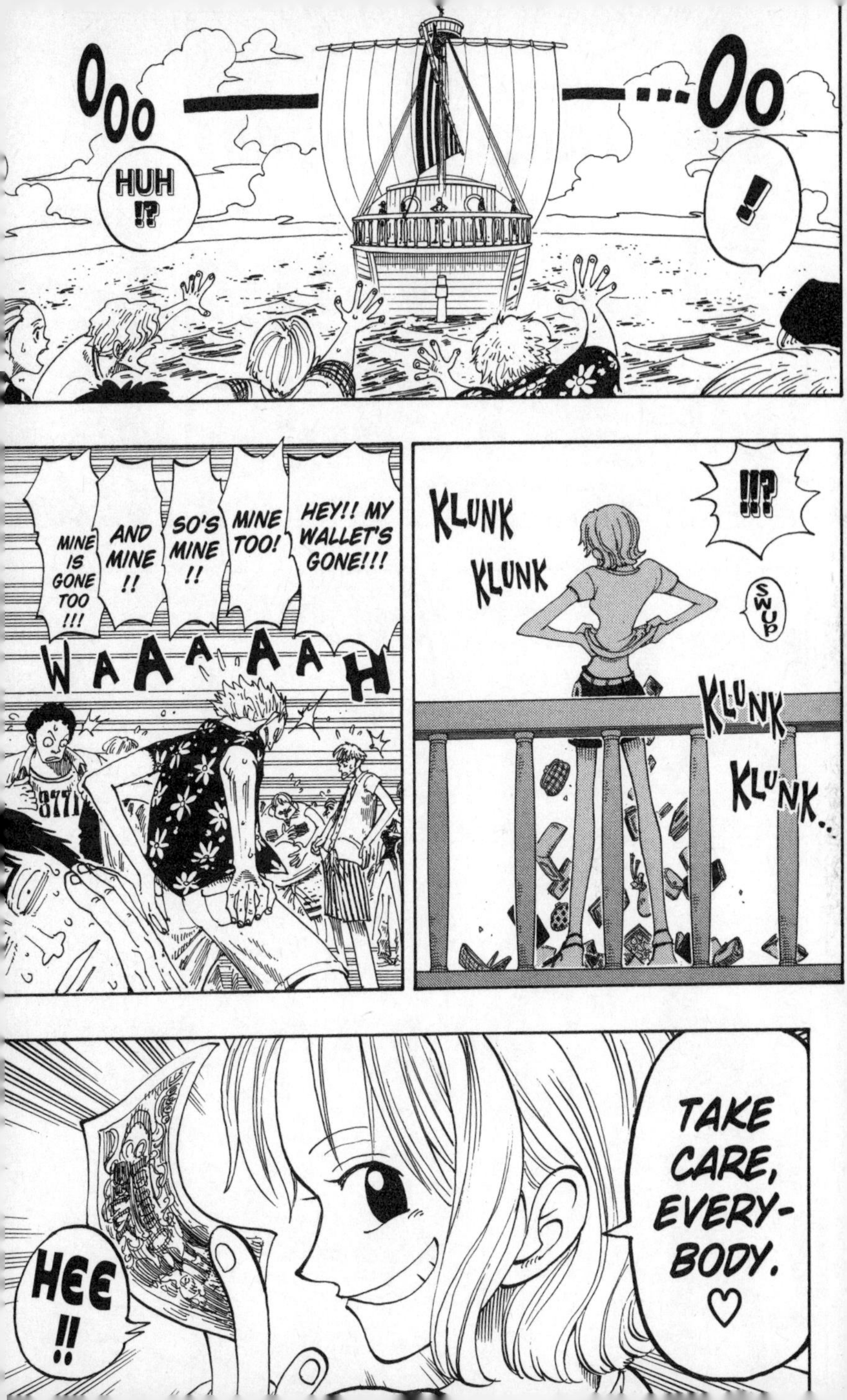
OOO————...OO
!
HUH!?
!!?
SWUP
KLUNK
KLUNK
KLUNK
KLUNK...
HEY!! MY WALLET'S GONE!!!
MINE TOO!
SO'S MINE!!
AND MINE!!
MINE IS GONE TOO!!!
WAAAAAH
TAKE CARE, EVERYBODY. ♥
HEE!!

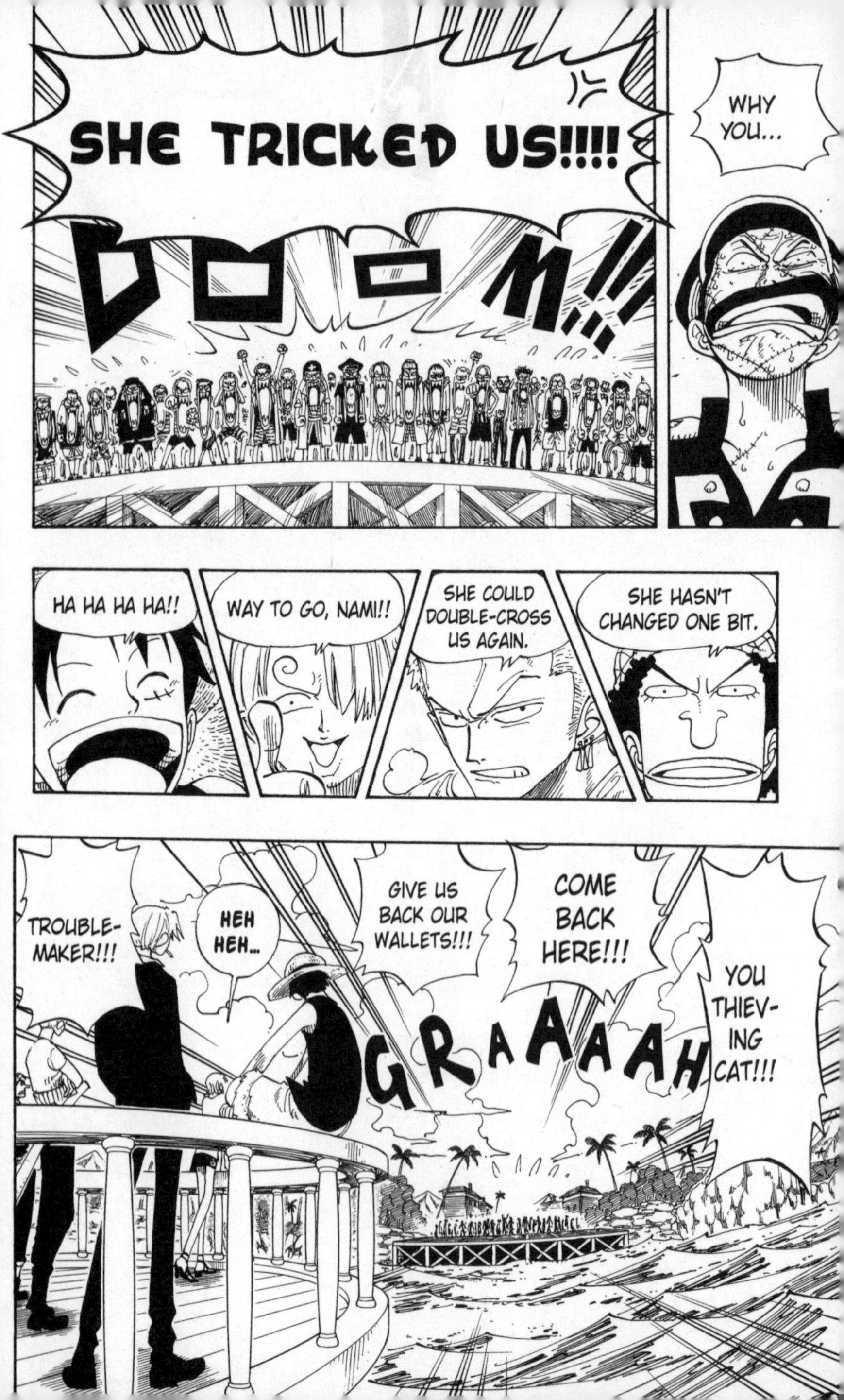
WHY YOU...
SHE TRICKED US!!!!
DOOOM!!!
SHE HASN'T CHANGED ONE BIT.
SHE COULD DOUBLE-CROSS US AGAIN.
WAY TO GO, NAMI!!
HA HA HA HA!!
YOU THIEV-ING CAT!!!
COME BACK HERE!!!
GIVE US BACK OUR WALLETS!!!
HEH HEH...
TROUBLE-MAKER!!!
GRAAAAH

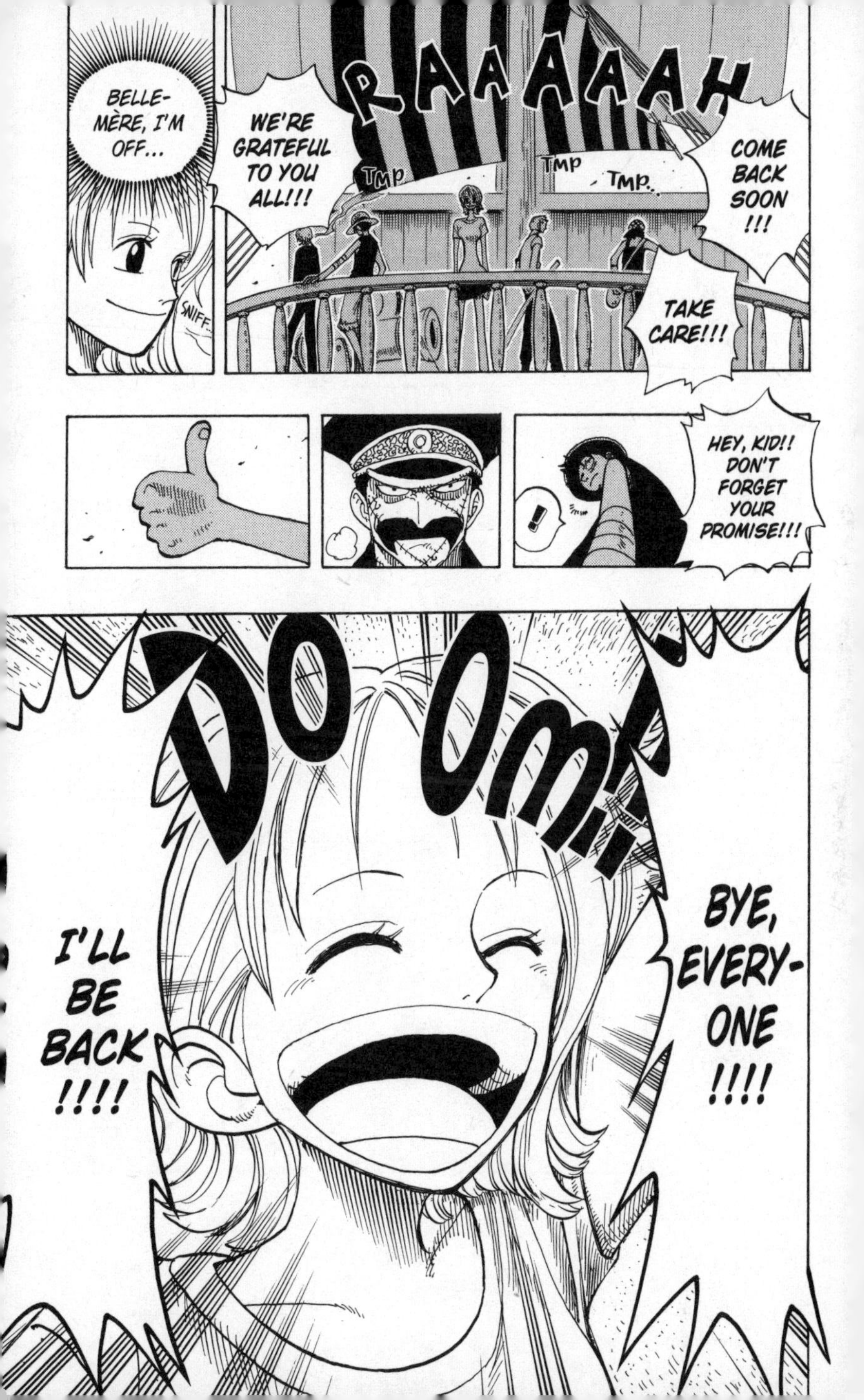
COME BACK SOON!!!
RAAAAAH
TMP
TMP
TMP..
TAKE CARE!!!
WE'RE GRATEFUL TO YOU ALL!!!
BELLE-MÈRE, I'M OFF...
SNIFF...
HEY, KID!! DON'T FORGET YOUR PROMISE!!!
!
BYE, EVERY-ONE!!!!
DOOM!!
I'LL BE BACK!!!!

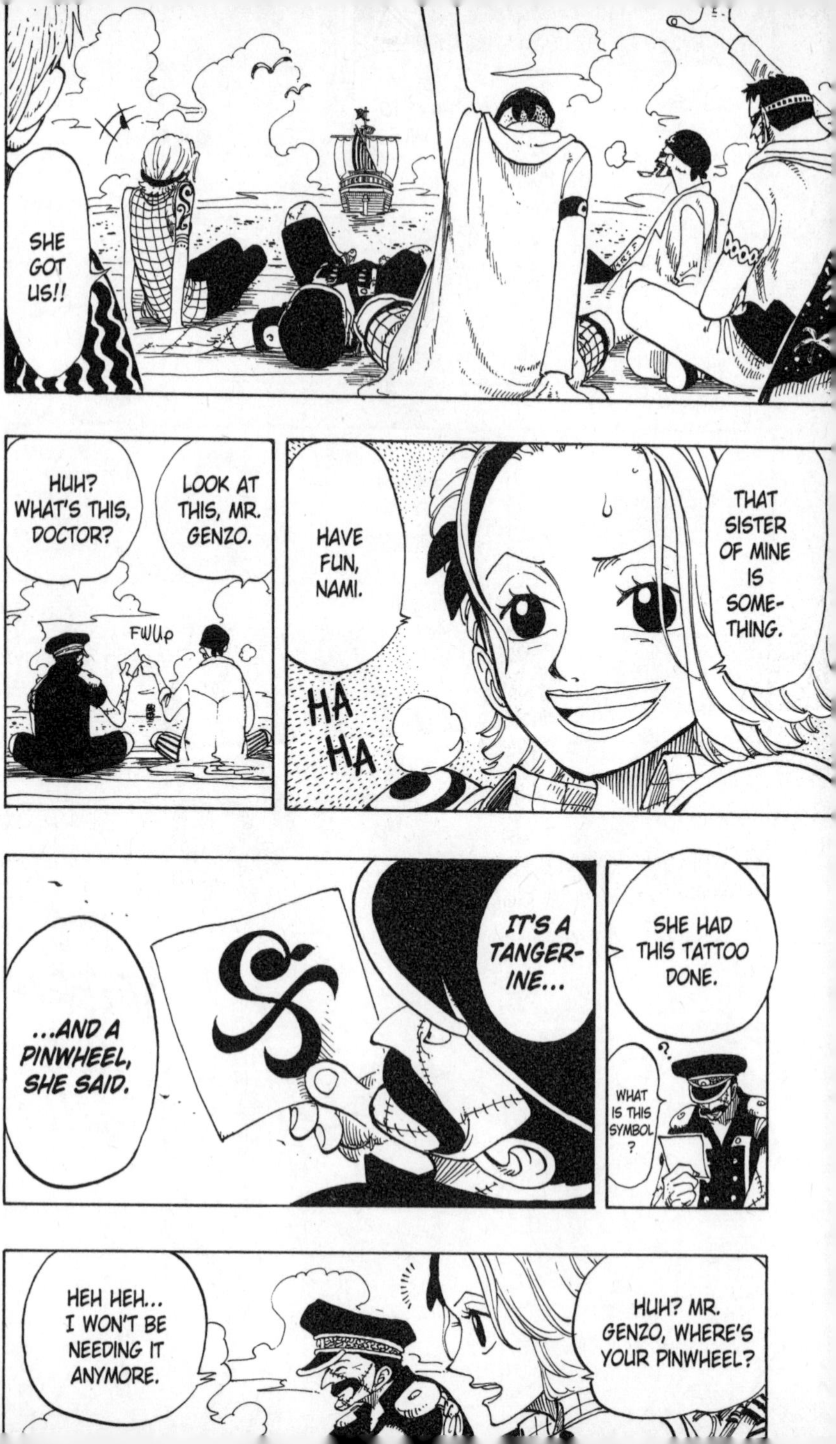
SHE GOT US!!
THAT SISTER OF MINE IS SOME-THING.
HAVE FUN, NAMI.
HA HA
LOOK AT THIS, MR. GENZO.
HUH? WHAT'S THIS, DOCTOR?
FWUP
SHE HAD THIS TATTOO DONE.
WHAT IS THIS SYMBOL?
IT'S A TANGER-INE...
...AND A PINWHEEL, SHE SAID.
HUH? MR. GENZO, WHERE'S YOUR PINWHEEL?
HEH HEH... I WON'T BE NEEDING IT ANYMORE.

4.

ⓒ Nami's room. It's clean.

Emergency exit (connects with the men's quarters, but isn't normally used).

Treasure chest (precious jewels, Nami's collection)

Bookcase

Desk

Hammock storage (Pull the rope and a hammock descends.)

Stairs (enter from storeroom)

Storage box for surveying and navigation tools

Bar

Grog

ⓒ It was built by a carpenter, Mr. Tell, before the ship left Coco Village.

ⓒ Merry (vol. 3, p. 148) designed this room for Usopp's friend Kaya, so it's nicely decorated.

Chapter 96:
THE MEANEST MAN IN THE EAST

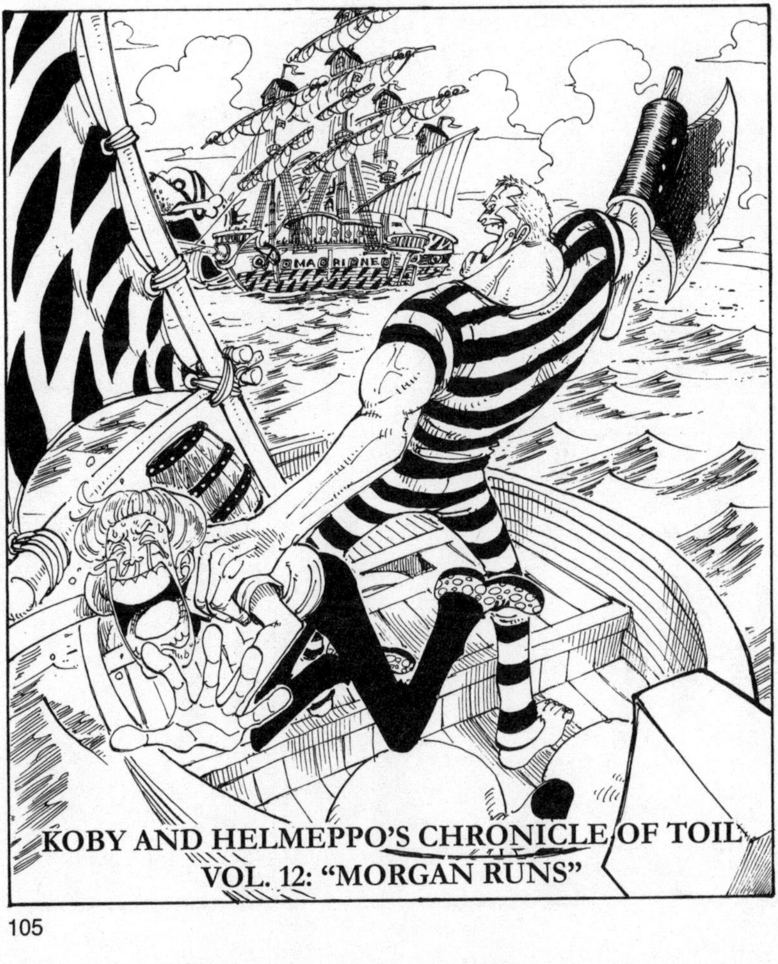
MAGRIONE
KOBY AND HELMEPPO'S CHRONICLE OF TOIL
VOL. 12: "MORGAN RUNS"

YOU'RE CHARGING TOO MUCH!

DID YOU RAISE THE PRICE AGAIN?

WHAT'S A NEWSPAPER OR TWO?

IF YOU RAISE IT AGAIN, I'M NOT BUYING FROM YOU ANYMORE.

KAW

KLINK!

NEWS PAPER

STOP SQUAWKING!! I'M TRYING TO DEVELOP THE ULTIMATE KILLER, THE PEPPER SAUCE STAR!!

...IT'S TIME TO MAKE MONEY FOR MYSELF. I DON'T WANT TO BE A PENNILESS PIRATE.

DON'T BE STUPID! NOW THAT ARLONG'S GONE...

ANYONE WHO GETS THIS IN HIS EYES...

DOOOM

YOU'RE DONE COLLECTING MONEY, AREN'T YOU?

IT ADDS UP IF YOU BUY ONE EVERY DAY.

KAW

NO!!

WHAT? CAN'T I HAVE JUST ONE!?

GAAA-AGH!!!

FWOOSH

AARGH!!!

HANDS OFF!!!

...WON'T STAND A CHANCE!!

KRASH!!

SPLASH!

AW, THANK YOU, SANJI. ♡

NAMI, I SHALL GUARD THIS GROVE WITH ALL THE LOVE IN MY HEART!!

DOOOM!!

THIS IS NAMI'S TANGERINE GROVE!! I WON'T LET YOU TOUCH THEM!!

FWUP!

OKAY. I'M IN TOO GOOD A MOOD TO FIGHT.

hee hee hee hee

THERE WAS ANOTHER COUP D'ÉTAT IN VIRA.

THE WORLD SURE IS IN TURMOIL.

FWUP!

YAY! WE'RE FINALLY SAILING FOR THE GRAND LINE!!

YEE-OWW!!

FWOOSH

SHE'S GOT HIM WRAPPED AROUND HER FINGER.

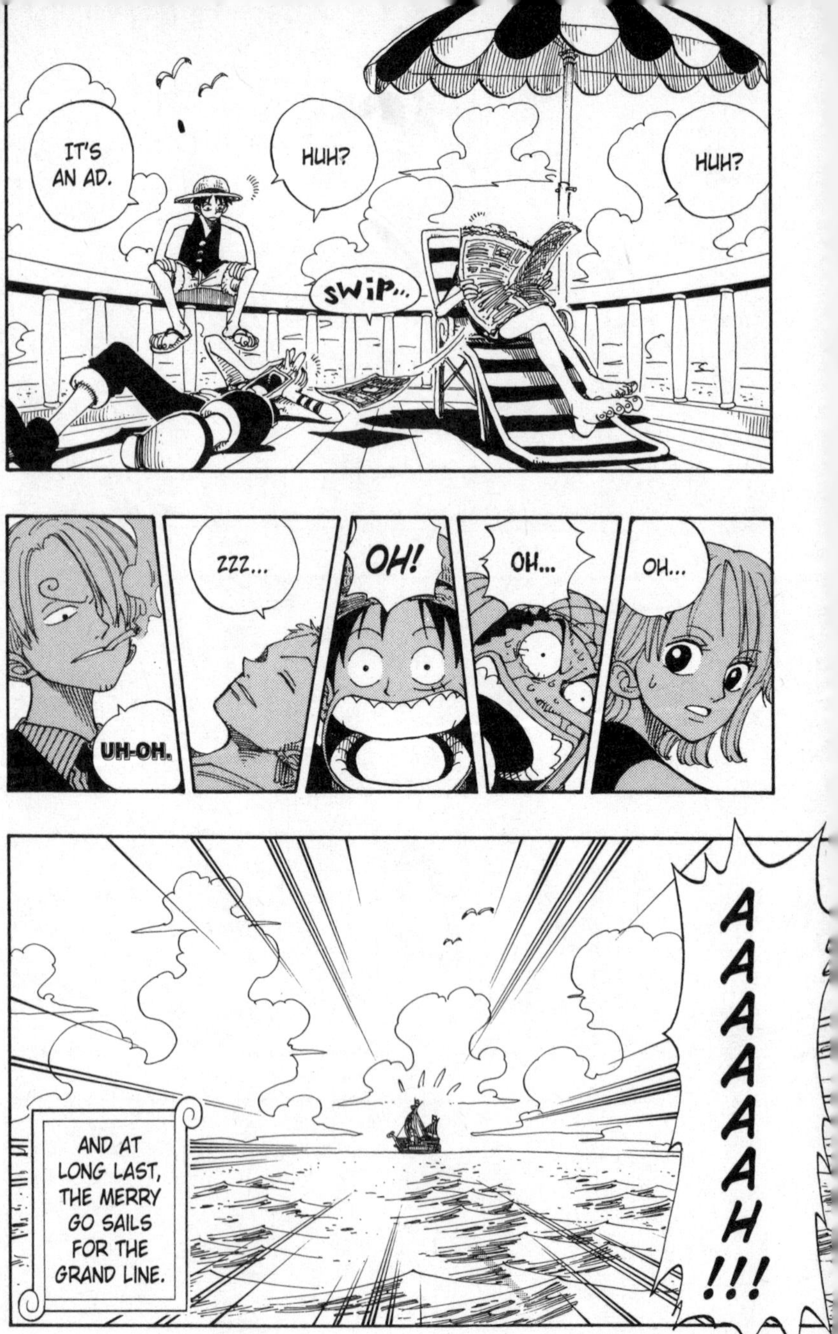
HUH?
HUH?
IT'S AN AD.
SWIP...
OH...
OH...
OH!
ZZZ...
UH-OH.
AAAAAAH!!!
AND AT LONG LAST, THE MERRY GO SAILS FOR THE GRAND LINE.

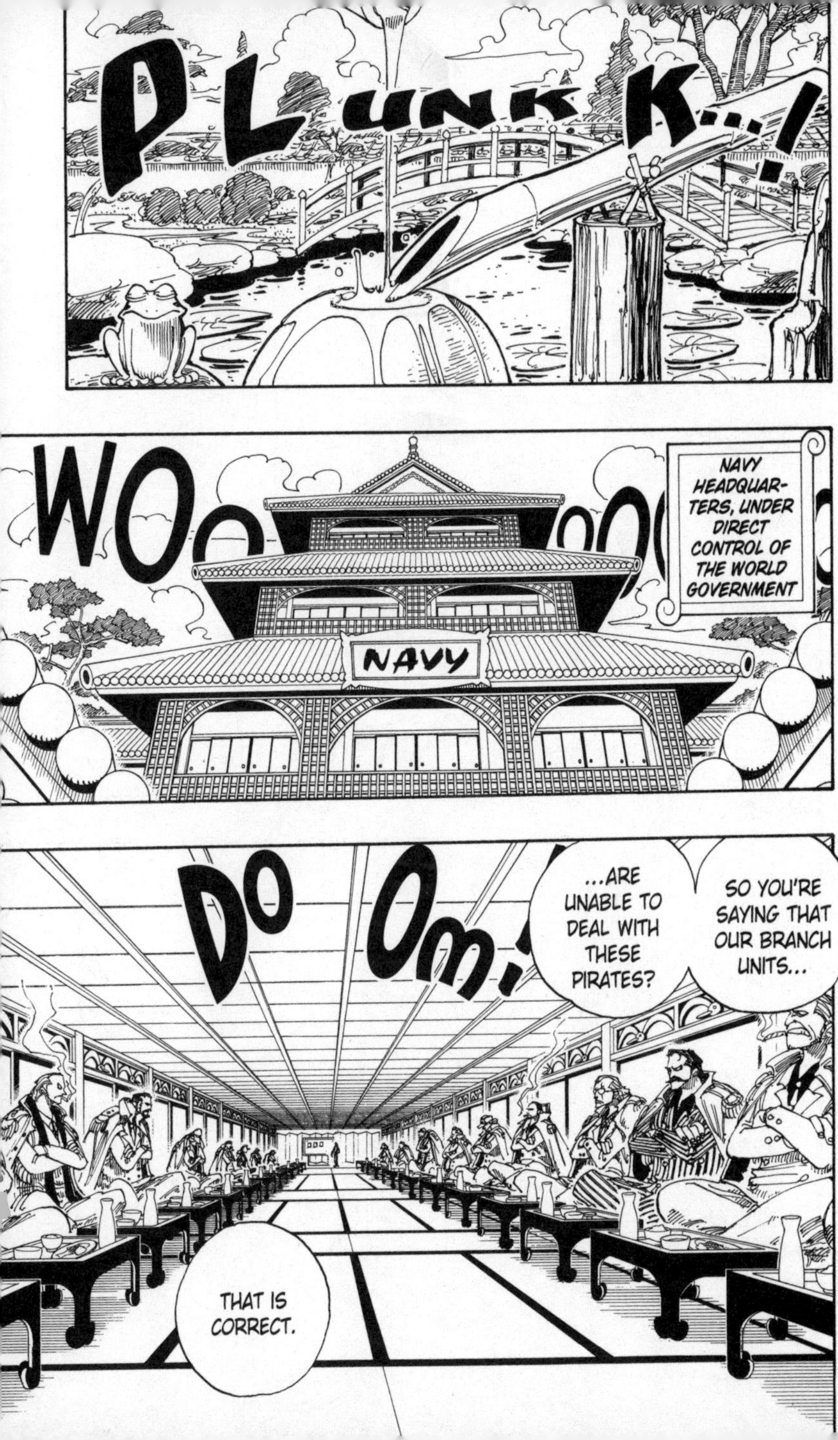
PLUNK K..!
WOO
NAVY HEADQUARTERS, UNDER DIRECT CONTROL OF THE WORLD GOVERNMENT
NAVY
DOOM!
SO YOU'RE SAYING THAT OUR BRANCH UNITS...
...ARE UNABLE TO DEAL WITH THESE PIRATES?
THAT IS CORRECT.

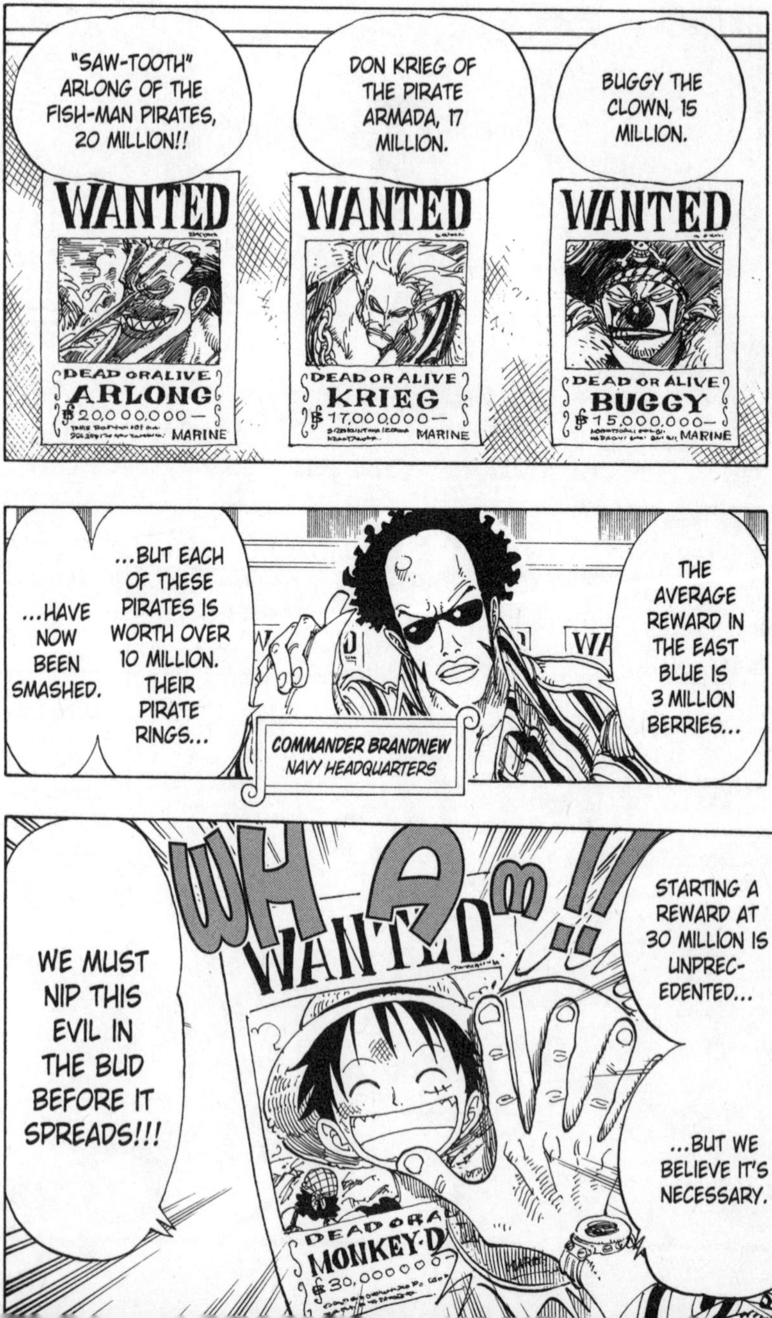
BUGGY THE CLOWN, 15 MILLION.
WANTED
DEAD OR ALIVE
BUGGY
฿15,000,000—
MARINE
DON KRIEG OF THE PIRATE ARMADA, 17 MILLION.
WANTED
DEAD OR ALIVE
KRIEG
฿17,000,000—
MARINE
"SAW-TOOTH" ARLONG OF THE FISH-MAN PIRATES, 20 MILLION!!
WANTED
DEAD OR ALIVE
ARLONG
฿20,000,000—
MARINE
THE AVERAGE REWARD IN THE EAST BLUE IS 3 MILLION BERRIES...
COMMANDER BRANDNEW
NAVY HEADQUARTERS
...BUT EACH OF THESE PIRATES IS WORTH OVER 10 MILLION. THEIR PIRATE RINGS...
...HAVE NOW BEEN SMASHED.
STARTING A REWARD AT 30 MILLION IS UNPRECEDENTED...
...BUT WE BELIEVE IT'S NECESSARY.
WHAM!!
WANTED
DEAD OR AL
MONKEY·D
฿30,000,000
WE MUST NIP THIS EVIL IN THE BUD BEFORE IT SPREADS!!!

THIS IS THE STRONG-HOLD OF LIBERTY. IN THIS AGE OF PIRATES, NO WEAKNESS IS PERMITTED HERE!!!

ANYONE WHO WANTS TO LEAVE IS FREE TO DO SO!!!

BO—OM!!

WOOO...

WE ARE JUSTICE!!!

IT'S NOT THE FAULT OF THE CITIZENS IF THEY FALL PREY TO CUT-THROATS!!

...IT'S UP TO US, THE NAVY, TO USE OUR MIGHT TO CRUSH THEM!!!

IF EVIL FORCES SAIL THE SEAS...

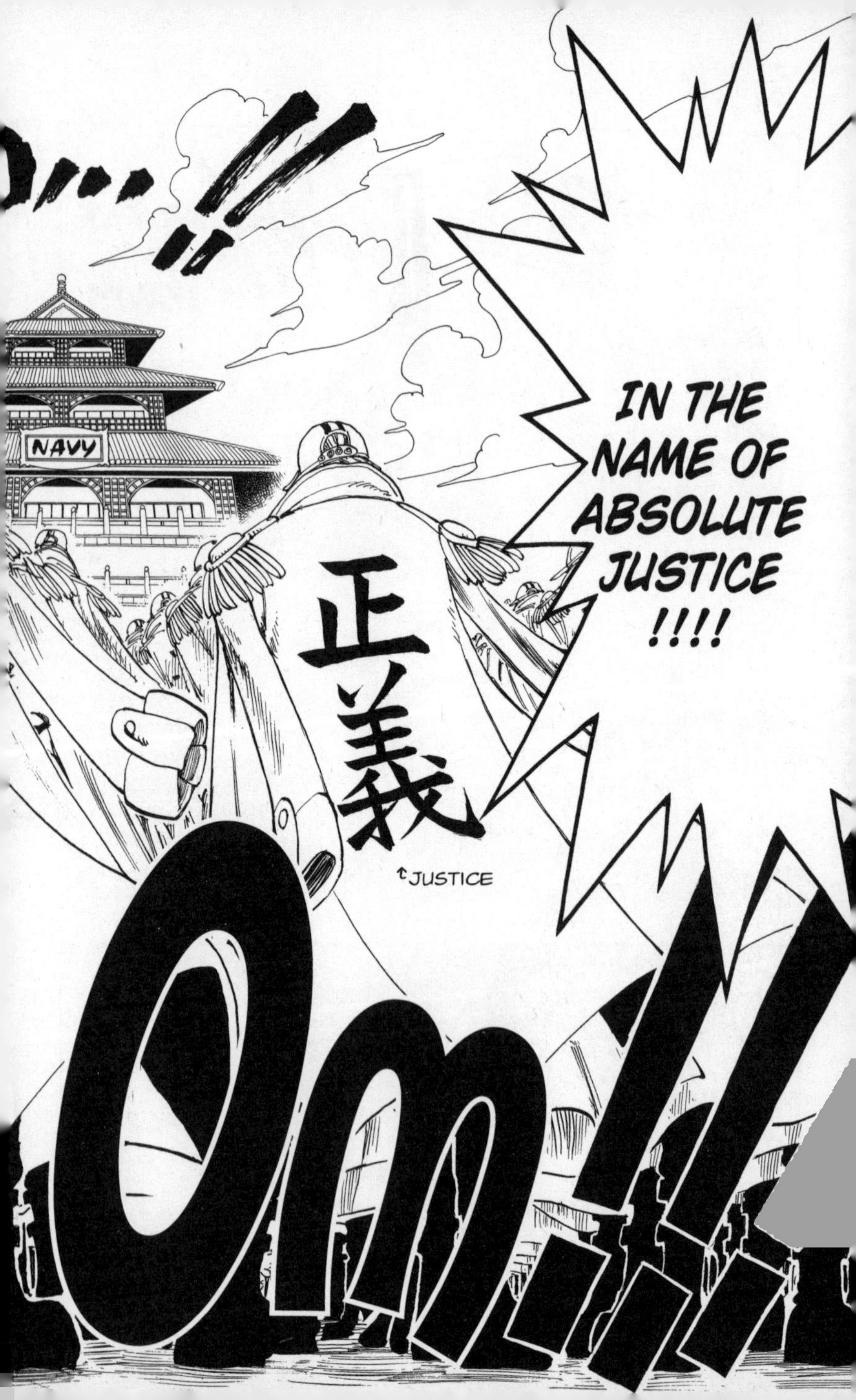
IN THE NAME OF ABSOLUTE JUSTICE !!!!
正義
JUSTICE
NAVY

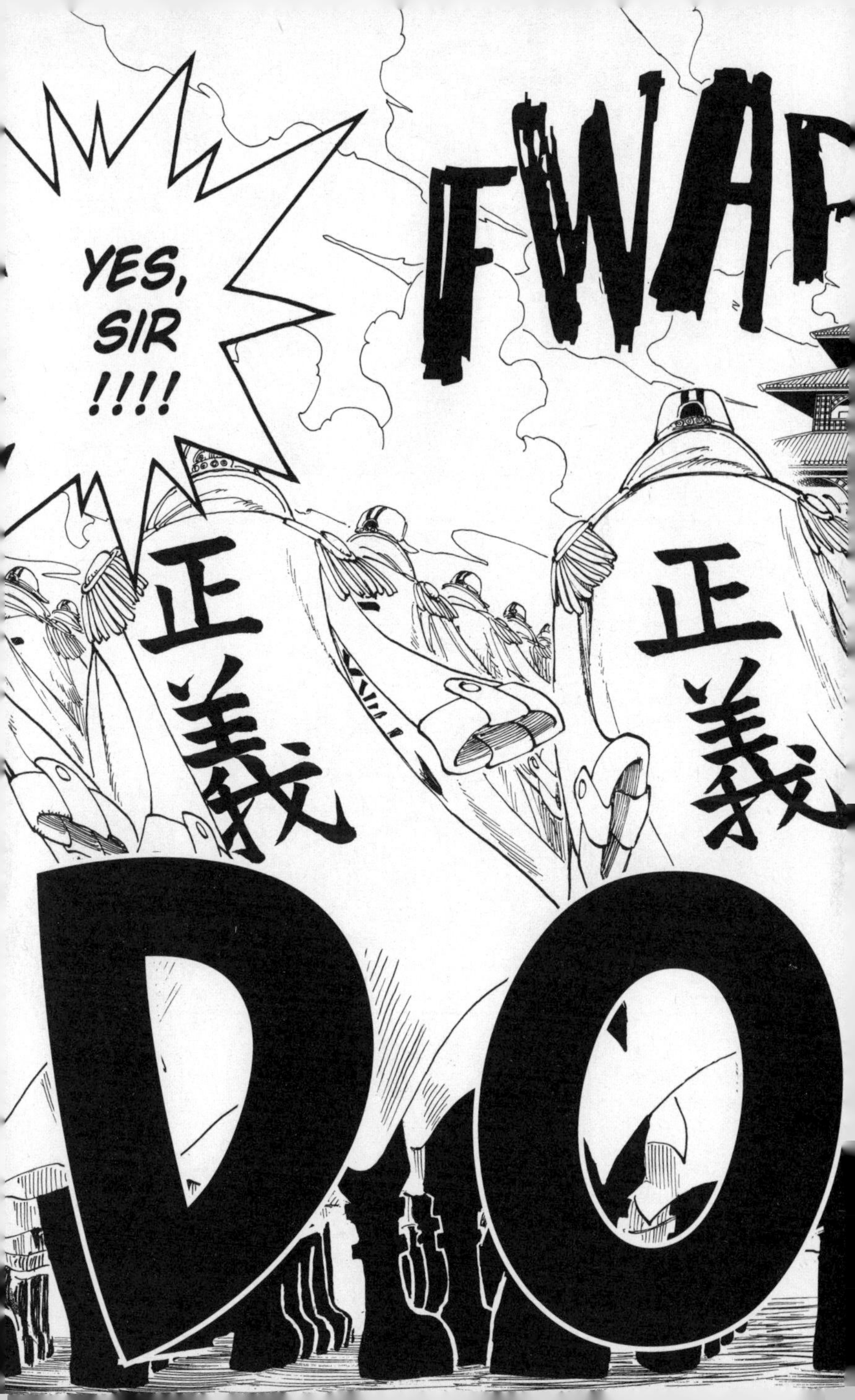
YES, SIR !!!!
FWAP
正義
正義
DO

THEY SAY WE'RE WORTH 30 MILLION BERRIES!!

WANTED
DEAD OR ALIVE
MONKEY D. LUFFY
30,000,000

HA HA HA HA!! WE'RE WANTED DEAD OR ALIVE!!

YOU'RE GRINNING LIKE AN IDIOT. IT'S NOTHING TO BRAG ABOUT.

LOOK!! I'M KNOWN ALL OVER THE WORLD!!

AT THAT PRICE, HEADQUARTERS IS PROBABLY INVOLVED. THE TOUGHEST BOUNTY HUNTERS ARE GOING TO COME AFTER YOU, TOO.

THE NAVY'S HUNTING YOU, LUFFY!!

AS USUAL, YOU GUYS HAVE NO IDEA HOW SERIOUS THIS IS.

DON'T BE JEALOUS! IF YOU GET TO BE A BIG SHOT, THEY MIGHT PUT YOU ON A POSTER TOO, EVEN IF YOU AREN'T A CAPTAIN.

HEY, THERE'S AN ISLAND.

YEAH!!

OKAY, LET'S SAIL FOR THE GRAND LINE, MEN!!

THIS IS NO TIME TO BE RELAXING IN THE EAST BLUE.

IF WE SEE THAT ISLAND...

THERE IT IS.

...THEN WE'RE APPROACHING THE GRAND LINE.

THE PIRATE KING, GOLD ROGER, WAS BORN THERE...

...AND EXECUTED THERE.

THAT'S WHERE THE FAMOUS ROGUETOWN IS.

THEY CALL IT "THE TOWN OF THE BEGINNING AND THE END."

WANT TO GO THERE?

IT'S WHERE THE PIRATE KING DIED!

ROGUE-
TOWN
TOWN OF
THE
BEGINNING
AND THE
END

Roguetown

DOOM

BLA
B
BLA
B

YACK
YACK

SO THIS IS
WHERE THE
AGE OF
PIRATES
BEGAN.

WOW!!
THIS
PLACE IS
HUGE!!

I GUESS
I'LL FIND
US SOME
EQUIPMENT.

I CAN PROBABLY GET
SOME GOOD COOKING
INGREDIENTS HERE.

And
some cute
chicks.

TMP TMP

RIGHT!!
I'M GOING
TO GO
SEE THE
EXECUTION
SCAFFOLD
!!

I'LL BE
GLAD TO
LEND YOU
SOME
MONEY...
AT 300%
INTEREST.

HEH
HEH

THERE'S
SOMETHING
I WANT TO
BUY TOO.

OUR BOSS IS IN JAIL, THANKS TO YOU LOT. NOW YOU'RE GOING TO PAY.

SO...YOU'RE NOT WITH THAT MONSTER TODAY, EH!?

YACK YACK

BLAH BLAH

BLAB

!

WELL, I'LL BE HAPPY TO TAKE YOU ON.

THEN YOU HAVEN'T HAD ENOUGH.

ALL RIGHT, THEN!!

WOOO——O

WHAT!? YOU WANT TO FIGHT US!!?

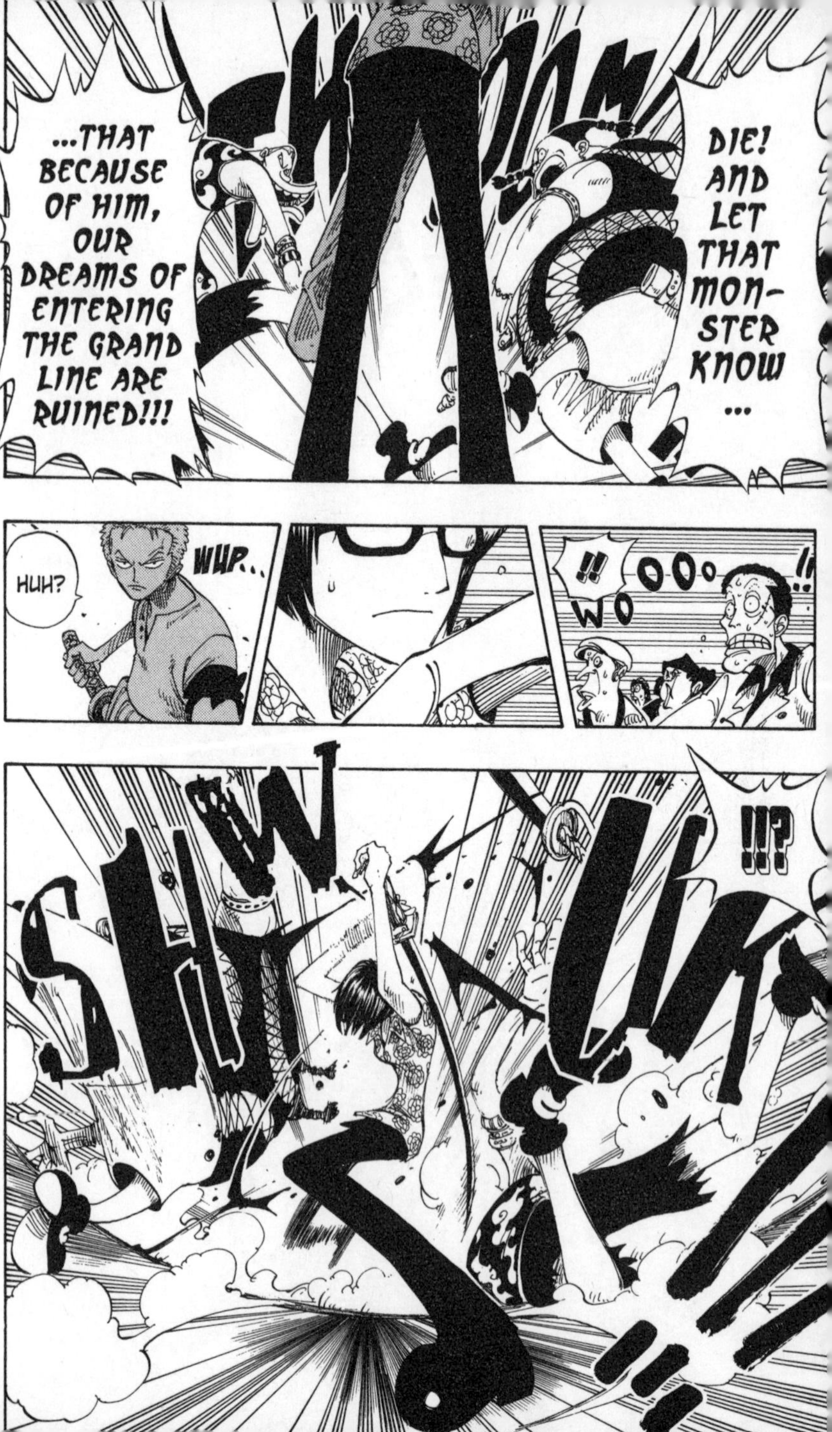
DIE! AND LET THAT MON-STER KNOW ...
...THAT BECAUSE OF HIM, OUR DREAMS OF ENTERING THE GRAND LINE ARE RUINED!!!
!!
WOOOO
!!
WUP...
HUH?
!!?

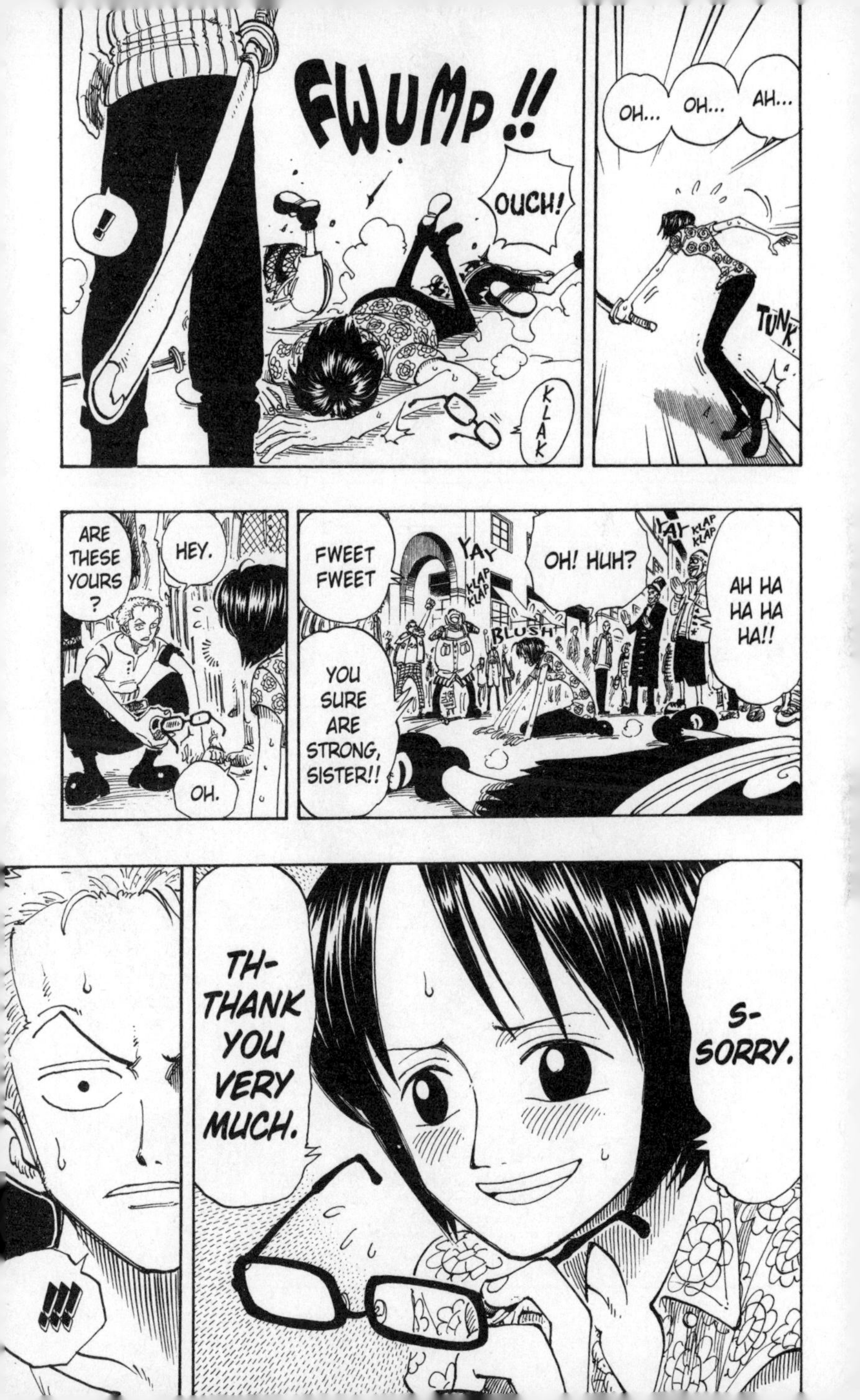
AH...
OH...
OH...
TUNK
FWUMP!!
OUCH!
KLAK
!
YAY
KLAP KLAP
AH HA HA HA HA!!
OH! HUH?
YAY
KLAP KLAP
FWEET FWEET
BLUSH
YOU SURE ARE STRONG, SISTER!!
HEY.
ARE THESE YOURS?
OH.
S-SORRY.
TH-THANK YOU VERY MUCH.
!!!

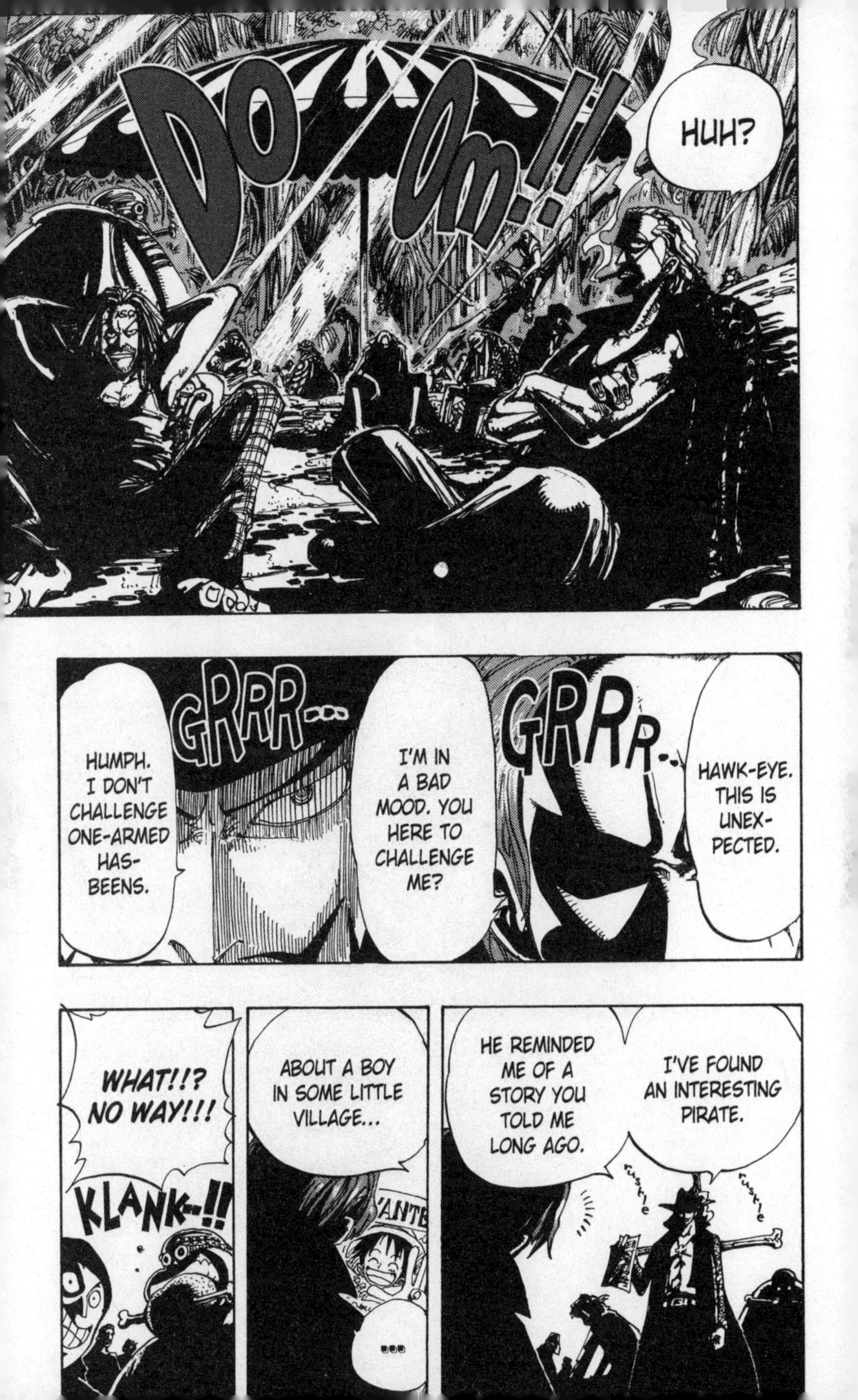

DOOM!!
HUH?
HAWK-EYE. THIS IS UNEX-PECTED.
GRRR..
I'M IN A BAD MOOD. YOU HERE TO CHALLENGE ME?
GRRR...
HUMPH. I DON'T CHALLENGE ONE-ARMED HAS-BEENS.
I'VE FOUND AN INTERESTING PIRATE.
rustle
rustle
HE REMINDED ME OF A STORY YOU TOLD ME LONG AGO.
ABOUT A BOY IN SOME LITTLE VILLAGE...
...
WHAT!!? NO WAY!!!
KLANK!!

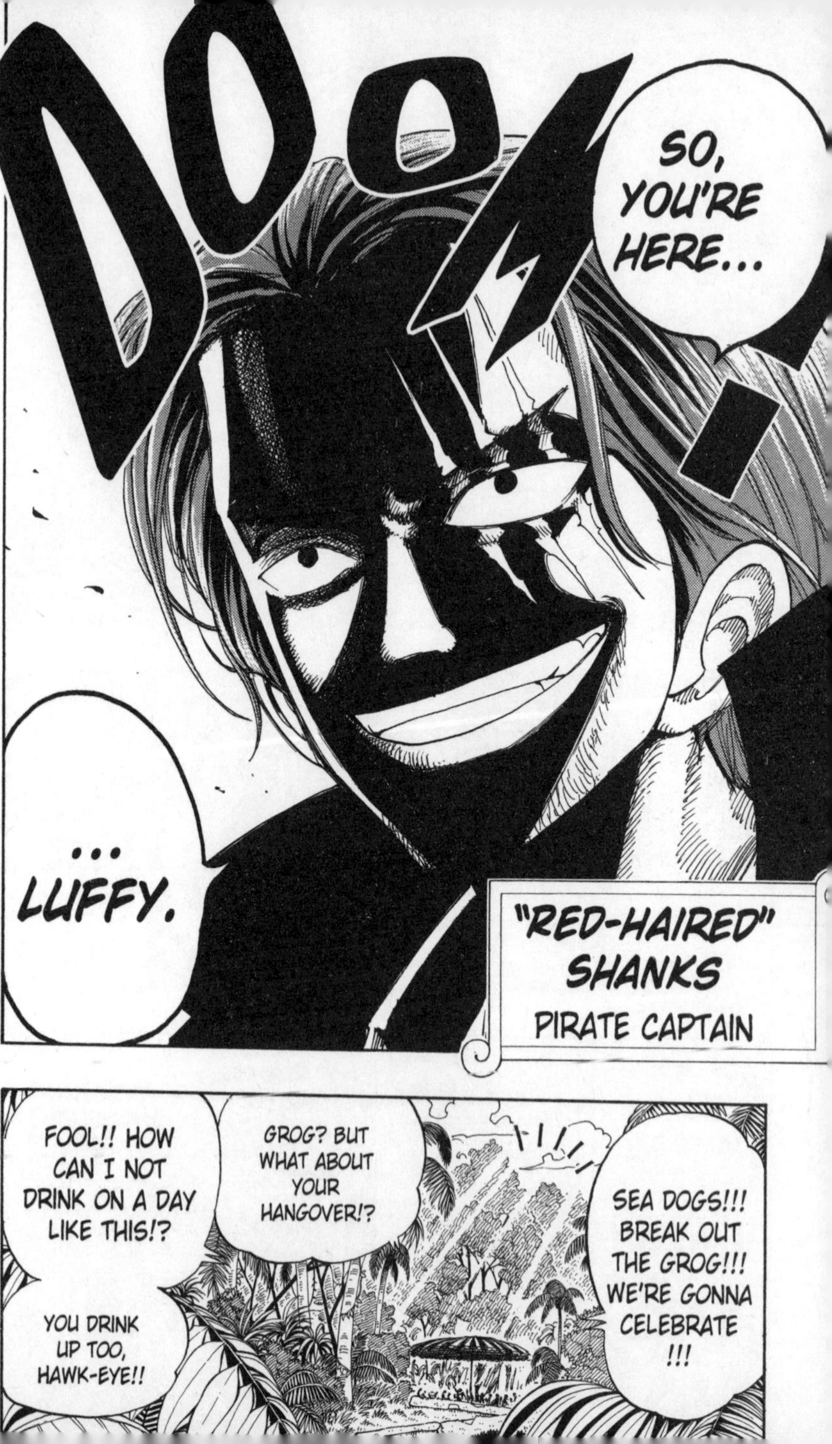
DOOM
SO, YOU'RE HERE...
... LUFFY.
"RED-HAIRED" SHANKS
PIRATE CAPTAIN
SEA DOGS!!! BREAK OUT THE GROG!!! WE'RE GONNA CELEBRATE !!!
GROG? BUT WHAT ABOUT YOUR HANGOVER!?
FOOL!! HOW CAN I NOT DRINK ON A DAY LIKE THIS!?
YOU DRINK UP TOO, HAWK-EYE!!

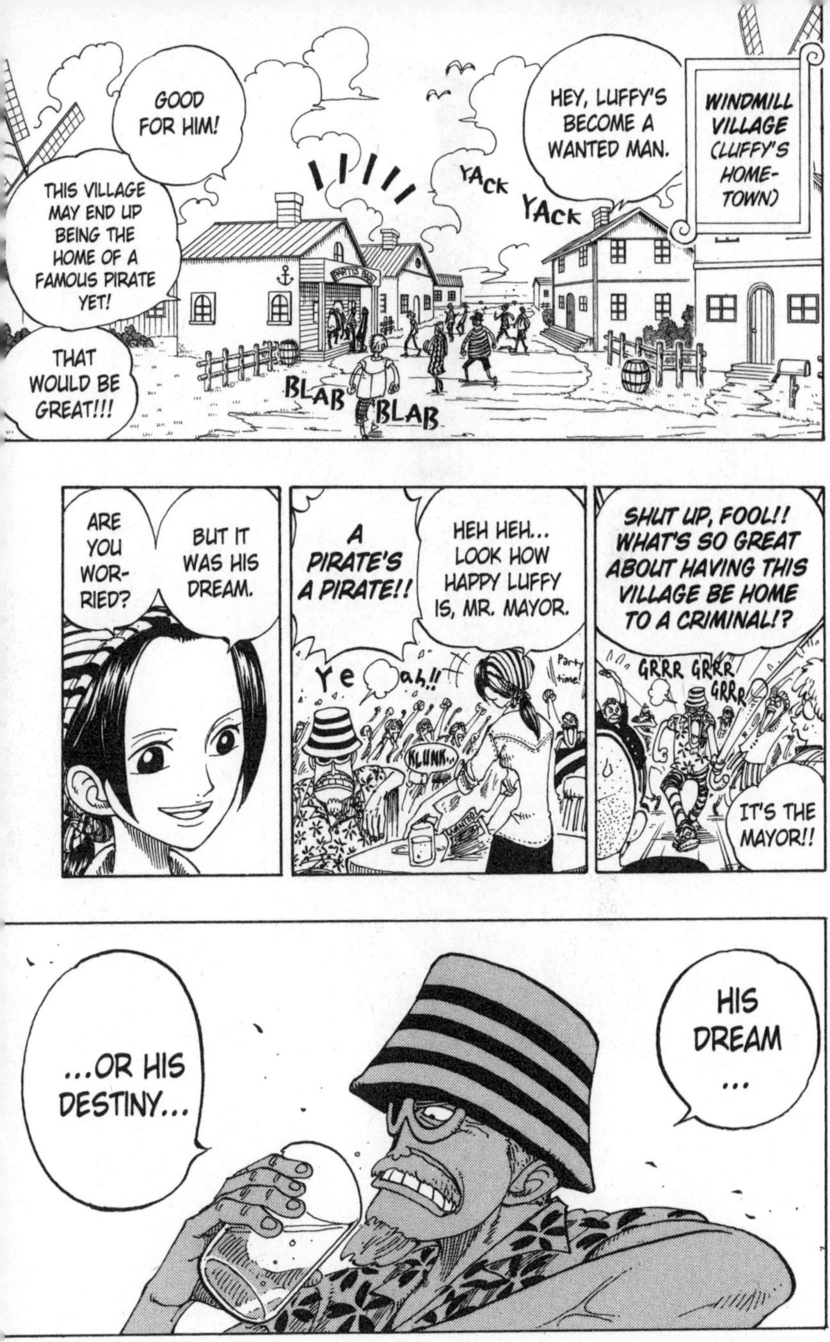
WINDMILL VILLAGE (LUFFY'S HOME-TOWN)
HEY, LUFFY'S BECOME A WANTED MAN.
YACK
YACK
GOOD FOR HIM!
THIS VILLAGE MAY END UP BEING THE HOME OF A FAMOUS PIRATE YET!
THAT WOULD BE GREAT!!!
BLAB
BLAB
SHUT UP, FOOL!! WHAT'S SO GREAT ABOUT HAVING THIS VILLAGE BE HOME TO A CRIMINAL!?
GRRR GRRR GRRR
IT'S THE MAYOR!!
HEH HEH... LOOK HOW HAPPY LUFFY IS, MR. MAYOR.
A PIRATE'S A PIRATE!!
Party time!
Yeah!!
KLUNK..
BUT IT WAS HIS DREAM.
ARE YOU WOR-RIED?
HIS DREAM ...
...OR HIS DESTINY...

Gun Deck & Anchor Rope Storage

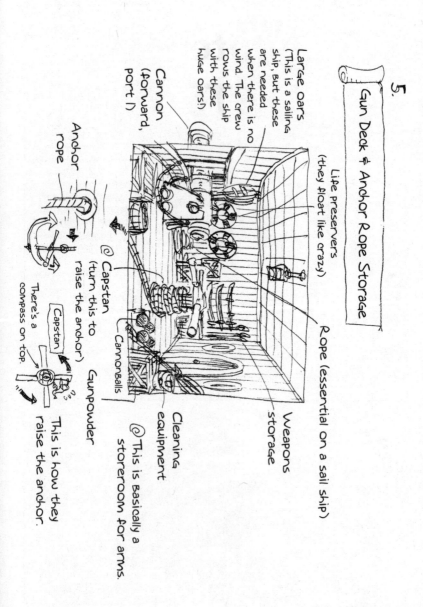

Large oars
(This is a sailing
ship, But these
are needed
when there is no
wind. The crew
rows the ship
with these
huge oars!)

Cannon
(forward,
port !)

Life preservers
(they float like crazy)

Rope (essential on a sail ship)

Weapons
storage

Cleaning
equipment

@ This is Basically a
storeroom for arms.

@ Capstan
(turn this to
raise the anchor)

Gunpowder

Cannonballs

Anchor
rope

Capstan

There's a
compass on top.

This is how they
raise the anchor.

Chapter 97:
KITETSU III

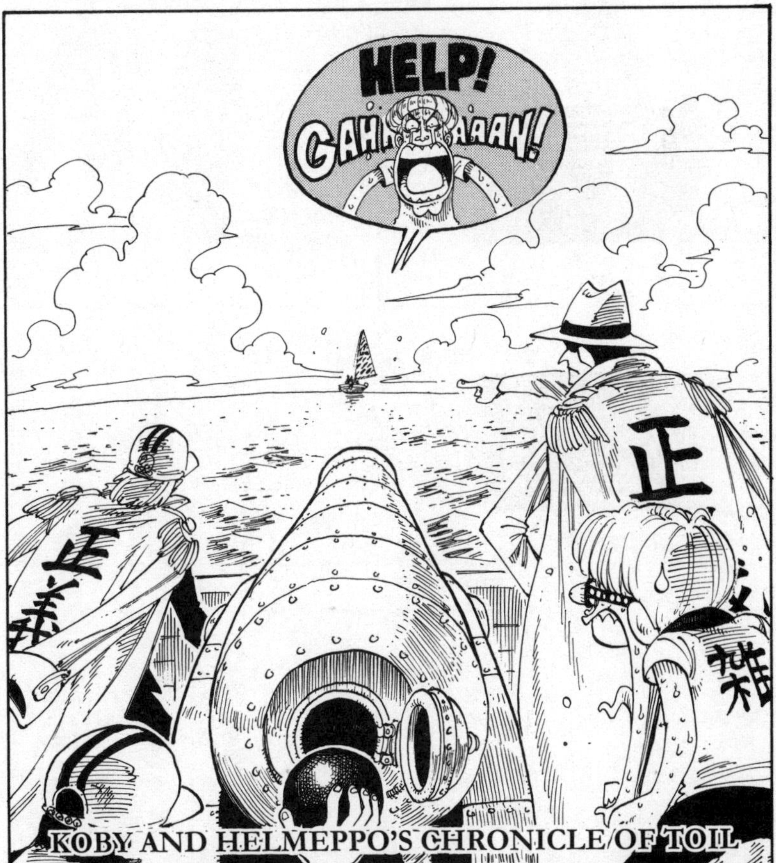
HELP!
GAHAAAAN!
KOBY AND HELMEPPO'S CHRONICLE OF TOIL
VOL. 13: "ARTILLERY ATTACK"

DOOM!!!

THE EXECUTION SCAFFOLD...

YACK YACK

BLAB BLAB

BLAB BLAB

...WAS EXECUTED.

THAT'S WHERE GOLD ROGER...

YACK YACK

THAT'S IT.

...DIED RIGHT THERE.

BLAB BLAB

YACK YACK

THE GREATEST PIRATE OF ALL TIME...

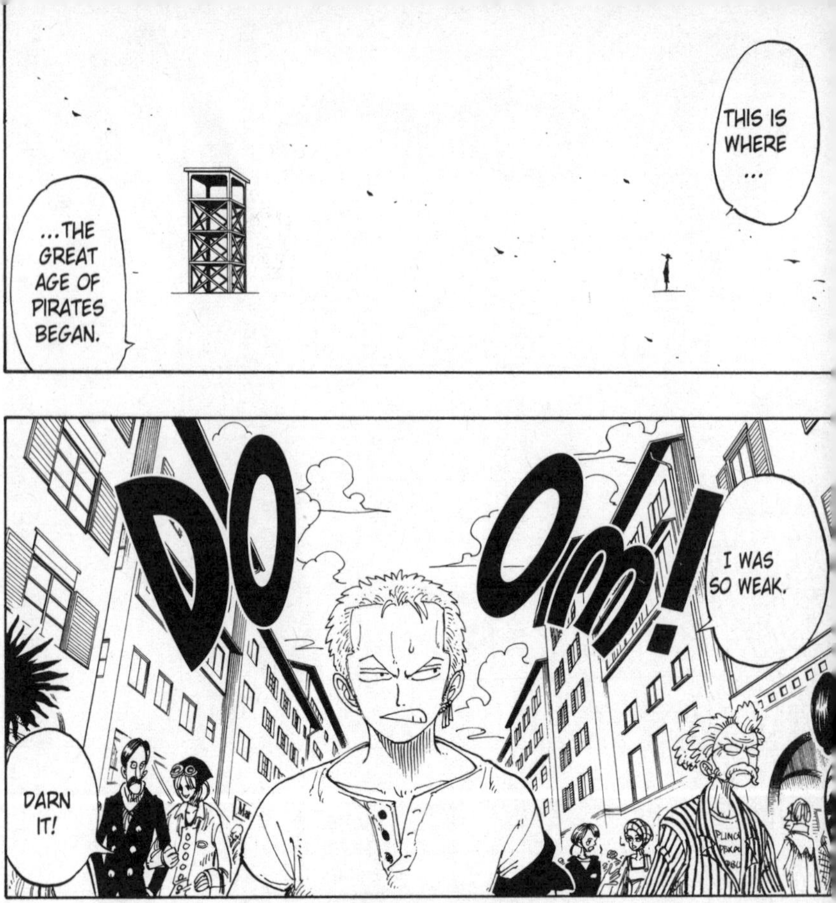
THIS IS WHERE ...
...THE GREAT AGE OF PIRATES BEGAN.
DOOM!
I WAS SO WEAK.
DARN IT!
STILL...
I-I'M SORRY.
IT'S UNCANNY HOW MUCH SHE LOOKS LIKE KUINA.
Like two peas in a pod.
AND SHE'S EVEN A SWORDS-MAN!
YACK YACK
I GUESS FEMALE SWORDSMEN DO EXIST.
I DOUBT I'LL SEE HER AGAIN, THOUGH.
BLAB BLAB
STILL, I WAS WEAK.

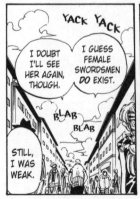

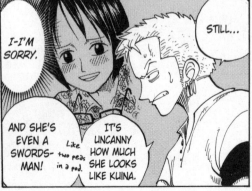

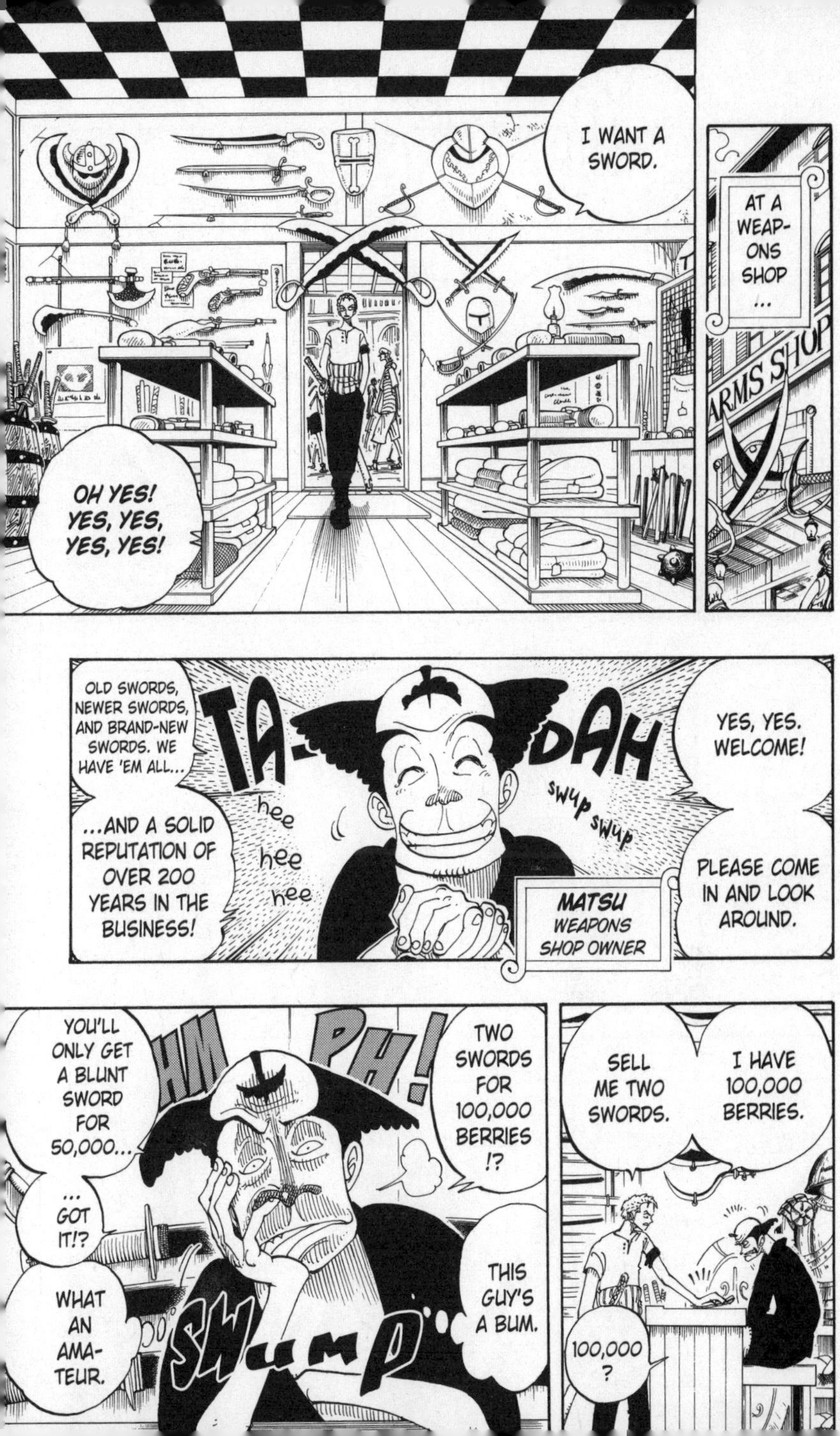
AT A WEAPONS SHOP...
ARMS SHOP
I WANT A SWORD.
OH YES! YES, YES, YES, YES!
YES, YES. WELCOME!
PLEASE COME IN AND LOOK AROUND.
TA-DAH
MATSU WEAPONS SHOP OWNER
swup swup
hee hee hee
OLD SWORDS, NEWER SWORDS, AND BRAND-NEW SWORDS. WE HAVE 'EM ALL...
...AND A SOLID REPUTATION OF OVER 200 YEARS IN THE BUSINESS!
I HAVE 100,000 BERRIES.
SELL ME TWO SWORDS.
100,000?
TWO SWORDS FOR 100,000 BERRIES!?
HMPH!
THIS GUY'S A BUM.
YOU'LL ONLY GET A BLUNT SWORD FOR 50,000...
...GOT IT!?
WHAT AN AMATEUR.
SHUMP

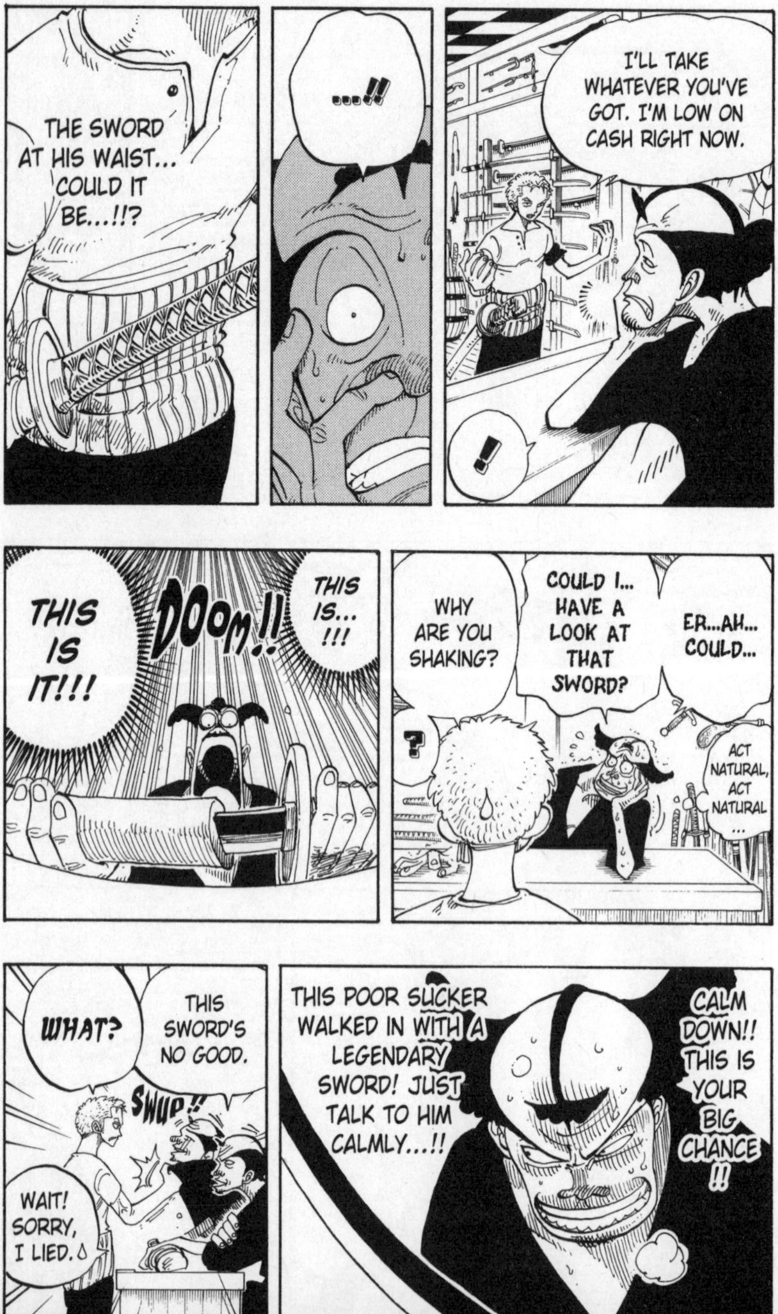
I'LL TAKE WHATEVER YOU'VE GOT. I'M LOW ON CASH RIGHT NOW.
!
...!!
THE SWORD AT HIS WAIST... COULD IT BE...!!?
ER...AH... COULD...
COULD I... HAVE A LOOK AT THAT SWORD?
WHY ARE YOU SHAKING?
ACT NATURAL, ACT NATURAL ...
?
THIS IS... !!!
DOOM!!
THIS IS IT!!!
CALM DOWN!! THIS IS YOUR BIG CHANCE !!
THIS POOR SUCKER WALKED IN WITH A LEGENDARY SWORD! JUST TALK TO HIM CALMLY...!!
THIS SWORD'S NO GOOD.
WHAT?
SWUP!!
WAIT! SORRY, I LIED.

HUH? WHAT ARE YOU TALKING ABOUT?

ER... FORGET THAT.

500,000 BERRIES THEN!!!

I'LL GIVE YOU 200,000 BERRIES FOR IT.

THEN YOU'LL HAVE 300,000 AND YOU CAN BUY THREE SWORDS FOR 100,000 BERRIES EACH!

LOOK HERE, FRIEND. MAYBE WE CAN WORK AROUND YOUR LACK OF FUNDS.

THIS SWORD IS NOTHING SPECIAL, BUT IT MIGHT BE WORTH *SOMETHING.*

LISTEN...

...THIS SWORD ISN'T FOR SALE AT ANY PRICE.

HOW CAN HE REFUSE !!?

I'LL GIVE YOU 650,000 BERRIES FOR IT!

GAAAH

WHAT THE HECK !?

I ALMOST HAVE HIM!

DON'T SAY IT!! DON'T SAY IT!!!

WHAT'S SHE DOING HERE!?

COULD IT BE...!!?

GULP!!

WHOA !!! THAT SWORD !!!

...THE WADO ICHIMONJI, THE STRAIGHT ROAD OF PEACE!!

THIS IS...

SURE, THAT'S ITS NAME...BUT IT'S NO GREAT SHAKES.

LOOK AT THIS BLADE!

!?

"WADO" WHAT!?

JUST LOOK RIGHT HERE! THIS SWORD'S WORTH 10 MILLION BERRIES!!

TH ROB! THROB!! THROB!!!

"NO GREAT SHAKES"!? ARE YOU NUTS!? THIS IS ONE OF THE GREAT 21!! IT'S A FAMOUS SWORD!!

YOU'RE HERE TO PICK UP AUTUMN RAIN RIGHT!? I'VE POLISHED IT!!

DAMAGING YOUR BUSINESS!? I'M SORRY! DID I SAY SOMETHING WRONG!?

WHY, YOU... I'LL SUE YOU FOR DAMAGING MY BUSINESS!!!

YOU IDIOT! WHY'D YOU HAVE TO TELL HIM THAT!!?

EEK! WHOA! OH!

WHAT'S A NOVICE LIKE YOU DOING WITH A FAMOUS SWORD, ANYWAY?

WHAM!!

I'VE NEVER SEEN SUCH A BEAUTIFUL SWORD! I COULDN'T HELP MYSELF!!

BUT SHE'S RIGHT. THAT SWORD IS WASTED ON SOMEONE LIKE YOU WHO DOESN'T KNOW ITS VALUE.

THAT IDIOT GIRL SAVED YOU.

IT *IS* A FAMOUS SWORD!!

WHAT ARE YOU DOING!!?

KLAK KLAK KRASH!!

AAAH!!

LEAVE THAT SWORD AND GET OUT!!

I MET YOU ON THE STREET EARLIER!

HUH!?

PICK TWO.

THERE ARE SWORDS WORTH 50,000 BERRIES IN THAT BARREL.

WHAT'S HE SO MAD ABOUT?

BOUNTY HUNTER?

HAVEN'T YOU HEARD OF HIM? HIS NAME'S RORONOA ZOLO.

THREE SWORDS AT ONCE, HUH? JUST LIKE THAT BOUNTY HUNTER!

YOU MUST LIKE SWORDS!

THAT'S UNFOR-GIVABLE!!

USING A SWORD TO MAKE MONEY...

BUT IT'S AN EVIL NAME!!

THAT'S THE NAME OF A MASTER SWORDSMAN WHO'S FAMOUS THROUGHOUT THE EAST BLUE.

I KNOW THE NAME WELL.

AND MOST OF THE WORLD-FAMOUS SWORDS ARE IN THEIR HANDS.

ALL THE FAMOUS SWORDSMEN ARE EITHER PIRATES OR BOUNTY HUNTERS.

WHY IS THERE SO MUCH EVIL IN THE WORLD TODAY!?

THOSE SWORDS MUST BE CRYING.

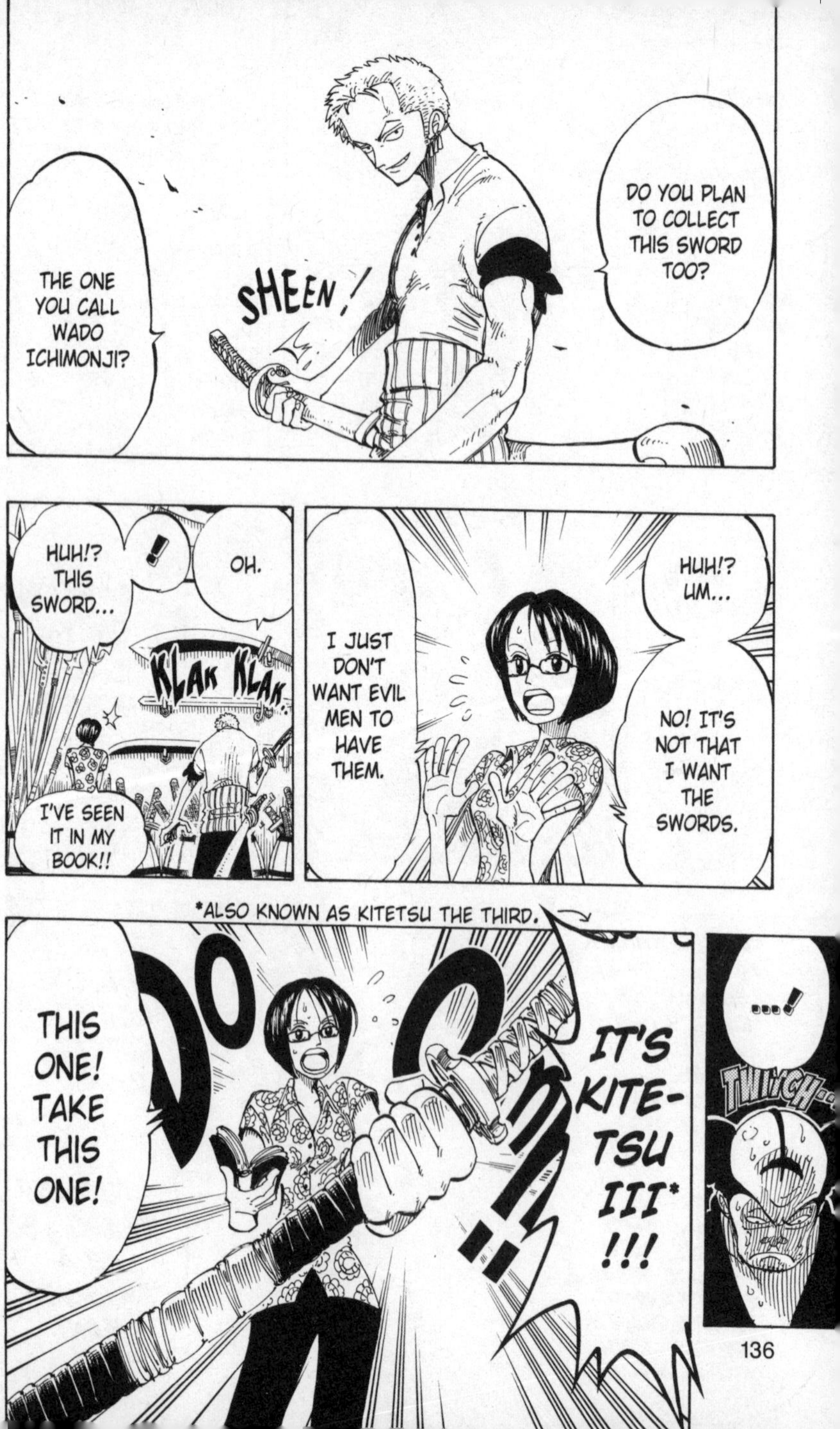
DO YOU PLAN TO COLLECT THIS SWORD TOO?
SHEEN!
THE ONE YOU CALL WADO ICHIMONJI?
HUH!? UM...
NO! IT'S NOT THAT I WANT THE SWORDS.
I JUST DON'T WANT EVIL MEN TO HAVE THEM.
OH.
!
HUH!? THIS SWORD...
KLAK KLAK
I'VE SEEN IT IN MY BOOK!!
...!
TWITCH...
IT'S KITE-TSU III* !!!
THIS ONE! TAKE THIS ONE!
*ALSO KNOWN AS KITETSU THE THIRD.

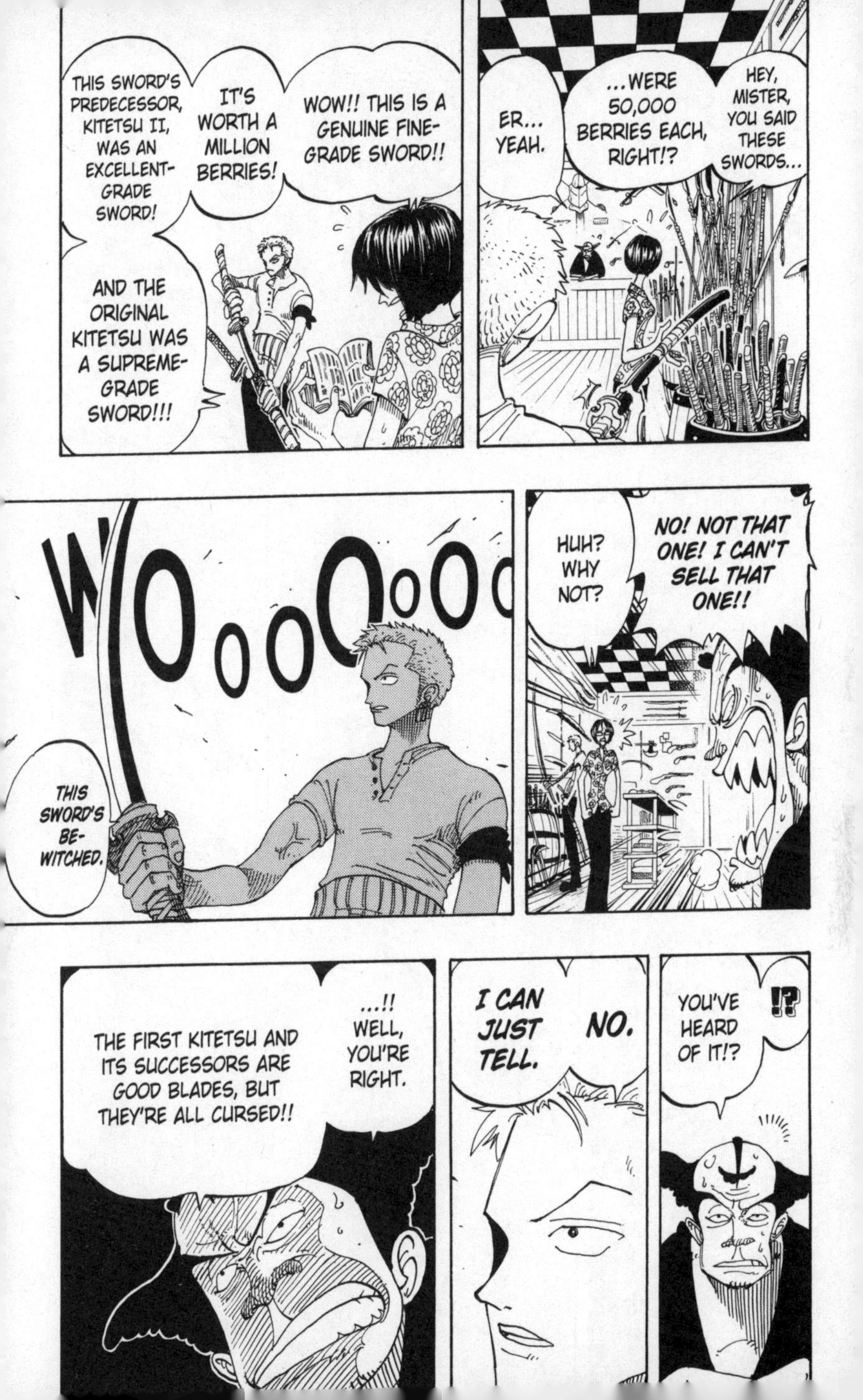
HEY, MISTER, YOU SAID THESE SWORDS...
...WERE 50,000 BERRIES EACH, RIGHT!?
ER... YEAH.
WOW!! THIS IS A GENUINE FINE-GRADE SWORD!!
IT'S WORTH A MILLION BERRIES!
THIS SWORD'S PREDECESSOR, KITETSU II, WAS AN EXCELLENT-GRADE SWORD!
AND THE ORIGINAL KITETSU WAS A SUPREME-GRADE SWORD!!!
NO! NOT THAT ONE! I CAN'T SELL THAT ONE!!
HUH? WHY NOT?
WOOOOOOOO
THIS SWORD'S BE-WITCHED.
!?
YOU'VE HEARD OF IT!?
NO.
I CAN JUST TELL.
...!! WELL, YOU'RE RIGHT.
THE FIRST KITETSU AND ITS SUCCESSORS ARE GOOD BLADES, BUT THEY'RE ALL CURSED!!

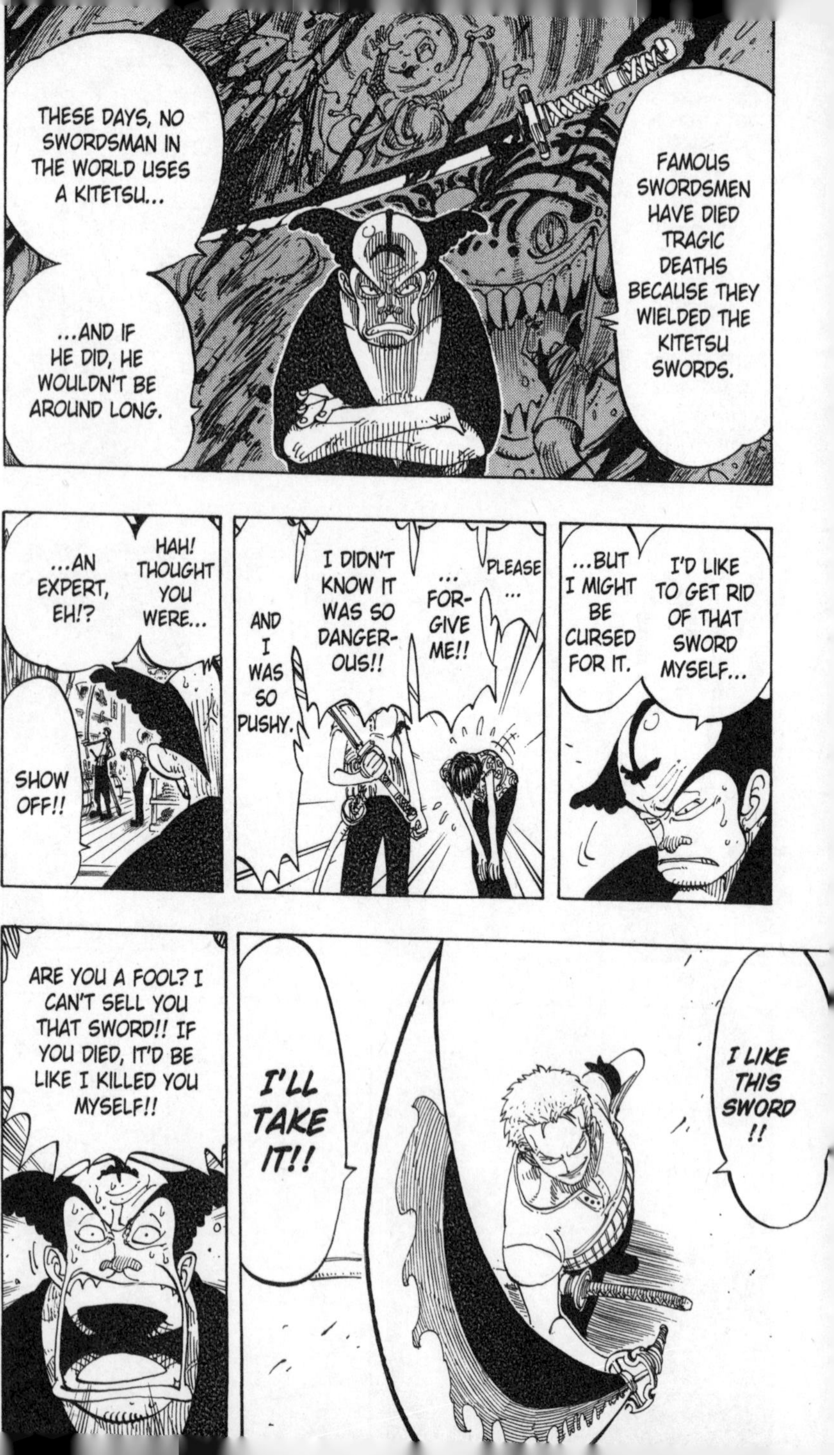
FAMOUS SWORDSMEN HAVE DIED TRAGIC DEATHS BECAUSE THEY WIELDED THE KITETSU SWORDS.
THESE DAYS, NO SWORDSMAN IN THE WORLD USES A KITETSU...
...AND IF HE DID, HE WOULDN'T BE AROUND LONG.
I'D LIKE TO GET RID OF THAT SWORD MYSELF...
...BUT I MIGHT BE CURSED FOR IT.
PLEASE ...
... FOR-GIVE ME!!
I DIDN'T KNOW IT WAS SO DANGER-OUS!!
AND I WAS SO PUSHY.
HAH! THOUGHT YOU WERE...
...AN EXPERT, EH!?
SHOW OFF!!
I LIKE THIS SWORD !!
I'LL TAKE IT!!
ARE YOU A FOOL? I CAN'T SELL YOU THAT SWORD!! IF YOU DIED, IT'D BE LIKE I KILLED YOU MYSELF!!

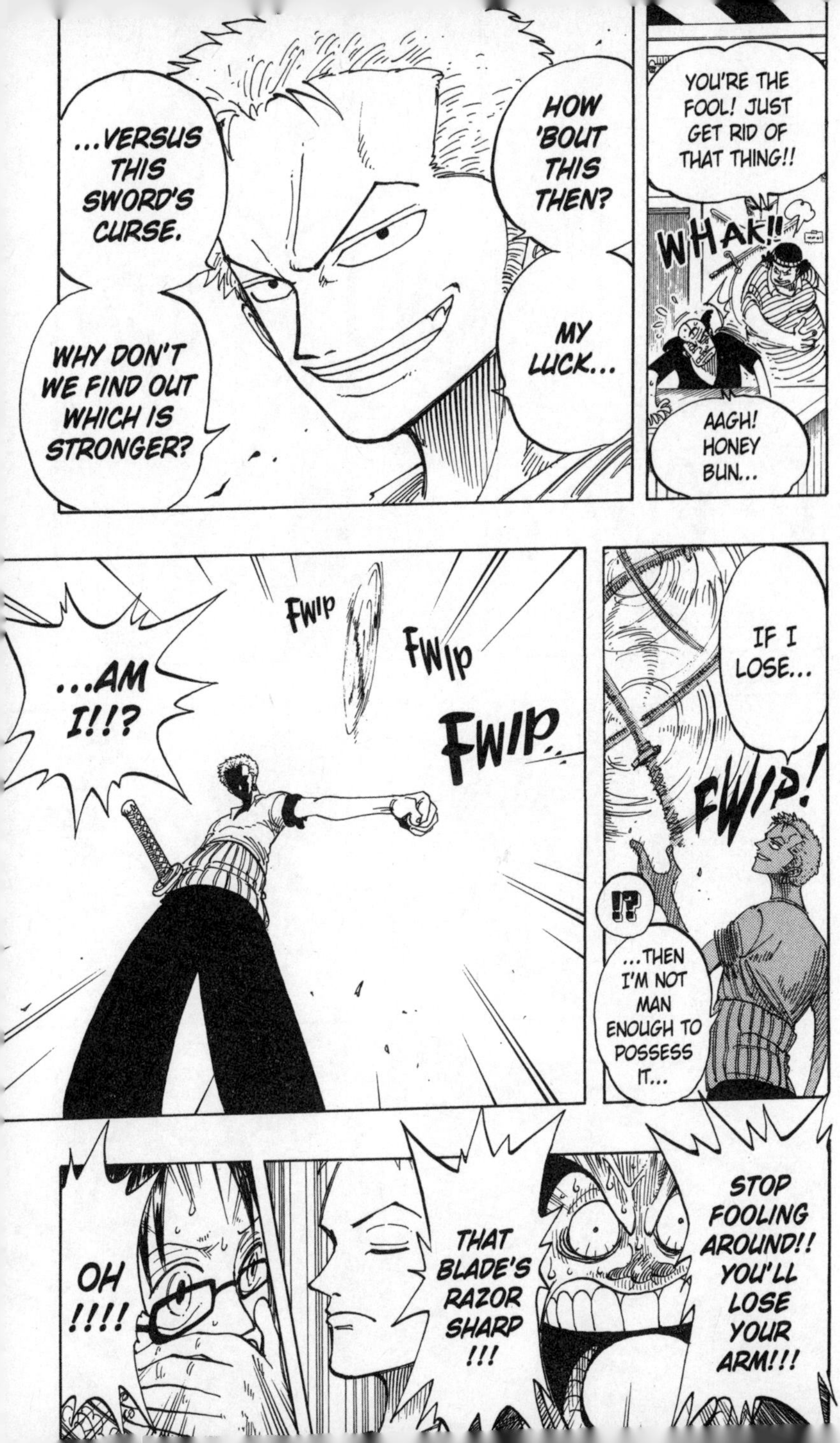
YOU'RE THE FOOL! JUST GET RID OF THAT THING!!
WHAK!!
AAGH! HONEY BUN...
HOW 'BOUT THIS THEN?
MY LUCK...
...VERSUS THIS SWORD'S CURSE.
WHY DON'T WE FIND OUT WHICH IS STRONGER?
IF I LOSE...
FWIP!
!?
...THEN I'M NOT MAN ENOUGH TO POSSESS IT...
FWIP
FWIP
FWIP
...AM I!!?
STOP FOOLING AROUND!! YOU'LL LOSE YOUR ARM!!!
THAT BLADE'S RAZOR SHARP!!!
OH !!!!

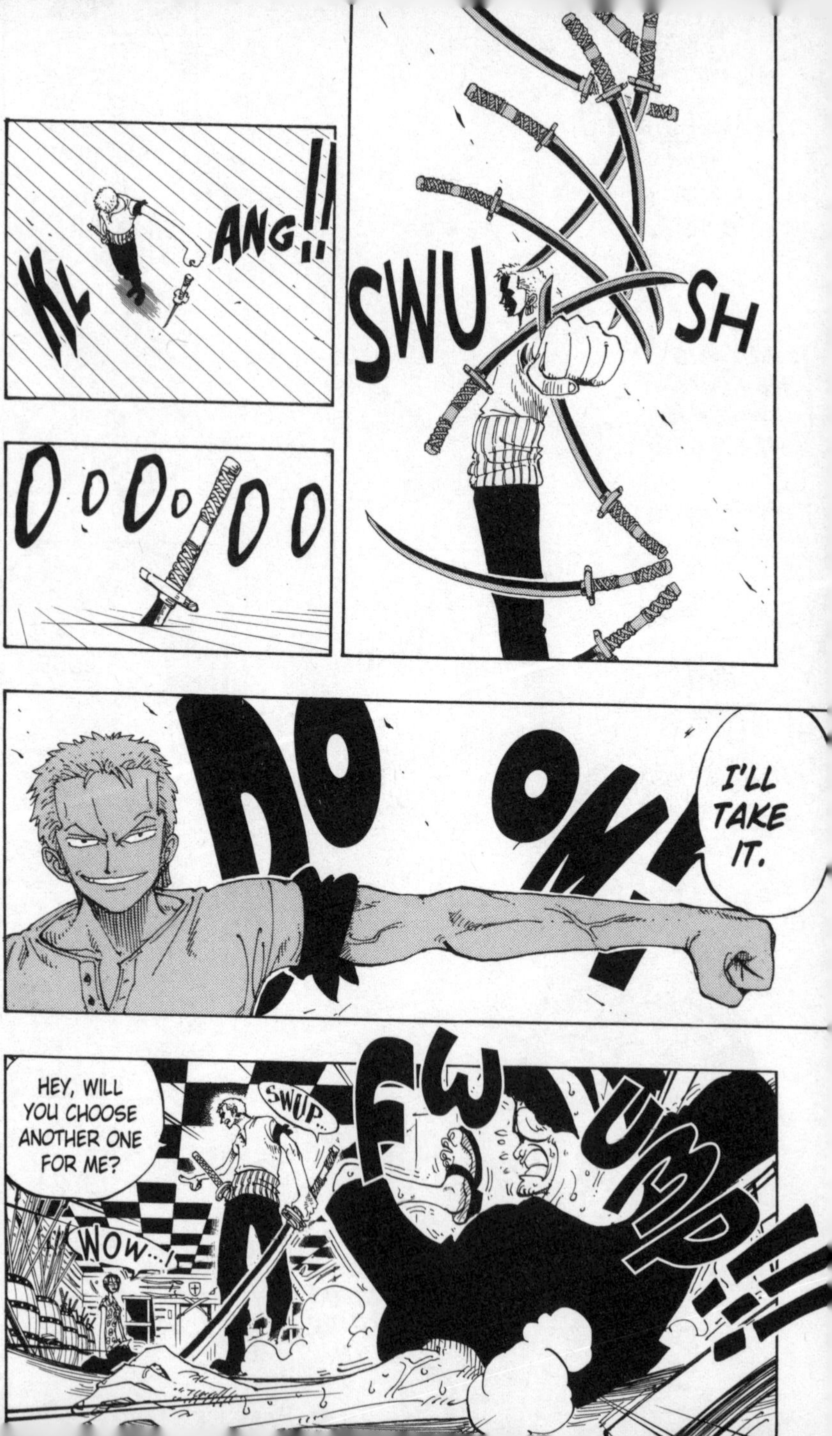
SWUSH
KLANG!!
DOOOOOO
DOOM
I'LL TAKE IT.
FWUMP!!
SWUP...
HEY, WILL YOU CHOOSE ANOTHER ONE FOR ME?
WOW...!

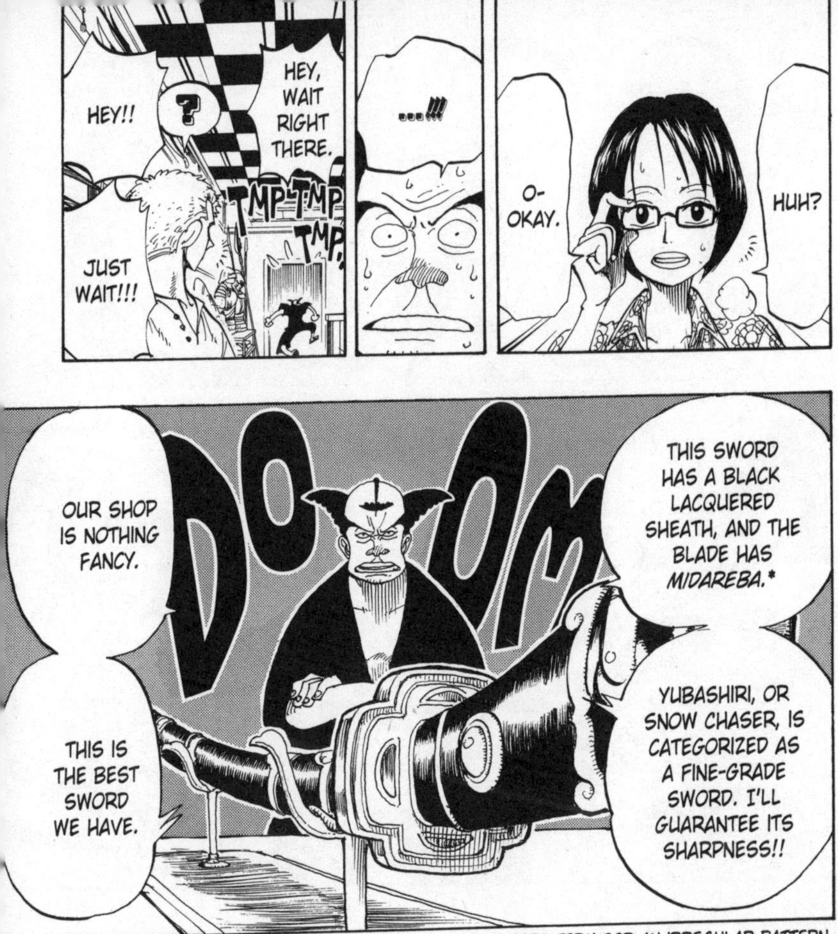
HUH?
O-OKAY.
...!!!
HEY, WAIT RIGHT THERE.
HEY!!
?
TMP TMP TMP,
JUST WAIT!!!
DOOM
THIS SWORD HAS A BLACK LACQUERED SHEATH, AND THE BLADE HAS *MIDAREBA.**
YUBASHIRI, OR SNOW CHASER, IS CATEGORIZED AS A FINE-GRADE SWORD. I'LL GUARANTEE ITS SHARPNESS!!
OUR SHOP IS NOTHING FANCY.
THIS IS THE BEST SWORD WE HAVE.

*A SWORD TERM FOR AN IRREGULAR PATTERN.

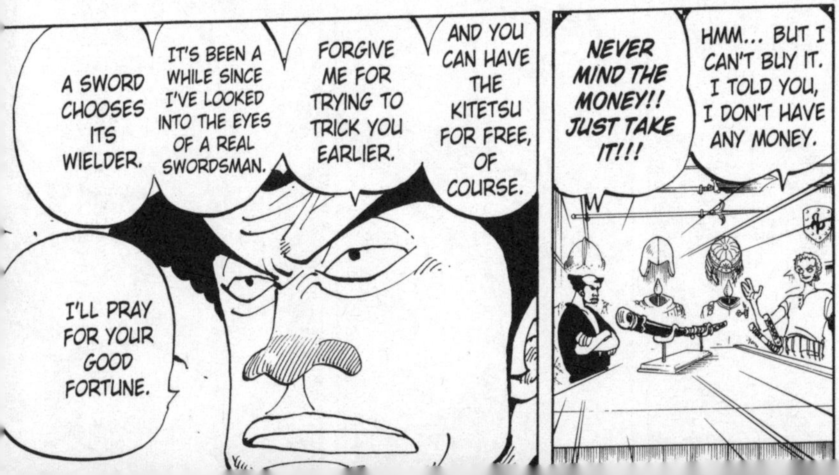
HMM... BUT I CAN'T BUY IT. I TOLD YOU, I DON'T HAVE ANY MONEY.
NEVER MIND THE MONEY!! JUST TAKE IT!!!
AND YOU CAN HAVE THE KITETSU FOR FREE, OF COURSE.
FORGIVE ME FOR TRYING TO TRICK YOU EARLIER.
IT'S BEEN A WHILE SINCE I'VE LOOKED INTO THE EYES OF A REAL SWORDSMAN.
A SWORD CHOOSES ITS WIELDER.
I'LL PRAY FOR YOUR GOOD FORTUNE.

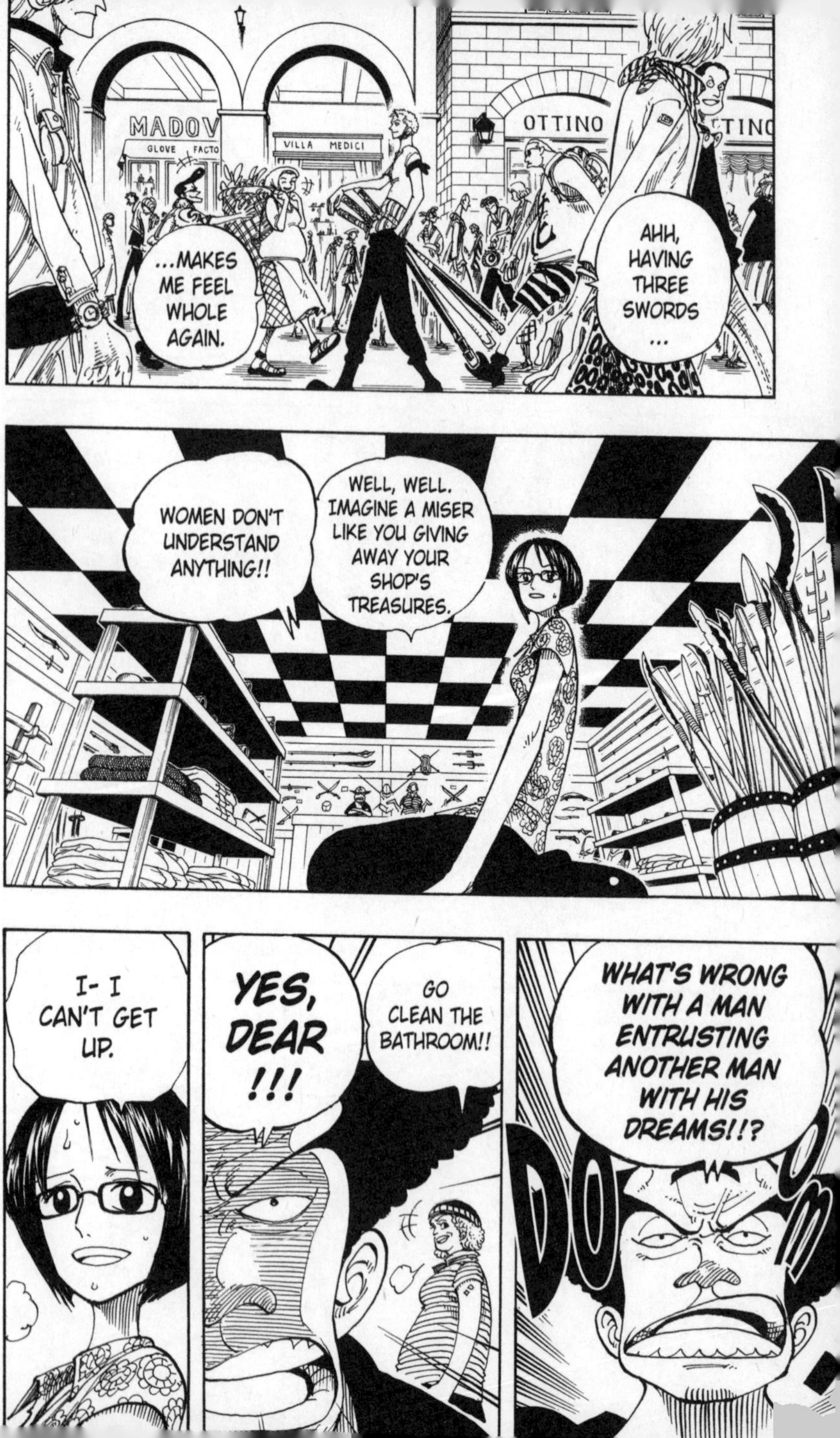
OTTINO
AHH, HAVING THREE SWORDS ...
VILLA MEDICI
MADOV
GLOVE FACTO
...MAKES ME FEEL WHOLE AGAIN.
WELL, WELL. IMAGINE A MISER LIKE YOU GIVING AWAY YOUR SHOP'S TREASURES.
WOMEN DON'T UNDERSTAND ANYTHING!!
WHAT'S WRONG WITH A MAN ENTRUSTING ANOTHER MAN WITH HIS DREAMS!!?
GO CLEAN THE BATHROOM!!
YES, DEAR !!!
I- I CAN'T GET UP.

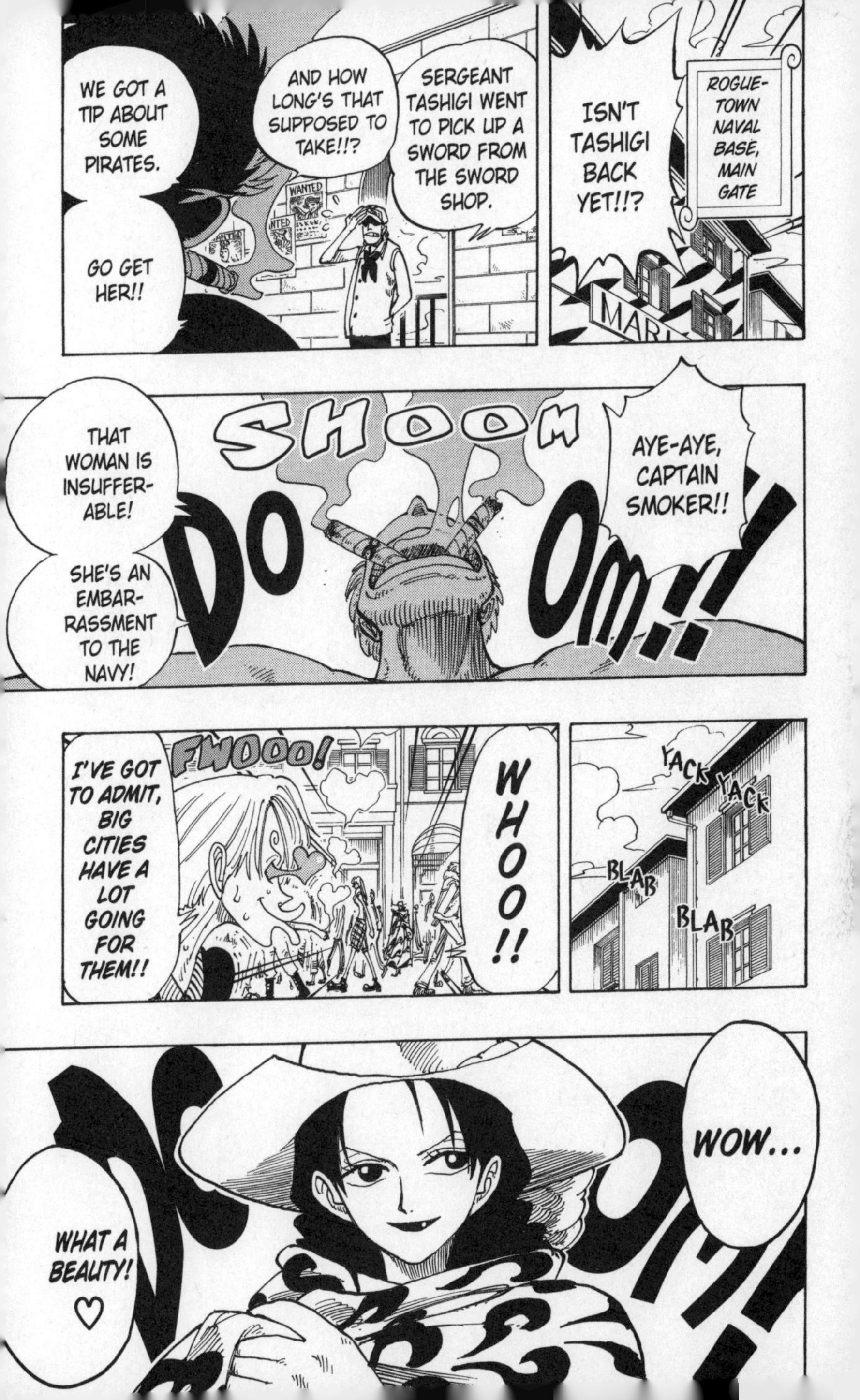
ROGUE-TOWN NAVAL BASE, MAIN GATE
ISN'T TASHIGI BACK YET!!?
SERGEANT TASHIGI WENT TO PICK UP A SWORD FROM THE SWORD SHOP.
AND HOW LONG'S THAT SUPPOSED TO TAKE!!?
WE GOT A TIP ABOUT SOME PIRATES.
GO GET HER!!
AYE-AYE, CAPTAIN SMOKER!!
SHOOM
DOOM!!
THAT WOMAN IS INSUFFERABLE!
SHE'S AN EMBARRASSMENT TO THE NAVY!
YACK YACK
BLAB
BLAB
WHOOO!!
FWOOO!
I'VE GOT TO ADMIT, BIG CITIES HAVE A LOT GOING FOR THEM!!
WOW...
WHAT A BEAUTY! ♡

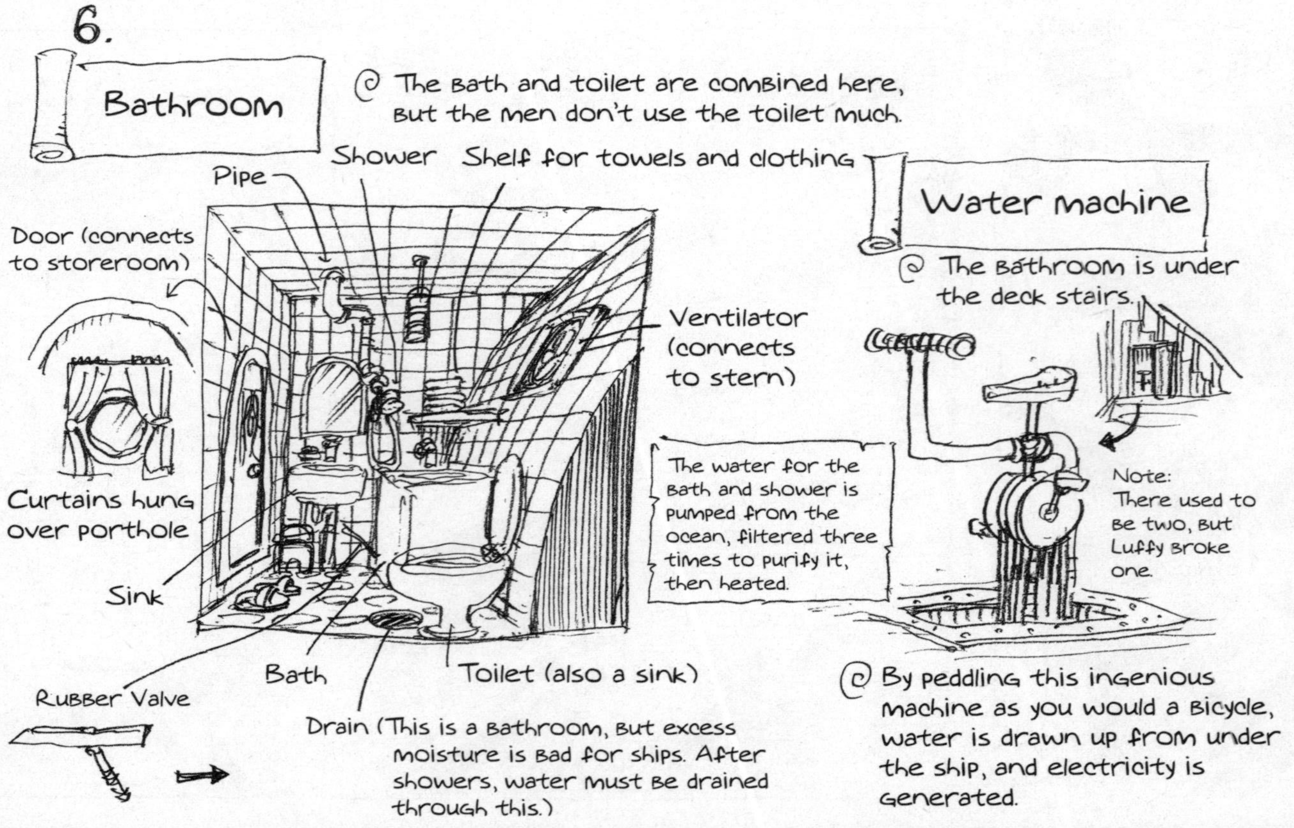
6.
Bathroom
@ The Bath and toilet are combined here, But the men don't use the toilet much.
Shower
Shelf for towels and clothing
Pipe
Door (connects to storeroom)
Curtains hung over porthole
Sink
Bath
Rubber Valve
Toilet (also a sink)
Drain (This is a Bathroom, But excess moisture is Bad for ships. After showers, water must Be drained through this.)
Ventilator (connects to stern)
The water for the Bath and shower is pumped from the ocean, filtered three times to purify it, then heated.
Water machine
@ The Bathroom is under the deck stairs.
Note: There used to Be two, But Luffy Broke one.
@ By peddling this ingenious machine as you would a Bicycle, water is drawn up from under the ship, and electricity is generated.

Chapter 98: DARK CLOUDS

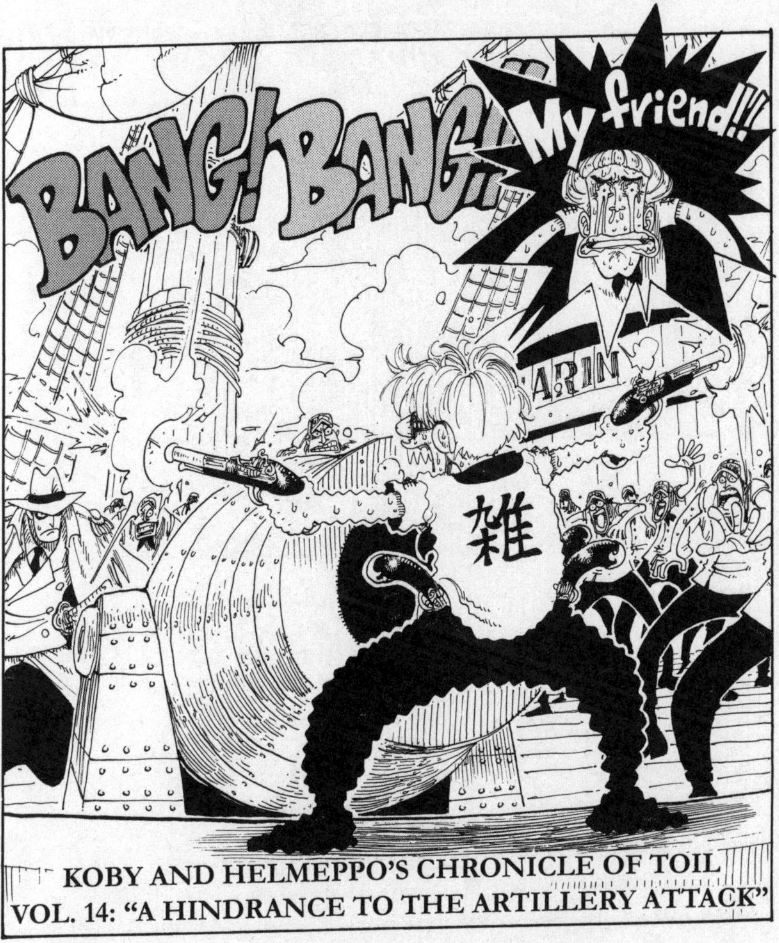
My friend!!!
BANG! BANG!!
雑

KOBY AND HELMEPPO'S CHRONICLE OF TOIL
VOL. 14: "A HINDRANCE TO THE ARTILLERY ATTACK"

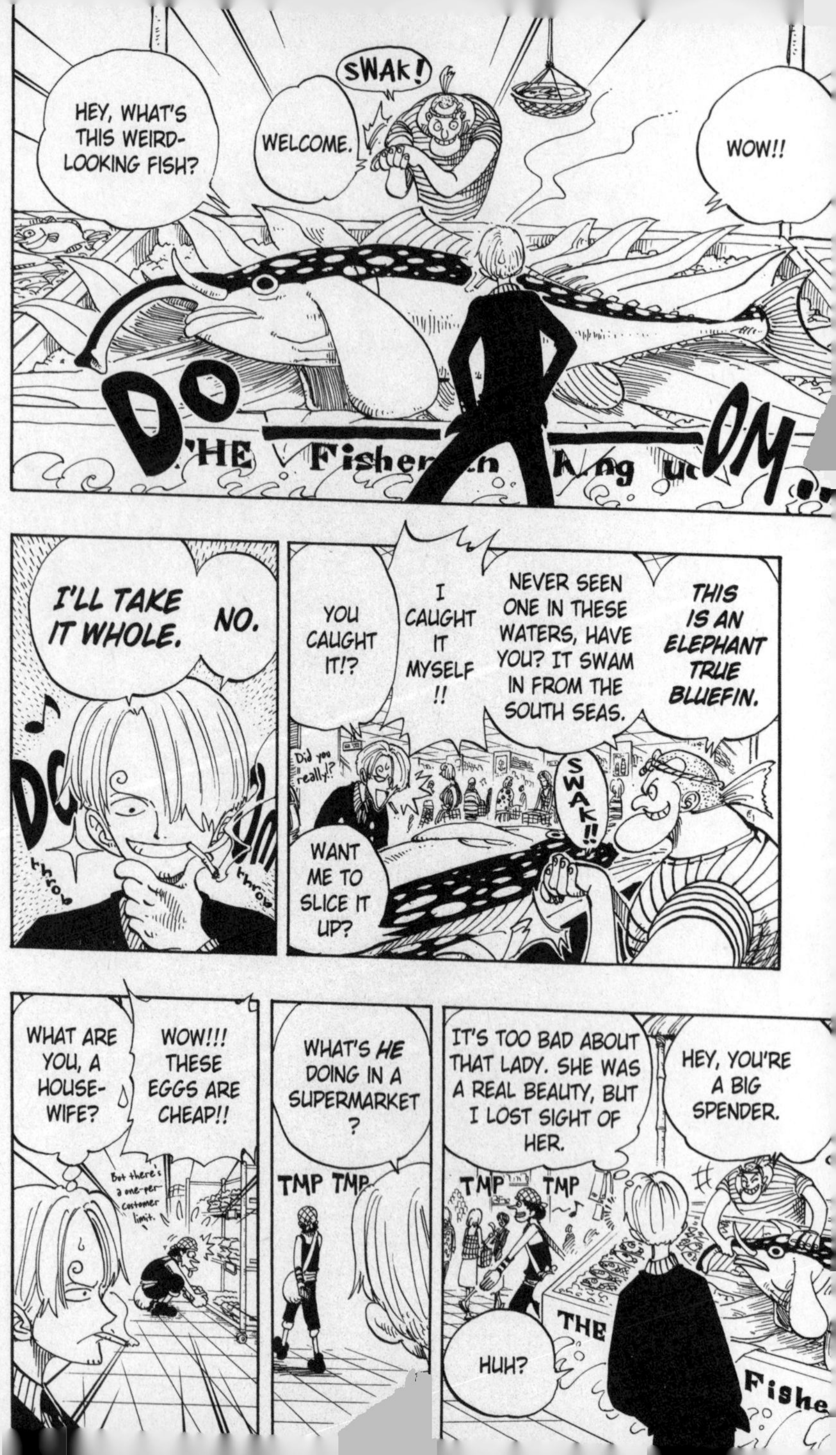
WOW!!
SWAK!
WELCOME.
HEY, WHAT'S THIS WEIRD-LOOKING FISH?
DO
OM
THE
Fisher
THIS IS AN ELEPHANT TRUE BLUEFIN.
NEVER SEEN ONE IN THESE WATERS, HAVE YOU? IT SWAM IN FROM THE SOUTH SEAS.
I CAUGHT IT MYSELF!!
YOU CAUGHT IT!?
Did you really!?
SWAK!!
WANT ME TO SLICE IT UP?
NO.
I'LL TAKE IT WHOLE.
throb throb
HEY, YOU'RE A BIG SPENDER.
IT'S TOO BAD ABOUT THAT LADY. SHE WAS A REAL BEAUTY, BUT I LOST SIGHT OF HER.
TMP TMP
HUH?
THE
Fishe
WHAT'S HE DOING IN A SUPERMARKET?
TMP TMP
WOW!!! THESE EGGS ARE CHEAP!!
But there's a one-per-customer limit.
WHAT ARE YOU, A HOUSE-WIFE?

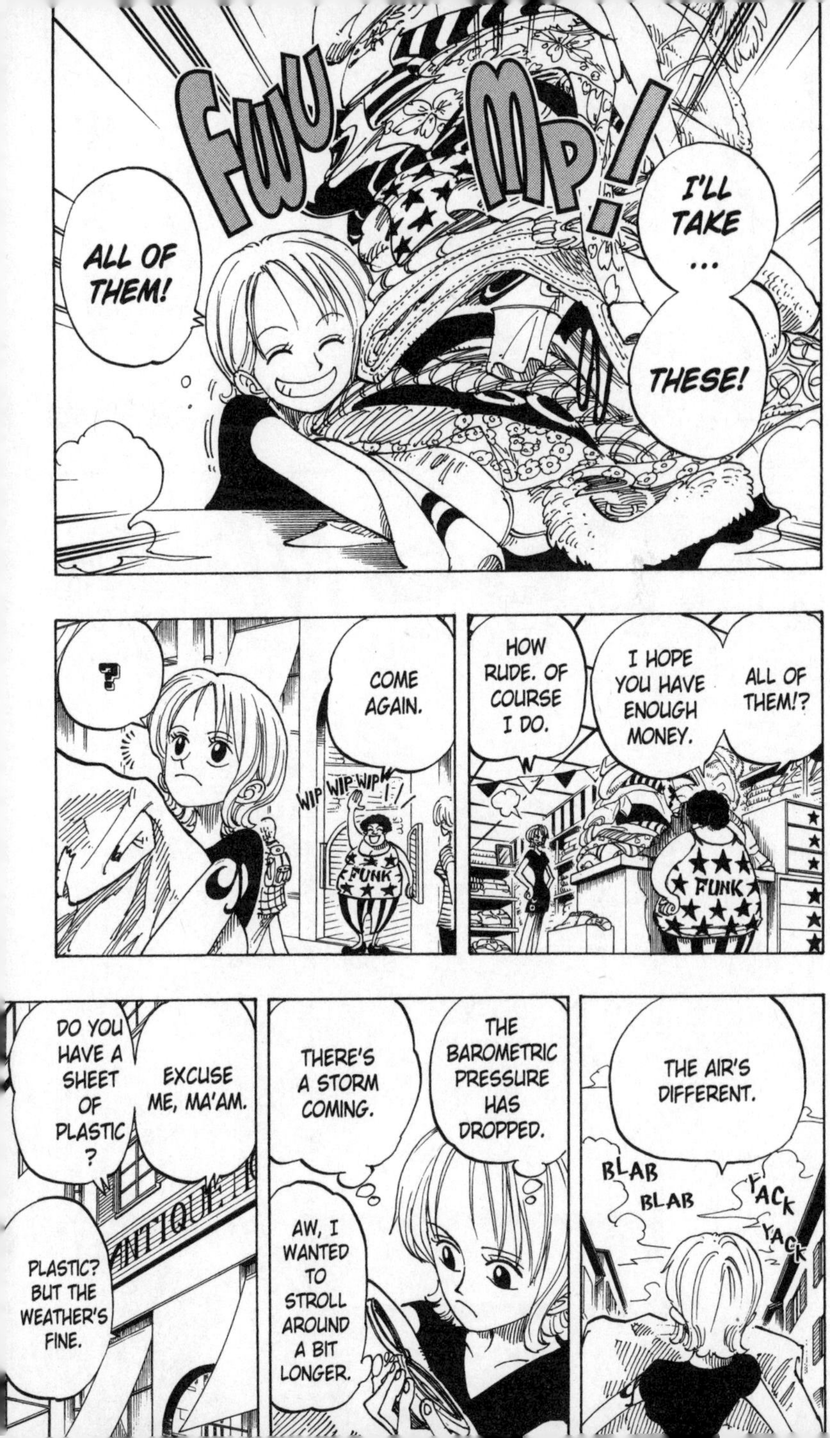
FWUUMP!
I'LL TAKE ... THESE!
ALL OF THEM!
ALL OF THEM!?
I HOPE YOU HAVE ENOUGH MONEY.
HOW RUDE. OF COURSE I DO.
FUNK
COME AGAIN.
WIP WIP WIP
FUNK
?
THE AIR'S DIFFERENT.
YACK YACK
BLAB BLAB
THE BAROMETRIC PRESSURE HAS DROPPED.
THERE'S A STORM COMING.
AW, I WANTED TO STROLL AROUND A BIT LONGER.
EXCUSE ME, MA'AM.
DO YOU HAVE A SHEET OF PLASTIC?
ANTIQUE
PLASTIC? BUT THE WEATHER'S FINE.

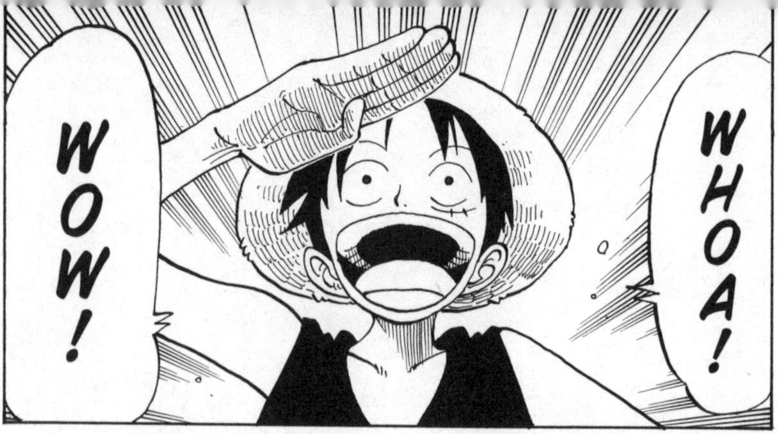
WHOA!
WOW!

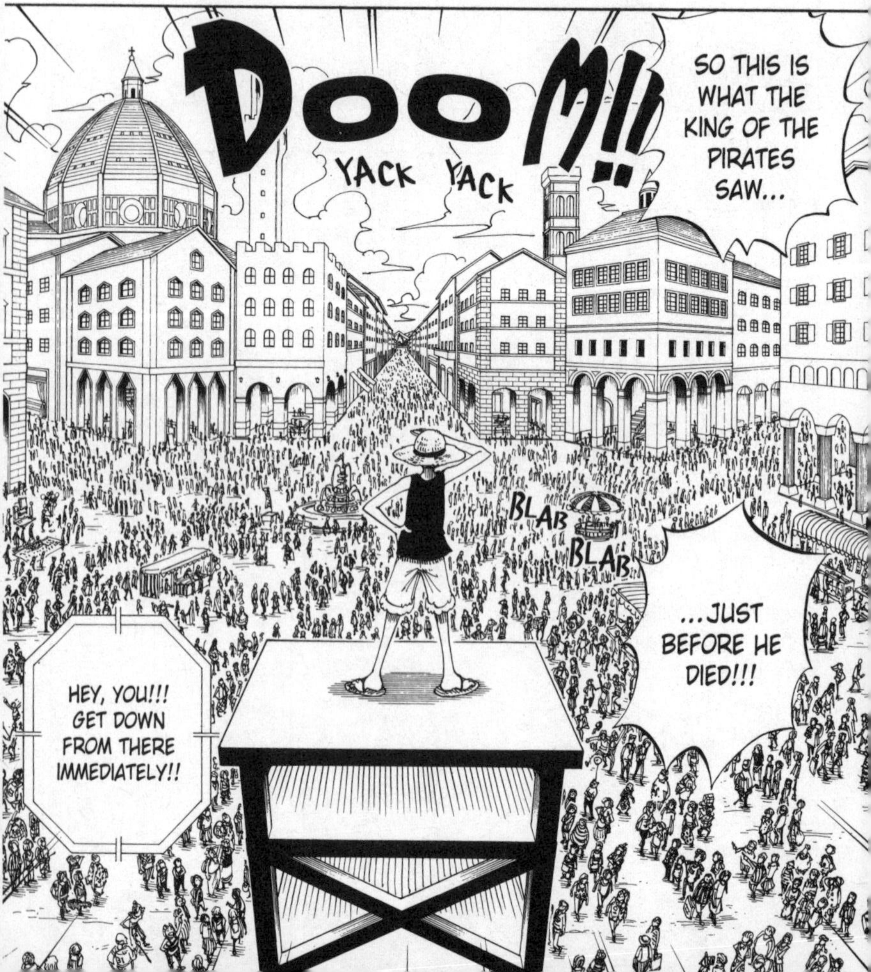
DOOM!!
SO THIS IS WHAT THE KING OF THE PIRATES SAW...
YACK YACK
BLAB BLAB
...JUST BEFORE HE DIED!!!
HEY, YOU!!! GET DOWN FROM THERE IMMEDIATELY!!

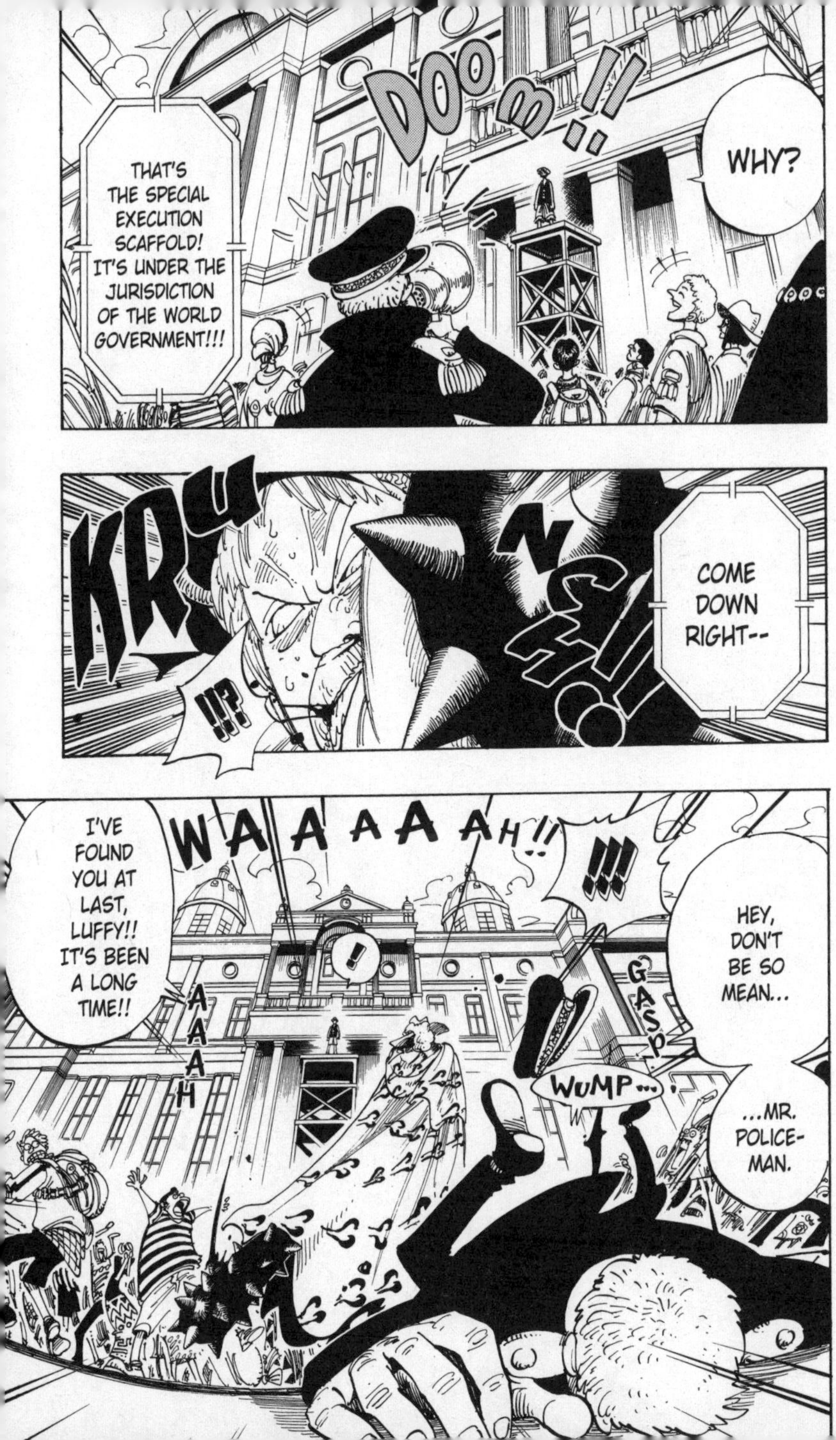
WHY?
DOOM!!
THAT'S THE SPECIAL EXECUTION SCAFFOLD! IT'S UNDER THE JURISDICTION OF THE WORLD GOVERNMENT!!!
COME DOWN RIGHT--
KRUNCH!!
!!?
HEY, DON'T BE SO MEAN...
...MR. POLICE-MAN.
GASP
WUMP...
!!!
WAAAAAH!!
!
AAAAH
I'VE FOUND YOU AT LAST, LUFFY!! IT'S BEEN A LONG TIME!!

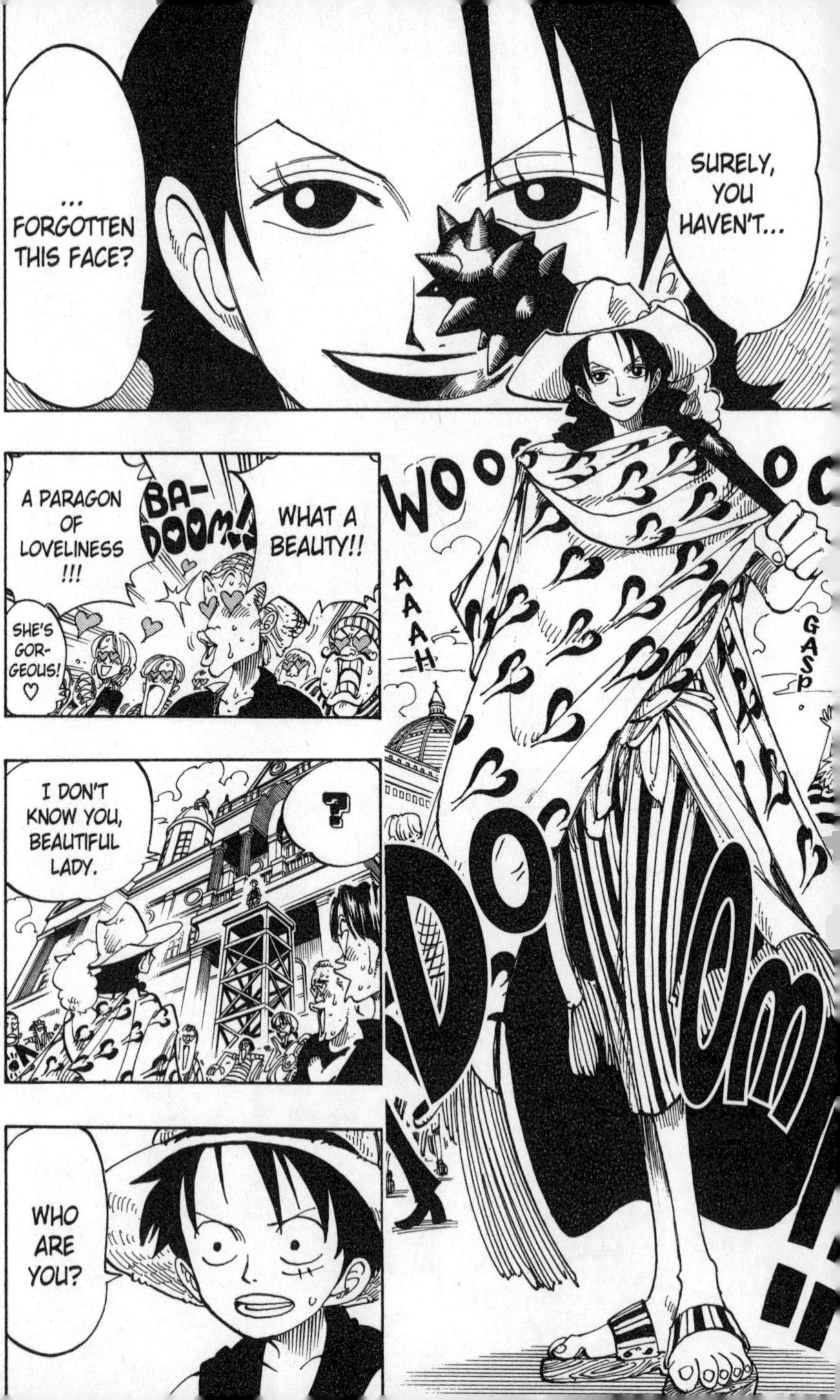
SURELY, YOU HAVEN'T...
... FORGOTTEN THIS FACE?
WOO
AAAH
GASP
DOOOM!!
BA-DOOM!!
WHAT A BEAUTY!!
A PARAGON OF LOVELINESS !!!
SHE'S GOR-GEOUS! ♡
?
I DON'T KNOW YOU, BEAUTIFUL LADY.
WHO ARE YOU?

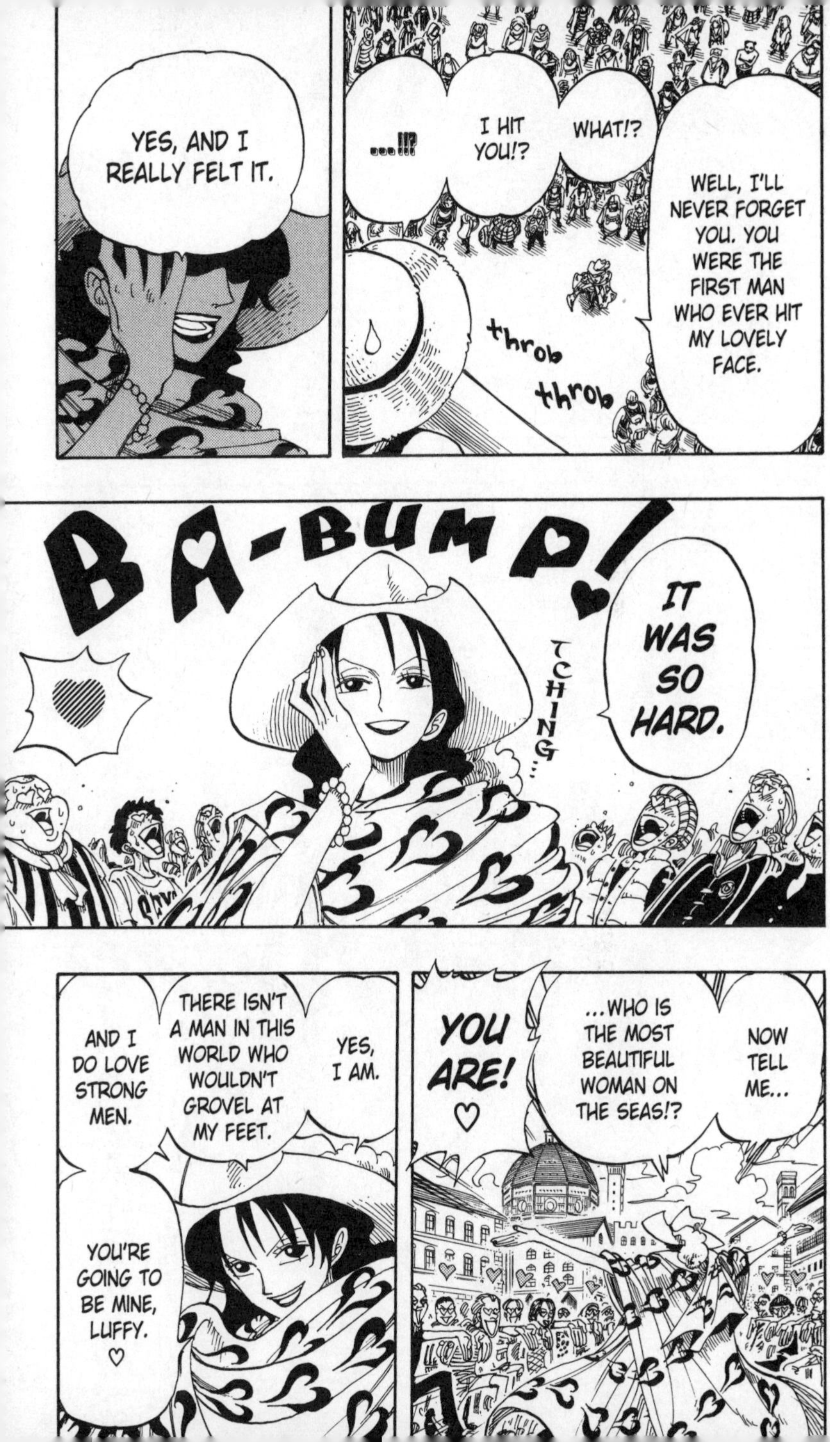
WELL, I'LL NEVER FORGET YOU. YOU WERE THE FIRST MAN WHO EVER HIT MY LOVELY FACE.
WHAT!?
I HIT YOU!?
...!!?
throb
throb
YES, AND I REALLY FELT IT.
BA-BUMP!
IT WAS SO HARD.
TCHING...
NOW TELL ME...
...WHO IS THE MOST BEAUTIFUL WOMAN ON THE SEAS!?
YOU ARE! ♡
YES, I AM.
THERE ISN'T A MAN IN THIS WORLD WHO WOULDN'T GROVEL AT MY FEET.
AND I DO LOVE STRONG MEN.
YOU'RE GOING TO BE MINE, LUFFY. ♡

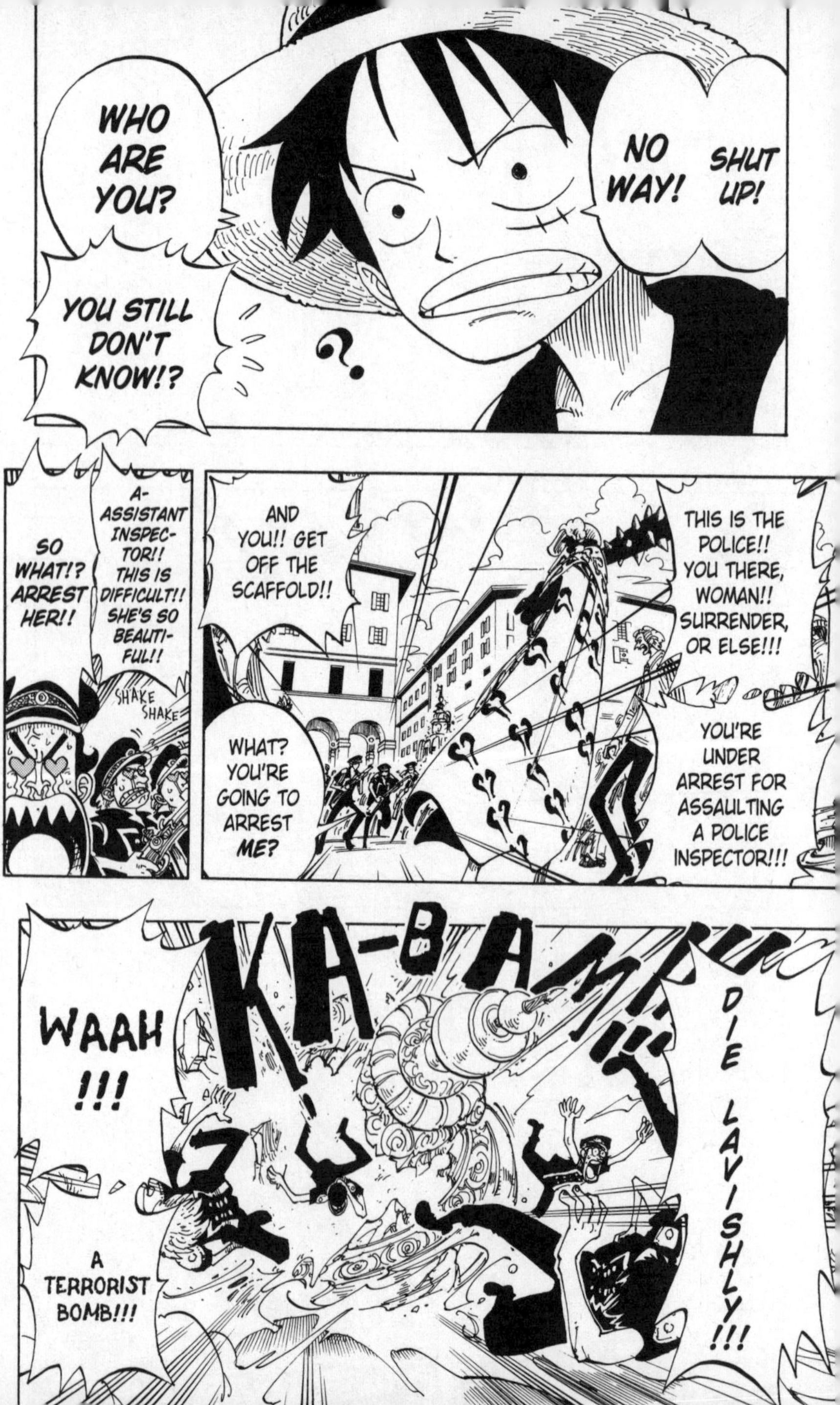
NO WAY! SHUT UP!
WHO ARE YOU?
YOU STILL DON'T KNOW!?
?
THIS IS THE POLICE!! YOU THERE, WOMAN!! SURRENDER, OR ELSE!!!
YOU'RE UNDER ARREST FOR ASSAULTING A POLICE INSPECTOR!!!
AND YOU!! GET OFF THE SCAFFOLD!!
WHAT? YOU'RE GOING TO ARREST ME?
A-ASSISTANT INSPECTOR!! THIS IS DIFFICULT!! SHE'S SO BEAUTIFUL!!
SO WHAT!? ARREST HER!!
SHAKE SHAKE
DIE LAVISHLY!!!
KA-BAM!!
WAAH!!!
A TERRORIST BOMB!!!

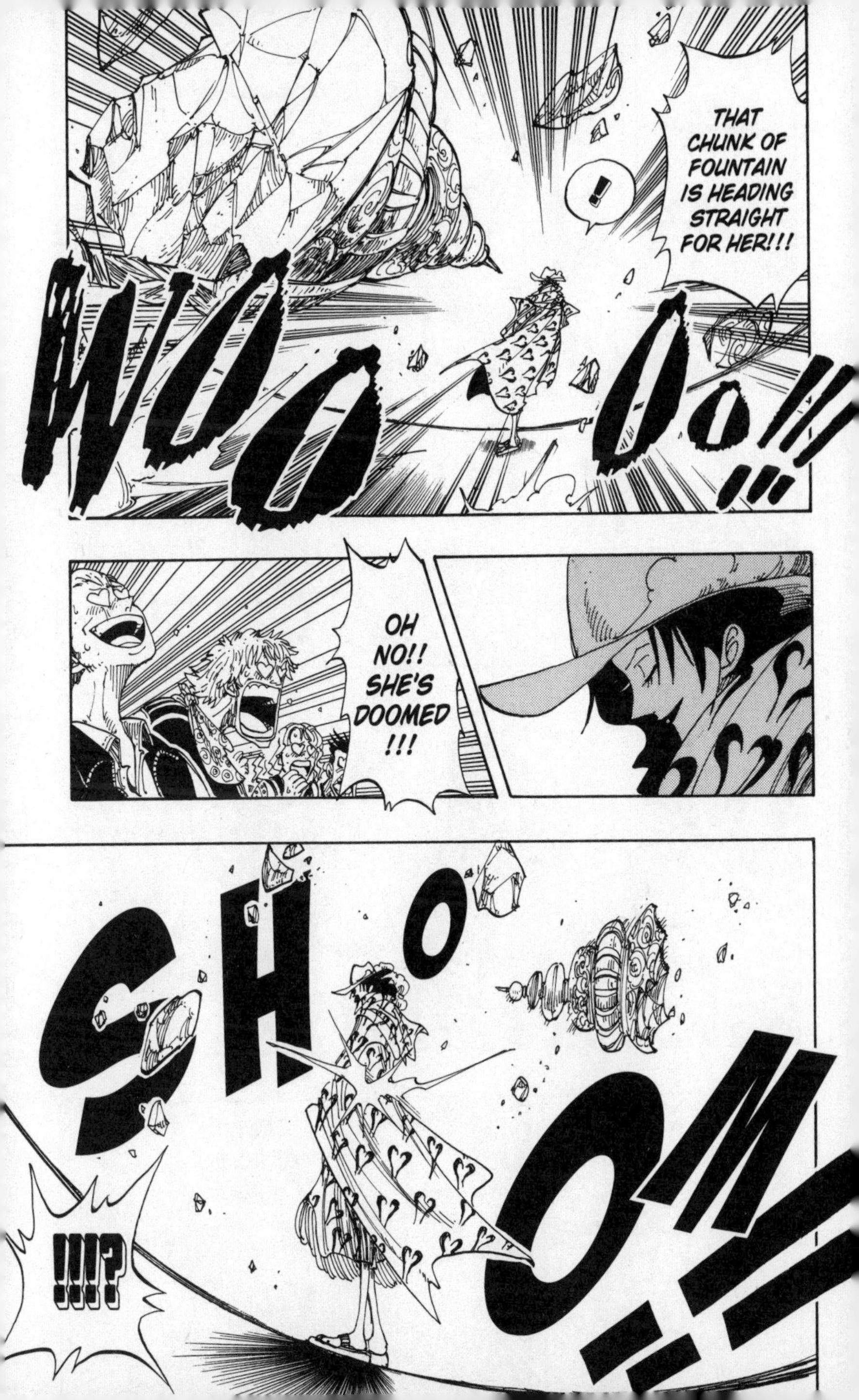
THAT CHUNK OF FOUNTAIN IS HEADING STRAIGHT FOR HER!!!
!
WOOOOO!!!!!
OH NO!! SHE'S DOOMED!!!
SHOOM!!
!!!?

...WHAT WAS THAT?

HEY! LOOK OUT!

WHAT HAPPENED!!? THE FOUNTAIN WENT RIGHT PAST HER!!

...CAN NEVER BE MARRED. YOU NEEDN'T WORRY.

WOOOOOO

PARDON THE SPECTACLE, BUT HER SMOOTH, SILKY SKIN...

DOOOM!!

I AM THE EXQUISITE LADY ALVIDA!!

YOU LOOK KINDA DIFFERENT...

REALLY?

RIGHT HERE!! IT'S ME!!

YOU SILLY FOOL!!

ALVIDA!? WHERE IS SHE!?

I PARTOOK OF THE SLIP-SLIP FRUIT!!

NOW MY BEAUTIFUL SKIN CANNOT BE MARRED BY ANY ATTACK!!!

HEH HEH! NICE OF YOU TO NOTICE!

I ATE THE DEVIL FRUIT AND TRANSFORMED!!!

...WAS BARELY ENHANCED. HOWEVER, AS YOU SAID...

SADLY, MY BEAUTY...

WE TEAMED UP IN ORDER TO FIND YOU.

...THERE'S SOMEONE YOU MUST DEFEAT FIRST!!

BUT IF YOU'RE GOING TO BECOME MY MAN...

AND HERE HE IS!!!

I DON'T THINK THAT'S IT.

...I DO LOOK A BIT DIFFERENT!! MY FRECKLES ARE GONE!!

KLAP KLAP!!

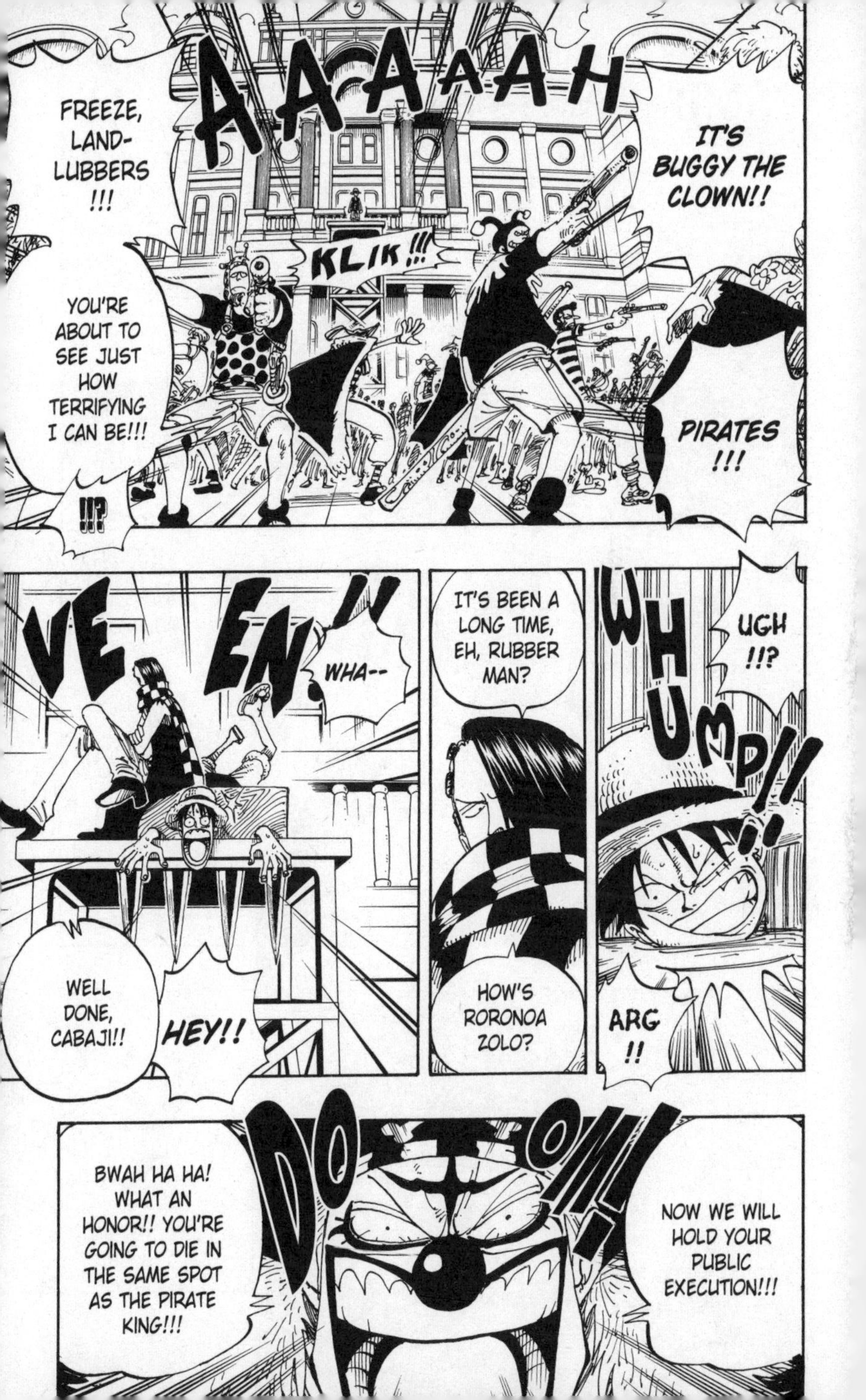
IT'S BUGGY THE CLOWN!!
PIRATES!!!
AAAAAH
KLIK!!!
FREEZE, LAND-LUBBERS!!!
YOU'RE ABOUT TO SEE JUST HOW TERRIFYING I CAN BE!!!
!!?
UGH!!?
WHUMP!!
ARG!!
IT'S BEEN A LONG TIME, EH, RUBBER MAN?
HOW'S RORONOA ZOLO?
WHA--
WELL DONE, CABAJI!!
HEY!!
NOW WE WILL HOLD YOUR PUBLIC EXECUTION!!!
BWAH HA HA! WHAT AN HONOR!! YOU'RE GOING TO DIE IN THE SAME SPOT AS THE PIRATE KING!!!

SSSS——ss

kiak

CAPTAIN SMOKER!! TERRIBLE NEWS!!!

MARINE

KLUNK

KRAK!!

KLUNK KLUNK!!

PIRATES ARE CAUSING A DISTURBANCE AT THE EXECUTION SCAFFOLD!!!

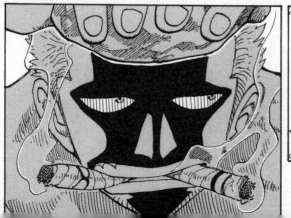

UH...

THE PIRATES ARE--!!

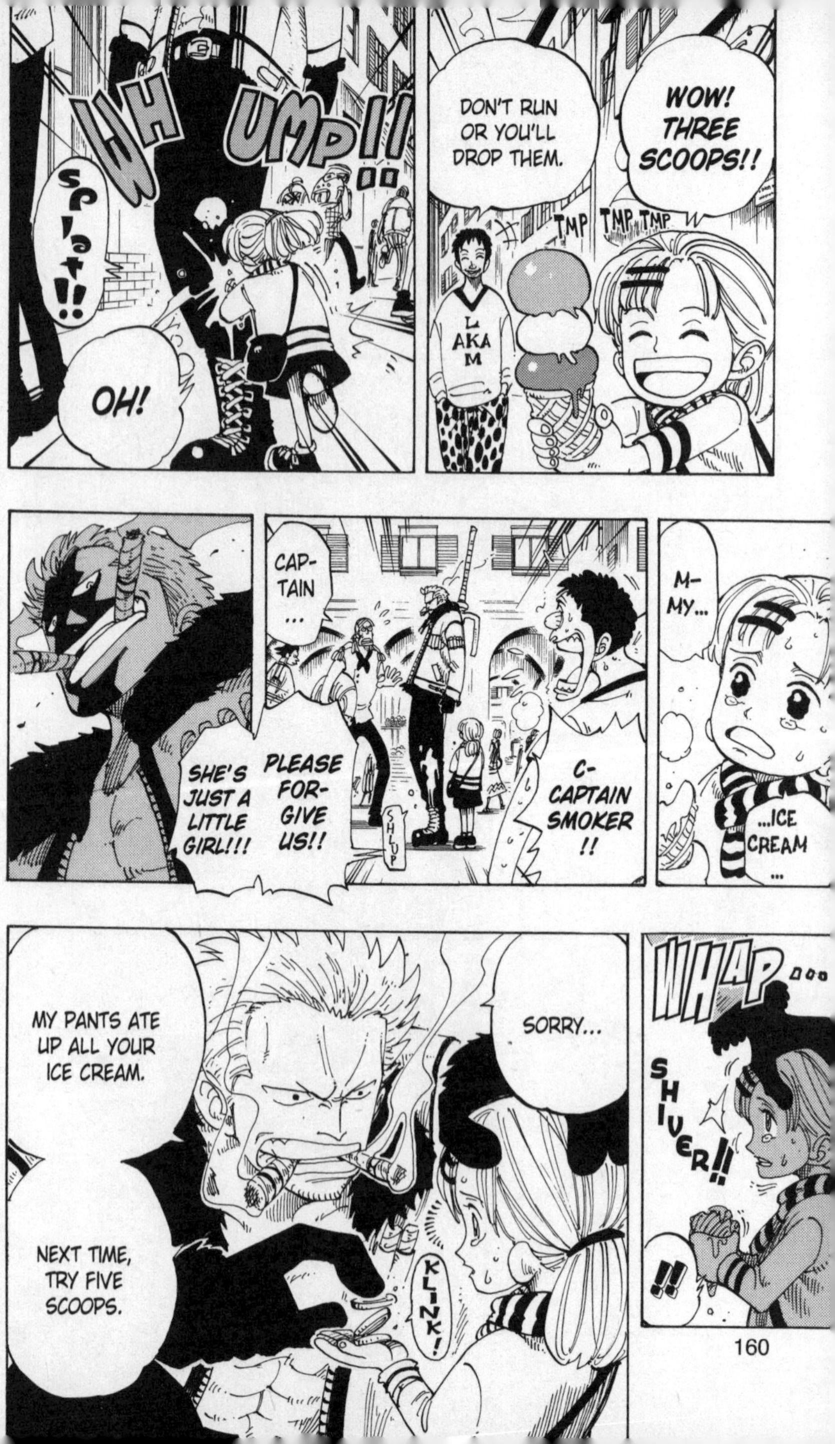
WOW! THREE SCOOPS!!
DON'T RUN OR YOU'LL DROP THEM.
TMP TMP TMP
WHUMP!!
SPLAT!!
OH!
M-MY...
...ICE CREAM...
C-CAPTAIN SMOKER!!
CAPTAIN...
PLEASE FORGIVE US!!
SHE'S JUST A LITTLE GIRL!!!
SHLUP
WHAP...
SHIVER!!
!!
SORRY...
MY PANTS ATE UP ALL YOUR ICE CREAM.
NEXT TIME, TRY FIVE SCOOPS.
KLINK!

MASTER CHIEF, HERE'S YOUR JACKET.

OH, THANK YOU, CHIEF.

I'M SORRY!! I'LL GET READY RIGHT AWAY!

TASHIGI!!!! WHERE HAVE YOU BEEN!!?

CAPTAIN SMOKER, SORRY I'M LATE!!

OH...THANK YOU. I'M SO SORRY.

TMP TMP TMP TMP

YOU MEAN MORE SO THAN USUAL!!?

FORGIVE ME.

I'M A LITTLE OFF TODAY.

YES, SIR!

C'MON. THERE'S A DISTURBANCE AT THE SQUARE!!

MASTER CHIEF PETTY OFFICER TASHIGI
NAVY HEADQUARTERS

...HAS THINNED OUT A LOT.

TMP TMP

?

THE CROWD...

WHY DO I HAVE TO CARRY THE HEAVY END!?

YOU CAME ALONG AT JUST THE RIGHT TIME, USOPP.

BY THE WAY, I SAW A STRANGELY DRESSED MAN RIDING A LION EARLIER.

I'D BETTER RETURN TO THE SHIP RIGHT AWAY.

THE AIR PRESSURE HAS DROPPED DANGEROUSLY LOW.

HUH?

BA-

AH.

DUMP

OH.

!!

ISN'T IT SUPPOSED TO BE RIGHT HERE?

HE SAID HE WANTED TO SEE THE EXECUTION SCAFFOLD.

SO? WHERE IS HE?

7.

⊙ Captain's chair

⊙ Luffy seems to like this chair. He's always sitting in it.

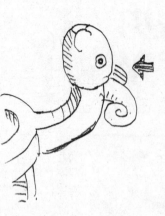

⊙ He can't swim, so why would he sit in a spot like this? Who knows? But he seems happy, so what's wrong with that?

Nami's Tangerine Grove

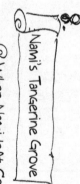

⊙ When Nami left Coco Village, she took three of Belle-Mère's tangerine trees with her.

⊙ Nami tends this little orchard.

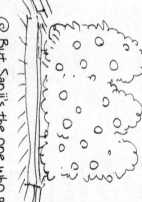

⊙ But Sanji's the one who protects the trees from tangerine snatchers (like Luffy).

⊙ The tangerines are supposed to be very sweet.

Chapter 99:
LUFFY DIED

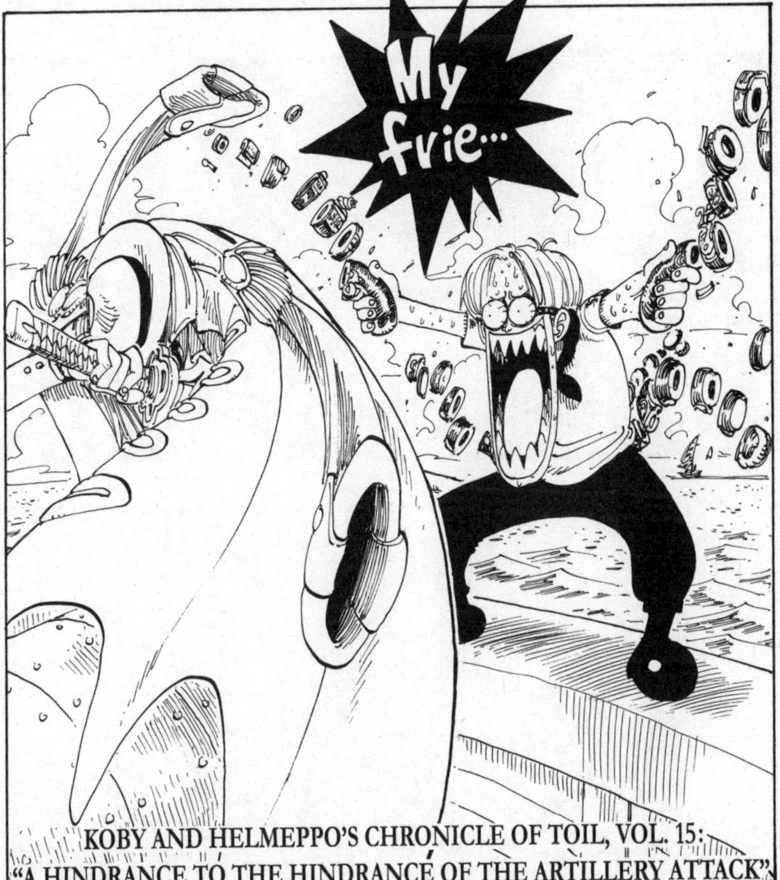
My frie...
KOBY AND HELMEPPO'S CHRONICLE OF TOIL, VOL. 15:
"A HINDRANCE TO THE HINDRANCE OF THE ARTILLERY ATTACK"

LEGENDS THAT ENDURE IN THE FUTURE...

...WERE EVENTS THAT TOOK PLACE IN THE DISTANT PAST.

WOOOOO

DOOOM!

FOR THAT, HE WILL BE EXECUTED IN GRAND STYLE!!!

THE CRIMINAL, M.D. LUFFY, IS GUILTY OF GETTING ON HIS HIGH HORSE AND UPSETTING ME!

BWAH HA HA HA HA HA

HOLD IT RIGHT THERE, YOU PIRATES!!!

HOORAY!!

SO CHEER IN GRAND STYLE!!!

BANG! BANGBANG!!!

WE HAVE BIGGER FISH TO FRY RIGHT NOW.

WE COULD HELP HIM!! AFTER ALL, I DID KILL ONE OF THE BIG FISH OF THE FISH-MEN!!

WHAT GOOD CAN WE DO THERE!?

HEY, WHAT'S THE BIG RUSH!?

RRMMMBB...

BIGGER FISH?

WE SHOULD GO BACK TO THE SQUARE AND HELP LUFFY!

WHAT!!?

A STORM'S GOING TO HIT THIS ISLAND.

HEY!! WAIT UP!!!

OH! THIS REALLY *IS* IMPORTANT!!

IF THERE'S A COMMOTION IN THE SQUARE, THERE'LL BE SOLDIERS.

THIS IS THE CALM BEFORE THE STORM!!

AND I SAW DARK CLOUDS IN THE EASTERN SKY.

THE AIR PRESSURE AND TEMPERATURE HAVE BEEN STEADILY DROPPING.

THWUMP!!

...WHAT'LL WE DO IF WE TRY TO ESCAPE AND THE BOAT'S GONE!!?

169

BUT IF WE WAIT...

WHAT'S YOUR HURRY, FOOL?

SHOULD WE ATTACK, SIR?

A DISPUTE BETWEEN PIRATES, EH?

...LET A PIRATE ESCAPE FROM OUR CITY?

RRMMM BB...

HAVE WE EVER...

...SURROUND BUGGY, ALVIDA AND THE REST OF THEM.

NOW LISTEN, WHEN LUFFY'S HEAD ROLLS...

WE'LL LET THOSE PIRATES KILL EACH OTHER.

THEN SHUT UP.

N-NO, NEVER!!

IT'LL MAKE OUR JOB EASY!!

IDIOT! AS IF I'D SPARE YOU!!!

PLEASE DON'T KILL ME!

I'M SORRY!

I'll never do it again

WOoOooo

SO MUCH FOR THE MAN I WAS GOING TO...

HMPH. THIS IS WHAT HAPPENS TO THOSE WHO DEFY US.

AW WELL, NEVER MIND THAT.

...

NO ONE WANTS TO HEAR IT.

YOU HAVE A BIG AUDIENCE.

ANY LAST WORDS?

...

WHAT A DREAMER.

HERE, OF ALL PLACES?

THOOM

DID HE SAY "KING OF THE PIRATES" !!?

WHAT !!?

STOP THE EXECU- TION !!!!

WHAM!

UGH!! U-UGH !!!

WHAM!!

IS THAT ALL YOU HAVE TO SAY, RUBBERHEAD!!?

BUT YOU'RE A SECOND TOO LATE!!

SO YOU'VE COME, ZOLO.

SANJI!!!! ZOLO!!!

HELP!!!

IT'S RORONOA ZOLO!

WHAT'S GOING ON!?

...AND HIS PIRATES!!!

ZOLO'S WORKING WITH THAT MONKEY GUY...

WHAT!!?

ER... BUT...

THE BOUNTY HUNTER? WHAT GREAT TIMING!!

RORONOA ZOLO!? HERE!?

IT'S THAT GUY!!!

!!!

GOT IT!!

TEAR DOWN THE SCAFFOLD!!

EEK

AAAH

AAAH

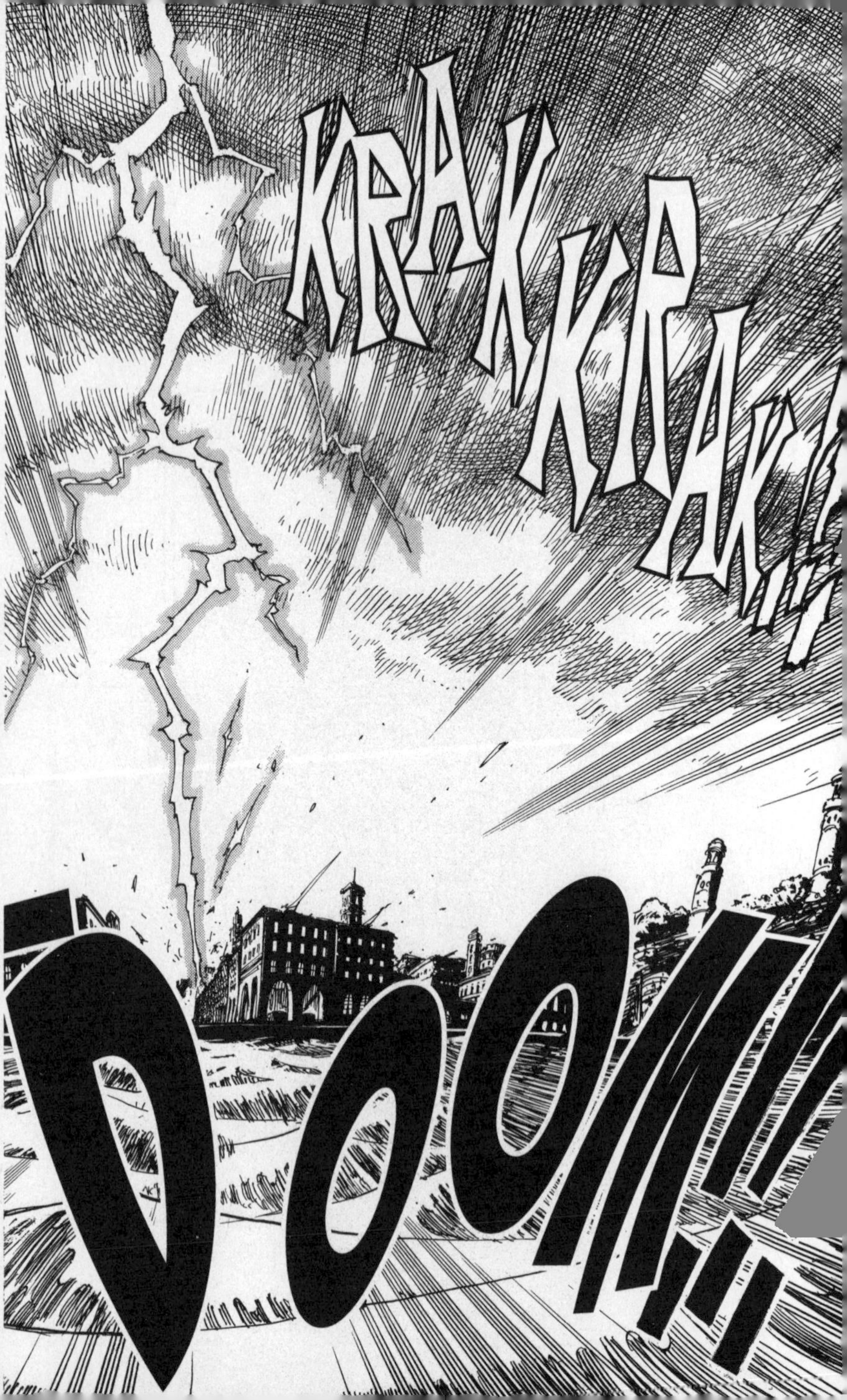
KRAK KRAK...!!
DOOM...!!

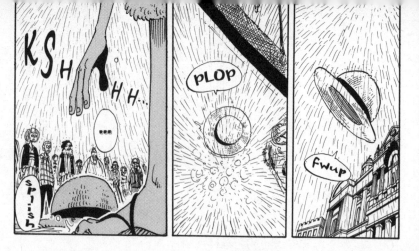

LUCKY ME.

SPLOP

HA HA HA HA! I'M ALIVE.

DON'T TALK NONSENSE. LET'S GET OUTTA HERE.

WE'RE NOT IN THE CLEAR YET.

KLANK

THANK GOODNESS.

DO YOU BELIEVE IN A HIGHER POWER?

RUN FOR IT !!!

RAAAH

HEY, WHICH WAY!?

HERE THEY COME !!

SURROUND THE SQUARE AND CAPTURE THE PIRATES!!

DOOM !!

HE SAW HIS DEATH, ACCEPTED IT AND LAUGHED!!

IN THAT MOMENT HE ACCEPTED HIS FATE.

THAT'S NOT IT!!!

WHY DID HE LAUGH? DID HE KNOW HE'D BE RESCUED?

WELL, THAT MONKEY LAUGHED!!!

...EVERY MAN TREMBLES IN FEAR, HOWEVER TOUGH HE IS.

LAUGH!? WHEN FACED WITH CERTAIN DEATH...

SOLDIER, DID YOU EVER SEE A PIRATE LAUGH RIGHT BEFORE HIS EXECUTION?

CAPTAIN!! THE PIRATE ROUND-UP IS...

TWENTY-TWO YEARS AGO, ANOTHER MAN LAUGHED ON THAT VERY SPOT.

HE WAS GOLD ROGER, KING OF THE PIRATES!!!

WOooOoo

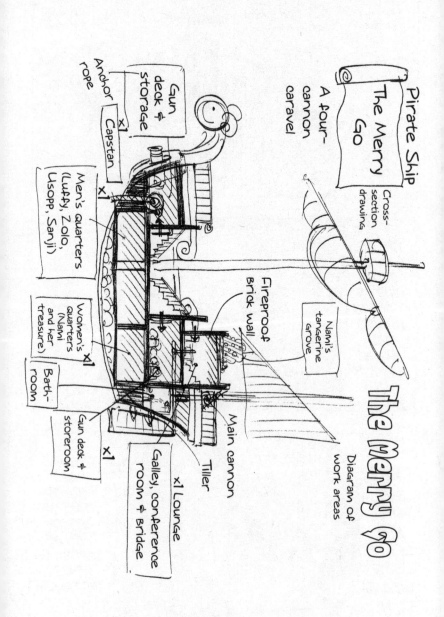

Pirate Ship

The Merry Go

Cross-section drawing

A four-cannon caravel

The Merry Go

Diagram of work areas

Gun deck & storage

Anchor rope

x1 Capstan

Men's quarters (Luffy, Zolo, Usopp, Sanji) x1

Women's quarters (Nami and her treasure) x1

Bath-room

Fireproof Brick wall

Nami's tangerine grove

Main cannon

Tiller

Gun deck & storeroom x1

x1 Lounge Galley, conference room & Bridge

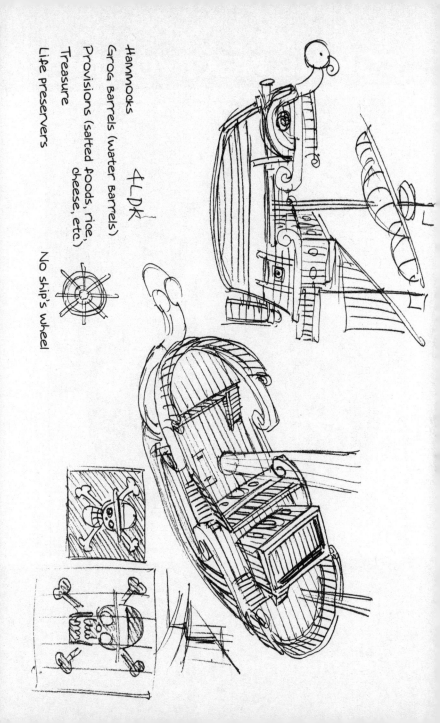

Hammocks

Grog barrels (water barrels)

Provisions (salted foods, rice, cheese, etc.)

Treasure

Life preservers

4LDK

No ship's wheel

COMING NEXT VOLUME:

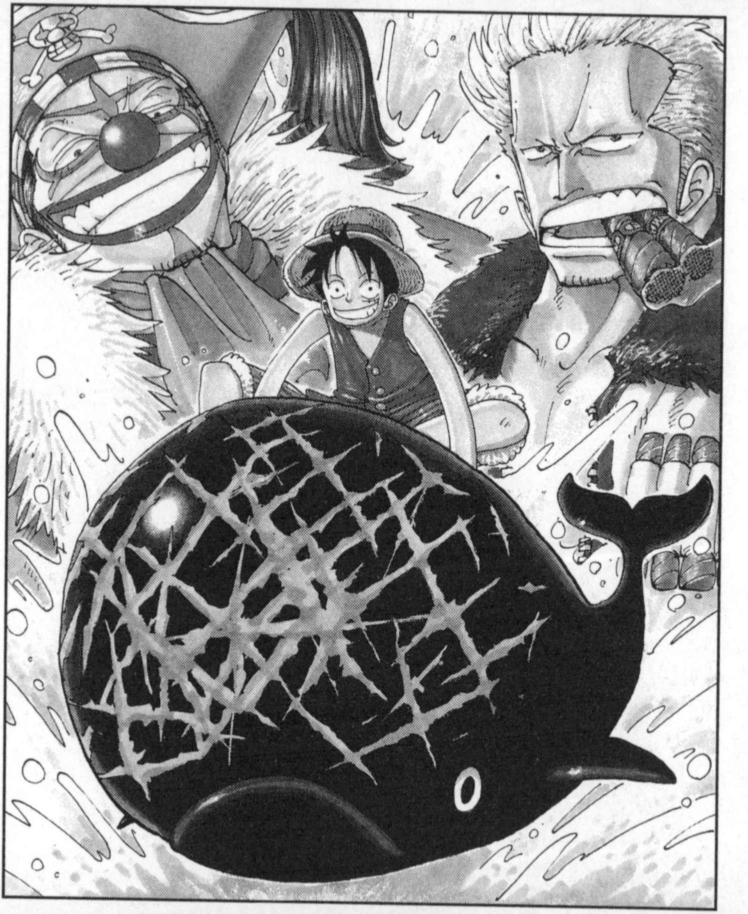

Luffy and his crew are bound for the Grand Line at last, with both newfound enemies and old ones in hot pursuit. Braving a terrible storm, the Straw Hat Pirates make their way toward what they believe is the entrance to the famed sea. But Nami's map is pointing straight up the side of a mountain!

ON SALE NOW!

Story and Art by

KOYOHARU GOTOUGE

In Taisho-era Japan, kindhearted Tanjiro Kamado makes a living selling charcoal. But his peaceful life is shattered when a demon slaughters his entire family. His little sister Nezuko is the only survivor, but she has been transformed into a demon herself! Tanjiro sets out on a dangerous journey to find a way to return his sister to normal and destroy the demon who ruined his life.

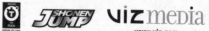

MY HERO ACADEMIA
IZUKU MIDORIYA WANTS TO BE A HERO MORE THAN ANYTHING, BUT HE HASN'T GOT AN OUNCE OF POWER IN HIM. WITH NO CHANCE OF GETTING INTO THE U.A. HIGH SCHOOL FOR HEROES, HIS LIFE IS LOOKING LIKE A DEAD END. THEN AN ENCOUNTER WITH ALL MIGHT, THE GREATEST HERO OF ALL, GIVES HIM A CHANCE TO CHANGE HIS DESTINY...
MY HERO ACADEMIA
KOHEI HORIKOSHI
RATED T FOR TEEN
ratings.viz.com
SHONEN JUMP
viz media
www.viz.com
BOKU NO HERO ACADEMIA © 2014 by Kohei Horikoshi/SHUEISHA Inc.

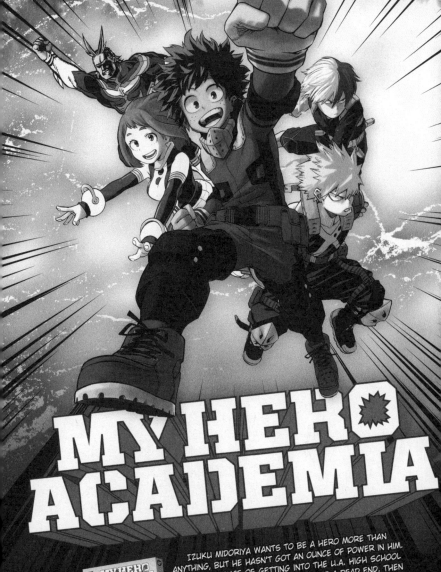

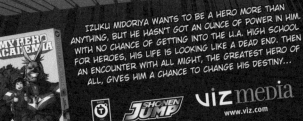

You're Reading in the Wrong Direction!!

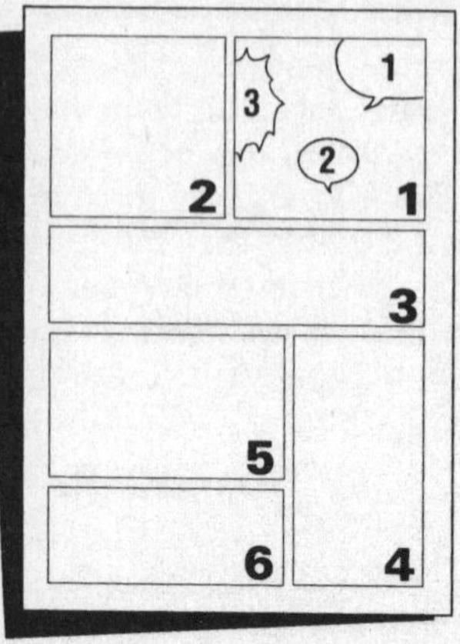
1
2
3
1
2
3
4
5
6

Whoops! Guess what? You're starting at the wrong end of the comic!

...It's true! In keeping with the original Japanese format, **One Piece** is meant to be read from right to left, starting in the upper-right corner.

Unlike English, which is read from left to right, Japanese is read from right to left, meaning that action, sound effects and word-balloon order are completely reversed... something which can make readers unfamiliar with Japanese feel pretty backwards themselves. For this reason, manga or Japanese comics published in the U.S. in English have sometimes been published "flopped"–that is, printed in exact reverse order, as though seen from the other side of a mirror.

By flopping pages, U.S. publishers can avoid confusing readers, but the compromise is not without its downside. For one thing, a character in a flopped manga series who once wore in the original Japanese version a T-shirt emblazoned with "M A Y" (as in "the merry month of") now wears one which reads "Y A M"! Additionally, many manga creators in Japan are themselves unhappy with the process, as some feel the mirror-imaging of their art skews their original intentions.

We are proud to bring you Eiichiro Oda's **One Piece** in the original unflopped format. For now, though, turn to the other side of the book and let the journey begin...!

–Editor

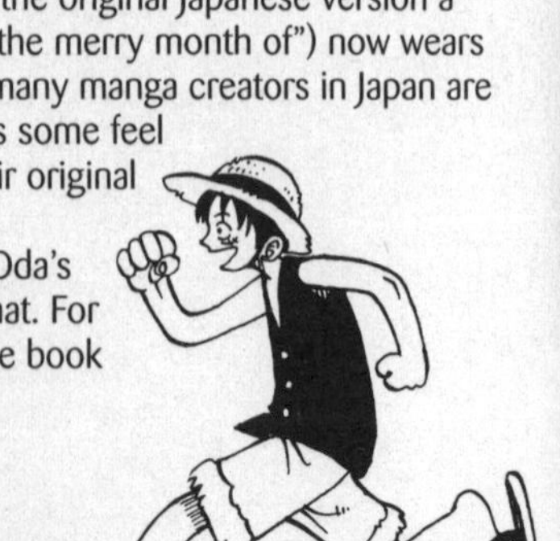